ALLEGORIES
OF
WRITING

SUNY Series,
The Margins of Literature

Mihai I. Spariosu, Editor

ALLEGORIES OF WRITING
The Subject of Metamorphosis

Bruce Clarke

STATE UNIVERSITY OF NEW YORK PRESS

Production by Ruth Fisher
Marketing by Nancy Farrell

Published by
State University of New York Press, Albany

© 1995 State University of New York

For information, address the State University of New York Press, State University Plaza, Albany, NY 12246

Library of Congress Cataloging-in-Publication Data
Clarke, Bruce, 1950–
   Allegories of writing : the subject of metamorphosis / Bruce
Clarke.
      p.   cm. — (SUNY series, the margins of literature)
   Includes bibliographical references and index.
   ISBN 0-7914-2623-8 (alk. paper). — ISBN 0-7914-2624-6 (pbk. :
alk. paper)
   1. Metamorphosis in literature.   I. Title.   II. Series.
PN56.M53C58   1995
809'.93353—dc20   94-48335
                                                             CIP

10 9 8 7 6 5 4 3 2 1

for Jona

CONTENTS

PREFACE

This is what determines the character of allegory as a form of writing.
It is a schema; and as a schema it is an object of knowledge, but
it is not securely possessed until it becomes a fixed schema: at one
and the same time a fixed image and a fixing sign.
—Walter Benjamin

Allegory imposes the temporal predicament it is about upon the theory
that would, in effect, deliver it from that predicament. Interpreting
allegory, we write it, and may take that writing for theory, delivering
us from time; constructing theories of allegory, we risk the fall
into mere allegoresis, denying our temporality.
—Rita Copeland and Stephen Melville

We begin to glimpse the process of allegorical interpretation as a kind
of scanning that, moving back and forth across the text, readjusts its
terms in constant modification of a type quite different from our
stereotypes of some static medieval or biblical decoding, and which one
would be tempted (were it not also an old-fashioned word!) to
characterize as dialectical.
—Fredric Jameson[1]

The epigraphs sketch the modern critical development of allegory
theory and indicate the danger as well as the promise for a theoretical reading of allegorical texts. There is a tension as well as an
accommodation between allegory and its theory. Allegory calls for
theory because it rewrites itself in another form—it produces its
own interpretation—and theoretical criticism calls forth allegorical
readings. But the theoretical reader of allegory may end up composing and imposing a mere allegoresis, a rhetorical doubling that
evades rather than engages history, a fixing of the flow of signification taken as the aim and the end of meaning. Copeland and
Melville (1991) have shown that allegorical reading cannot be simply set apart from allegorical writing as its dispensible, parasitical
supplement, for allegoresis regularly emerges from within narrative allegory, as when Dante has Virgil explicate the moral landscapes of the *Inferno*. However, intrusive rather than responsive
reading can result when critical tropes are fixed, hermeneutic
metaphors reified in service of closed interpretive systems.

Allegories of Writing: The Subject of Metamorphosis faces this
threat because it desires to theorize, and so pursues a constellation

of structural, rhetorical, psychoanalytical, and theological elements that reconfigure themselves throughout history *as* allegories. Generically, allegories are the narrative vehicles, not of waking experiences, but of dreams, and dreams are both in and outside of time. There is a transhistorical residuum to the topic of this study, insofar as the various ironies of metamorphic episodes dramatize our abiding human status as linguistic creatures. I have tried to counter the internal threat of allegorical ahistoricism, however, by keeping the argument mobile. Scanning a transcultural network of texts and pretexts, *Allegories of Writing* looks at metamorphic allegory through a kind of critical kaleidoscope.

The modern restitution of allegory's critical prestige took shape in Walter Benjamin's examination of the *Trauerspiel,* where he connected German baroque allegory to Western cultural history and to a metaphysical discourse on temporality. Benjamin's ideas were further developed in Hans-Georg Gadamer's *Truth and Method* and Paul de Man's "The Rhetoric of Temporality."[2] For Gadamer, an allegorical hermeneutics running counter to the strictures of symbolist poetics can retrieve and resitutate historical sense, whereas for de Man, the secure possession of allegorical meaning is always troubled by the dilemma, however authentic, of its temporal disjunctiveness. Fredric Jameson's (1991) revisionist criticism takes a postmodern turn by restructuring the ambivalence of the allegorical text, the inevitable slippages among its planes of meaning, in terms not of temporal but of spatial distance: "the allegorical, then . . . can be minimally formulated as the question posed to thinking by the awareness of incommensurable distances within its object of thought" (168). In these terms, the metamorphic body in a literary narrative—displaced in fictive time and space from its proper origin—is an allegory of the allegorical: the metamorphic agent is a personified text split into incompatible components.

Although previous studies of the topic have not remarked the fact, the secular Western literature of bodily metamorphosis is a species of allegorical writing. *Allegories of Writing* presents the first full synthesis of allegory theory and literary metamorphosis. The modern literature of metamorphosis—conveniently epitomized by Kafka's *Metamorphosis*—is directly descended from classical traditions. Moreover, there are important formal and thematic relations between the mode of allegory and the trope of metamorphosis. This study samples the multidimensional field of literary metamorphosis by constructing the complex ideological cosmos of metamorphic allegory, and then *scaling* that cosmos (to borrow a trope from chaos theory) to set up multiple relations among both its formal levels of signification and its successive temporal frames and cultural uses. This recursive cycling among metamorphic texts and their allegorical topics clarifies the cultural history of literary metamorphosis and renovates its structural networks, its critical resonances as a polyvalent allegorical device.

As Angus Fletcher has noted, "allegories are far less often the dull systems that they are reputed to be than they are symbolic power struggles."[3] And allegorical readings of the trope of human metamorphosis have always been political. The conservative reader takes physical metamorphoses to represent the maintenance of the soul's integrity under circumstances of extreme bodily alienation; the radical or resisting reader takes the same changes to sound the structural determinations of the decentered subject and narrate its performative transformations. This divergence in styles of interpretation parallels two divergent trends in the Western literature of metamorphosis: a tradition of Neoplatonic critical reading and a counter trend of ironic composition that exploits the subversive resonances of metamorphic episodes. This study examines both trends for the thematic architecture, the allegorical cosmos of metamorphic narratives across time, and for the temporal relations of particular pretexts to their dogmatic or parodic transformations.

Allegories of Writing is manifestly organized by thematic sequence, from the structure and history of metamorphic allegory to the interlocking topics of the subject: moral affect, economic transformation, allegorical monstrosity, and the problematic of gender. The latent form of the study, however, is traceable in the relations among four texts—Plato's *Phaedrus,* Apuleius's *Golden Ass,* Shakespeare's *A Midsummer Night's Dream,* and Keats's *Lamia.* Through these texts runs a definite line of historical connection. Apuleius read the *Phaedrus,* Shakespeare read Adlington's translation of the *Golden Ass,* and Keats read Shakespeare as well as Elizabethan and later translations of Homer, Ovid, and Apuleius. The other primary texts—Homer's *Odyssey,* Ovid's *Metamorphoses,* Milton's *Paradise Lost,* Coleridge's *Ancient Mariner,* Stevenson's *Jekyll and Hyde,* Kafka's *Metamorphosis,* Bulgakov's *Heart of a Dog,* Calvino's *Cosmicomics* and *t zero,* and García Márquez's *One Hundred Years of Solitude*—are arranged around this core not by relations of immediate influence but by their participation in the ironic literary deployment of metamorphic devices. I have not attempted to produce an encyclopedic treatment. Rather, I have tried to indicate and flesh out the theoretical and cultural breadth of the topic.

Chapter 1 establishes the primary structural connections between the mode of allegory and the trope of metamorphosis. It relates both allegory and metamorphosis to writing and translation, through brief examinations of the *Golden Ass, A Midsummer*

Night's Dream, Lamia, Jekyll and Hyde, and the *Metamorphosis*. Chapter 2 traces the history of metamorphic allegory from its classical inception in the philosophical reading of the epic to its postmodern status within the current scientific episteme. Chapter 3 shifts from textuality and history to psychoanalysis and political economy. Parables of psychosocial concerns animate a series of scenes from the *Odyssey*, the *Golden Ass, One Hundred Years of Solitude*, and *Jekyll and Hyde*. Chapter 4 reads literary metamorphs with regard to their monstrosity, the fall of nature into the daemonic forms of writing, by examining episodes of the *Phaedrus*, the *Metamorphosis*, the *Ancient Mariner, Heart of a Dog, Cosmicomics* and *t zero*. Finally, chapter 5 reprises most of the texts studied in *Allegories of Writing* as stories written over the dialectic of gender. In sum, *Allegories of Writing: The Subject of Metamorphosis* recovers, examines, and evaluates the critical force of metamorphic devices in Western writing.

I began to explore this topic shortly after taking my doctorate in 1980 at SUNY/Buffalo. In many ways *Allegories of Writing* is a product of the Buffalo English department of the 1970s. I would like to acknowledge my gratitude for the teaching fellowship that brought me there, for the openness and challenge of the program, and for the professors and friends who made that time memorable.

From Buffalo to Baton Rouge is a twenty-four hour ride. At Louisiana State University from 1980 to 1982 I had the good fortune to meet Bainard Cowan, Dan Fogel, and John May and to have their congenial support as I began to piece together some ideas about metamorphosis. Thanks to Gale Carrithers for keeping me afloat, and to the English Department's Philological Society for hearing an early paper on Plato and Keats.

At Texas Tech, John Samson and Doug Crowell have both made contributions too profound to enumerate. For manifold forms of encouragement and assistance, I would also like to thank Joel Weinsheimer, Jeff Smitten, Bob Markley, Bill Rossi, Jimmie Killingsworth, Laurie Churchill, Wendell Aycock, Leon Higdon, Don Rude, Sherry Ceniza, Tommy Barker, and Ernie Sullivan.

The manuscript has greatly benefitted from careful readings by Joel Reed, Jim Paxson, and Allen Miller. I am grateful, too, for the generous help of Charles Altieri, Irving Massey, Art Efron, John Kronick, David Wagenknecht, Eric Gould, Evelyn Hinz, Mike Walsh, John Morrow, Ron Schleifer, Kate Hayles, Bill Paulson, and Paul Harris. Finally, thanks as always to my wife, Donna.

Grateful acknowledgement is made to the Trustees of Boston University, for permission to use "Fabulous Monsters of Conscience:

Anthropomorphosis in Keats's *Lamia," Studies in Romanticism* 23:4 (Fall 1984); to *Mosaic,* for permission to use "Daemonic Anatomy: Embarrassment and Theft in Apuleius's *The Golden Ass," Mosaic* 21:2–3 (Spring 1988), in a special issue titled *Contexts: The Interdisciplinary Study of Literature;* and to the University of Hartford, for permission to use "Circe's Metamorphoses: Late Classical and Early Modern Allegorical Readings of the *Odyssey* and Ovid's *Metamorphoses," University of Hartford Studies in Literature* 21:2 (1989).

Excerpts from *t zero* by Italo Calvino © 1967 by Giulio Einaudi Editore, s.p.a., English translation by William Weaver copyright © 1969 by Harcourt Brace & Company and Jonathan Cape Limited, reprinted by permission of Harcourt Brace & Company.

Excerpts from *The Golden Ass* of Apuleius and translated by Robert Graves. Translation copyright © 1951 and copyright renewed © 1978 by Robert Graves. Reprinted by permission of Farrar, Straus & Giroux, Inc.

ABBREVIATIONS

AM   Apuleius. *Metamorphoses.* 2 vols. Ed. and trans. J. Arthur Hanson. Cambridge: Harvard University Press, 1989.

AW   ———. *The Works of Apuleius.* London: G. Bell and Sons, 1899.

CC   Calvino, Italo. *Cosmicomics.* Trans. William Weaver. New York: Harvest/HBJ, 1968.

ERW   Coleridge, Samuel Taylor. "The Rime of the Ancient Mariner." In David Perkins, ed. *English Romantic Writers.* New York: Harcourt, Brace, Jovanovich, 1967, 404–13.

GA   Apuleius. *The Transformations of Lucius Otherwise Known as The Golden Ass.* Trans. Robert Graves. New York: Farrar, Straus & Giroux, 1983.

GM   García Márquez, Gabriel. *One Hundred Years of Solitude.* Trans. Gregory Rabassa. New York: Avon, 1973.

GS   Apuleius. *On the God of Socrates.* AW 350–73.

HD   Bulgakov, Mikhail. *Heart of a Dog.* Trans. Mirra Ginsburg. New York: Grove Weidenfeld, 1968; rp. 1987.

HO   Homer. *The Odyssey.* Trans. Albert Cook. New York: Norton, 1974.

JH   Stevenson, Robert Louis. *The Strange Case of Dr. Jekyll and Mr. Hyde.* In *The Novels and Tales of Robert Louis Stevenson.* 27 vols. New York: Charles Scribners' Sons, 1902, 7:279–372.

KL   Keats, John. *The Letters of John Keats.* Ed. Hyder Edward Rollins. 2 vols. Cambridge: Harvard University Press, 1958.

KP   ———. *John Keats: Complete Poems.* Ed. Jack Stillinger. Cambridge: Harvard University Press, 1982.

L   Lucretius. *The Way Things Are: The De Rerum Natura of Titus Lucretius Carus.* Trans. Rolfe Humphries. Bloomington: Indiana University Press, 1969.

M   Kafka, Franz. *The Metamorphosis / Die Verwandlung*. Trans.
         Willa and Edwin Muir. New York: Schocken, 1948.

OH   Ovid. *The Metamorphoses*. Trans. Rolfe Humphries.
         Bloomington: Indiana University Press, 1968.

OS   Ovid. *Ovid's Metamorphosis Englished, Mythologized, and
         Represented in Figures by George Sandys* (1632). Ed. Karl
         K. Hulley and Stanley T. Vandersall. Lincoln: University
         of Nebraska Press, 1970.

P   Plato. *The Loeb Classical Library: Plato With an English
         Translation*. Cambridge: Harvard University Press.
         Phaedo, Phaedrus: vol. 1, trans. H. N. Fowler, 1960.
         Symposium: vol. 5, trans. W. R. M. Lamb, 1946.
         Timaeus: vol. 7, trans. R. G. Bury, 1952.

PL   Milton, John. *Paradise Lost*. 2nd ed. Ed. Scott Elledge. New
         York: Norton, 1993.

R   Plato. *The Republic*. Trans. Richard W. Sterling and William
         C. Scott. New York: Norton, 1985.

S   Shakespeare, William. *William Shakespeare: The Complete
         Works*. Ed. Alfred Harbage. Baltimore: Penguin, 1969.

SE   Freud, Sigmund. *The Standard Edition of the Complete
         Psychological Works of Sigmund Freud*. Ed. James
         Strachey et al. 23 vols. London: Hogarth Press, 1953–66.

TZ   Calvino, Italo. *t zero*. Trans. William Weaver. New York:
         Harvest/HBJ, 1969.

1. Writing as the Daemonic

"O Bottom, thou art changed! . . . Thou art translated!"
—*A Midsummer Night's Dream* 3.1.104–7

Of all the mythic occurrences to which literary characters can be subjected, bodily metamorphoses are at once the most drastic and the most typical. Mythic typicality places an allegorical frame around any literary metamorphic episode. For instance, although the precise significance of Gregor Samsa's transformation may be in doubt, we remain confident about the ultimate profundity of Kafka's *Metamorphosis*, just because it recalls the fate of so many other epic or Ovidian protagonists. In this sense alone, the *Metamorphosis* is an allegory of writing: it flaunts its own paradigmatic belatedness, its virtual location within the immeasurable line of metamorphic typology. Once Kafka chose to transpose a metamorphic fiction into the modern world, he could not go wrong, and the intrinsic comedy of his fable is bound up with the abiding literary instinct for miraculous transformation.[1]

Walter Benjamin associates baroque allegory with the melancholy of transcendental meaning and historical time: "In allegory," writes Benjamin (1985) with reference to the German *Trauerspiel*, "the observer is confronted with the *facies hippocratica* of history as a petrified, primordial landscape. Everything about history that, from the very beginning, has been untimely, sorrowful, unsuccessful, is expressed in a face—or rather in a death's head" (166).[2] The ludicrous juxtapositions of minds and bodies in metamorphic stories such as Kafka's complicate this scheme, however, for these narratives present parodic revisions or travesties of epic and theological solemnities. Whereas a mythic or scriptural metamorphosis may be the occasion for an awesome epiphany or revelation of the sacred, a literary metamorphosis cannot be taken completely seriously. Its manifest absurdity is already the most reliable indicator of allegorical irony, urging the reader to reconstruct the particular pretexts undergoing parodic transformation.

This is not to say that literary metamorphoses have nothing serious to tell us. On the contrary, fictive transformations of human bodies can represent the most dire and literal human issues. Embedded in the changes of Lucius, Bottom, Lamia, Dr. Jekyll,

1

and Gregor Samsa are grave matters of gender construction and sexual conflict; familial and class identity; economic, social, and cosmological structures; moral affects and intellectual ideals. The aim of this study is to codify and interrelate these levels of meaning in metamorphic stories. Still, all such material and spiritual significances are folded into and doubled over the ostensibly nonsensical surface of the fiction. Literary metamorphoses powerfully play upon the essential and potentially tragic disjunctiveness of allegorical form. They make the interfusion of sense and nonsense their textual sport.

This interfusion of the meaningless and the meaningful is also the condition of language, especially when it is set forth in the graphic body of writing. The transformation of spoken language or visual images *into* writing prefigures all the other transformations carried out by and in writing. The structural model of the sign as a composite of signifier and signified can be used to indicate the fundamental reciprocity of allegory and metamorphosis. To read a text as an allegory produces an inner transformation of its meaning, a substitution of signifieds, whereas the event of a bodily metamorphosis depicts an outer transformation, a substitution of signifiers. An allegory enforces a semantic or thematic translation of the lexical sense of a text; a metamorphosis brings about the literal rewriting of a character on the model of verbal translation from one language into another.

The critical recuperation of allegory that has taken its main impetus from the work of Benjamin has focused especially on its writing-like or scriptive character: "at one stroke the profound vision of allegory transforms things and works into stirring writing" (Benjamin 1985, 176). Insofar as translation is a paradigm of writing in general, metamorphosis in literature may be read as an allegory of writing and its effects—reading, (mis)interpretation, figuration, intertextual transmission, and so forth. The metamorphic changes represented within texts are allegories of the metamorphic changes *of* texts. Characters that produce or endure bodily metamorphoses personify the intermediary power of verbal translation, the powers of written scripts to bridge the gaps among dead and living languages and societies. Agents with metamorphic powers intervene in strange locales and foreign languages, cross over into alien registers. Similarly, elements in translated texts cross over verbal and cultural barriers, at the expense of the prior language and other formal qualities of the prior text. Yet metamorphic stories are eminently translatable. Fictions of bodily transformation retain their symbolic powers despite the alterations of the signifiers that narrate them.[3]

A literary metamorphosis typically exploits the mistakes and misrecognitions attending reading and writing. In the *Golden Ass*, the protagonist Lucius's metamorphosis into an ass instead of a bird immediately results from his girlfriend Fotis's misreading of the jars containing Pamphile's magical ointments. In *A Midsummer Night's Dream*, Puck transforms the affections of the quarreling lovers when he mistakes the "Athenian weeds" that render Demetrius interchangeable with Lysander, and Bottom's metamorphosis into a "monster" occurs in close proximity to Puck's comic "misprision." In both of these tales as well, the agent of metamorphosis is an elixir or *pharmakon,* as in Plato's famous metaphor for the ambivalent powers of writing. Near the end of the *Phaedrus,* Socrates relates that Thoth was the creator of numbers and arithmetic, geometry and astronomy, games of chance, as well as writing (§274d). Thoth submits his inventions to Ammon, to receive the Father's sign of approval. In defense of writing, Thoth tropes it as a *pharmakon.* Writing will be a miracle cure: "This invention, O king . . . will make the Egyptians wiser and will improve their memories; for it is an elixir of memory and wisdom that I have discovered" (*P* §274e). However, Ammon withholds his approval and declares that this drug will turn into a poison, deadening rather than spurring the memory, reducing living, inner wisdom to dead, outer simulacra (§274e–75b). Plato's metaphor of writing as a *pharmakon* is intended to structure values logocentrically, that is, to privilege insides over outsides. Yet as Derrida shows, the (non)virtue of the shifty *pharmakon* is to be indeterminate with regard both to its effect and to its position, neither entirely outside nor entirely inside.

The Greek counterpart of Thoth is Hermes, the most manifestly daemonic of the Olympian divinities. Hermes's proper attributes as a herald, messenger, guardian, and guide, an intermediary, as a secondary or filial term proclaiming an Other's (parental) word, parallel the standardized attributes of daemons in general. In the *Homeric Hymn to Hermes*, his innate talents include the gift of metamorphosis, which he uses to pass through a keyhole, to cross over stealthily from outside to inside after stealing Apollo's cattle, and the gift of persuasion, which he then uses to move Zeus to wink at his theft.[4] Both Thoth and Hermes are patrons of reading and writing, and accordingly, both bear a *pharmakon.* In Book 10 of the *Odyssey,* at Zeus's behest Hermes delivers to Odysseus the herb Moly, an antidote to protect him against Circe's metamorphic charm. Derrida notes some other parallels between Hermes and Thoth, not the least of which is their both being gods of death. "Like his Greek counterpart, Hermes,

whom Plato moreover never mentions, [Thoth] occupies the role of
messenger-god, of clever intermediary, ingenious and subtle enough
to steal, and always to steal away. The signifier-god."[5] Hermes has
a similar genius for impropriety, and comes to oversee a number of
disreputable agents and activities, stealthy operators and their acts:
thieves, merchants, alchemists, lovers, sophists, and rhetoricians,
and their economic, sexual, and linguistic commerce.[6]

In *A Midsummer Night's Dream,* Puck is not only the Cupid,
he is the Hermes, the metamorphic trickster of the text. Upon his
entrance, Puck tells us that he operates by means of the "slip":
"The wisest aunt, telling the saddest tale, / Sometime for three-foot
stool mistaketh me; / Then slip I from her bum, down topples she"
(*S* 2.1.51–53).[7] And when Oberon sends him to fetch the flower
"love-in-idleness" to concoct a love potion, Puck aligns with Hermes/
Thoth as the deliverer of a *pharmakon.* Moreover, the potion Puck
administers to Lysander, Demetrius, and Titania derives from the
mock-Ovidian metamorphosis of "a little western flower," upon which
fell an erotic daemonic power, "the bolt of Cupid" (2.1.166,165).[8]
The bearer of this *pharmakon* is a splendid figure for the aggressive comedy of metamorphic misprision.

John Keats's *Lamia* specifically concerns a triangle of stealthy
characters, and it brings the figure of Hermes together explicitly
with the story of a human metamorph. To motivate his Lamia
story, Keats conjures up the figure of Hermes and sends him in
search of an invisible nymph:

> . . . The ever-smitten Hermes empty left
> His golden throne, bent warm on amorous theft:
> From high Olympus had he stolen light
> On this side of Jove's clouds, to escape the sight
> Of his great summoner, and made retreat
> Into a forest on the shores of Crete. (*KP* 1.7–12)

Keats's image has Hermes already in stealthy flight, fleeing subservi-
ence to the Father, flying to the place of desire. "Hermes is constantly
underway: he is *enodios* ('by the road') and *hodios* ('belonging to a
journey'), and one encounters him on every path."[9] Keats's emphasis
on "amorous theft" is doubly accurate: Hermes was often found in
league with Aphrodite, to the point of virtual fusion in the figure of
Hermaphroditus. Hermes's association with a mythic androgyne underscores the propriety by which Keats brings Hermes forward as a
patron of transgressive and indeterminate erotic relations.

Reading Hermes's myth (in Keats's retelling) as an allegory of
writing, we find the dispossessed signified sliding away (the aban-

donment of the Father's word), as Hermes assumes primacy, asserts and enacts the arbitrary agency of the signifier, chasing desire down and along the syntagmatic chain. The patron of interpreters (*hermenes*) and textual intermediation (hermeneutics), Hermes oversees the script, as Hermes the guardian and guide of the dead oversees the crypt. Hermes the messenger personifies the medium of symbolic transmissions. Jane Harrison has drawn out the opposition in the figure of Hermes between the winged messenger and the ponderous, phallic stone Herm, "a rude pillar later surmounted by a head," to the point that a late-ancient fable "makes the god himself voice the dilemma: was he a tombstone, was he an immortal?"[10] Hermes's dual roles as a tombstone and a guide of departed souls are both underwritten by the circulatory structure of the linguistic sign: the signifier marks the spot where the signified died and entered the (s)crypt.[11] A suppresser or translator of semantic proprieties, an agent that ferries psyches or transfers unbound essences from one realm to another, that binds the dead to death, Hermes also personifies the trope—the brilliant, mercurial transfer of image and meaning from one term to another, from one order of signification to another. Counter to the Apollonian ideal of proper metaphor and the "light of truth," Hermes's genius concerns shady rhetoric: linguistic stealth, imposed allegoresis, verbal and graphic trickery, business contracts, skill at the oath. "Hermes is the master of the magic formulae which bind" (Brown 1969, 14).

Hermes knows the road to Hades; Keats at one point names him "the star of Lethe" (1.81). Following the aegis of Hermes, allegory goes to Hell. No trope can avoid some element of semantic impropriety; in this shifting light the trope is a potential curse, a stealthy appropriation of the essences of terms by other terms and the holding down of terms by other terms. A furtive trickster and thief, Hermes presides over the metempsychoses of linguistic agents, the displacements of semantic values. He grants illicit possessive desires; he promotes shady transfers.[12] Furthermore, the congruence in mythic personification between Hermes and Thoth underscores the daemonic status, the metamorphic nature of writing as such. In Derrida's exposition of Thoth as a figure for the filial, secondary, anti-authoritative or subversive position of writing in relation to the primary paternity of the spoken logos, Thoth personifies writing as daemonic. As scapegoat (*pharmakos*), wandering outcast, or stealthy outsider, the metamorph exemplifies the status of writing within a logocentric system.[13] Metamorphs such as Lucius, Lamia, or Mr. Hyde, are all hermetic characters met along the street or by the roadside.

Some literary metamorphoses emblematize their textuality simply by literalizing the *pharmakon*, reifying the agent of metamorphosis as something eaten or absorbed: the magical ointment Fotis misapplies to Lucius, or the juice of the flower "love-in-idleness" Puck uses to doctor the affections of the Athenian teenagers in *A Midsummer Night's Dream*.[14] In the *Strange Case of Dr. Jekyll and Mr. Hyde*, Jekyll's transcendental potion is also a textual trope. Its chromatic "turning" is an allegory of writing as metamorphosis. Stevenson describes the potion with an emphasis on what Dr. Lanyon literally terms the "metamorphoses" produced by its manufacture: "The mixture, which was at first of a reddish hue, began, in proportion as the crystals melted, to brighten in colour, to effervesce audibly, and to throw off small fumes of vapour. Suddenly and at the same moment, the ebullition ceased and the compound changed to a dark purple, which faded again more slowly to a watery green" (*JH* 347). Keats's invention of the Hermes episode that begins *Lamia* already marks it with a daemonic signifier, and the allegory of writing in the poem extends from Hermes to the character of Lamia herself. In traditional criticism, Lamia has often been taken as a figure for "literary romance" representing Keats's increasingly ambivalent attitude toward "the faery way of writing." Wandering from place to place and from body to body, the unfathered, unfathomable Lamia is a figure for any written discourse detached from its author and imposed upon by an interpretive authority—a dispossessed subject under the spell of another's word. Apollonius's final banishment of Lamia resonates with the Platonic demotion of writing in the *Phaedrus* and, more specifically, the exiling of Poetry in the *Republic*.

In the *Golden Ass*, a prominent anecdote early in the narrative dramatizes the linguistic dimension of literary metamorphosis. In a comic digression from the main plot of Lucius's metamorphic career, a character named Thelyphron gets mugged by a metonymy. First of all, as a center of mockery Thelyphron introduces Lucius's forthcoming role in the Festival of Laughter: both are the butt of cruel jesting, Thelyphron among the guests at one of Byrrhaena's banquets for having been beset upon and disfigured by Thessalian witches. A guest explains, "a fellow whose name I needn't mention got dreadfully bitten about the face by that hell pack" (*GA* 41). With this ironic glance at the speaker's name, commanded by Byrrhaena to deliver Lucius his story, Thelyphron begins. Once, when traveling through Larissa, he was so broke that he took a job guarding a corpse against nocturnal desecration. Although during the night he fell asleep, when he awoke the next day both he and the corpse seemed to be unmolested and Thelyphron collected his wage. But that afternoon during the last summons over the corpse, a grieving uncle accused the widow of poisoning her husband.

At this point an Egyptian necromancer proposed to solve the murder mystery by summoning the husband's shade back into his body, which could then testify in its own behalf. Soon enough, the corpse stirred and cried out accusations against the wife. It went on to explain that marauding witches had cast a sleeping spell on the student hired to stand guard, and had then called out the dead man's name—Thelyphron: "when they called: 'Thelyphron, Thelyphron, come!' he . . . offered his face for the mutilation that they intended for mine; and they nibbled off first his nose and then his ears." The living Thelyphron then confesses to Lucius, "I clapped my hand to my face . . . and my nose fell off; then I touched my ears, and they fell off too" (50). Byrrhaena's banquet bursts into laughter.[15]

Apuleius leaves the story of Thelyphron hanging there. Its purpose is not to indict the murderous wife's infidelity but to foreshadow Lucius's coming transformation. Thelyphron's "loss of face" adumbrates Lucius's own embarrassment, his total bodily dispossession by metamorphosis into an ass. With Thelyphron the occasion of transformative disfiguration is explicitly linguistic. He learns to his chagrin that he and the corpse he had contracted to guard have the same name.[16] Thus to his mortification, Thelyphron has been traduced by an adjacent signifier, double-crossed by the very arbitrariness of the vehicle of his own identity. Along with his wage, Thelyphron inherits another's physical misfortune. Some hermetic trickster positioned Thelyphron's name so that his person becomes a daemonic figure or allegorical vehicle for a corpse.

The linguistic counterpart of the spoken name is the written signature. Both are signifiers of proper identity and of the "propriety" by which one lays claim to personal possessions and social prestige. *Jekyll and Hyde* deploys a series of episodes in which socioeconomic motifs are woven into scenes of writing, particularly the writing of signatures. In Mr. Hyde the economic and the grammatological subtexts of the story collide.[17] Hyde is a walking chiasmus, an obscure crossroads, generated at the intersection where Dr. Jekyll in metamorphic disguise crosses and is crossed by a defenseless female. In the first chapter, "Story of the Door," Enfield recounts to Utterson an odd scene he had witnessed. It seems a "little man" had callously trampled a young girl who happened across his path from a "cross street" (284). Enfield had grabbed the malefactor, and the girl's indignant family demanded a sum of money. Enfield followed this throng to a back-alley doorway:

The next thing was to get the money; and where do you
think he carried us but to that place with the door?—
whipped out a key, went in, and presently came back
with the matter of ten pounds in gold and a cheque for
the balance . . . drawn payable to bearer and signed with
a name that I can't mention, though it's one of the points
of my story. . . . Yes, it's a bad story. For my man was a
fellow that nobody could have to do with, a really damnable man; and the person that drew the cheque is the
very pink of the proprieties. (285–86)

In the signature, writing coincides with a sign of personal
identity, a sign that can be either legitimately or illicitly dupli-
cated. In a practical context, fixing a signature to a financial document transforms personal identity into economic identity, producing
a tilt into the fluid indifferentiation of circulating currency. Checks
drawn on banks function when the bank credits the signature of
the drawer. But here, given the discrepancy between the bearer, a
"damnable man," and the unseen, as yet unnamed drawer, Enfield
is doubtful about the authenticity of the signature. The problem
Stevenson is proposing here may be stated: how can the signature
of someone who is not self-identical be credited? Hyde holds a check
on which two names are inscribed—one general sign of mobile
identity ("Bearer") and one signature of proper identity ("Jekyll").
Ostensibly this or any check authorizes a transfer of capital from
one account to another. However, in this case it authorizes a dubious circulation of the soul's gold from the official books of public
identity to a private slush fund. Through this business with the
check, Stevenson has already sketched out the actual state of affairs with Jekyll, as it will be unfolded by Utterson: Dr. Jekyll is
doctoring his own books, having set up a phony body, a dummy
corporation in the name of Edward Hyde. Jekyll has rigged his own
spiritual accounts, to secure illicit pleasures without incurring the
moral debts demanded by his conscientious economy.

The device of the dubious signature recurs several times once
Utterson sets out to get to the bottom of Jekyll's problems. In the
"Incident of the Letter" following the murder of Sir Danver Carew,
Utterson confronts Jekyll and speaks more truly than he yet knows,
asking, "You have not been mad enough to hide this fellow?" (311)
Jekyll responds by producing a letter

written in an odd, upright hand and signed "Edward
Hyde": and it signified, briefly enough, that the writer's
benefactor, Dr. Jekyll, whom he had long so unworthily

repaid for a thousand generosities, need labour under no alarm for his safety, as he had means of escape on which he placed a sure dependence. The lawyer liked this letter well enough. . . .

"Have you the envelope?" he asked.

"I burned it," replied Jekyll, "before I thought what I was about. But it bore no postmark. The note was handed in." (312)

But when Utterson asks who handed in the letter, the butler informs him that no messenger had appeared. Later Utterson shows a graphologist the "murderer's autograph" (314), Hyde's signature on the letter produced by Jekyll, and Jekyll's own signature. The expert compares them: "Well, . . . there's a rather singular resemblance; the two hands are in many points identical; only differently sloped" (315). Utterson jumps but lands just short of the proper conclusion: "'What!' he thought. 'Henry Jekyll forge for a murderer!'" (315)

The crucial detail here is an absence, the absence of the envelope in which a letter genuinely "handed in" would have arrived. Both signatures were in fact written by the same hand, and consequently there was no need of an envelope, an outer covering, upon which to inscribe the names of sender and receiver. There was no need of an actual conveyance between two persons, for in fact, both Jekyll and Hyde reside within the same envelope, and take turns "writing the signature" on that envelope. Ultimately, in *Jekyll and Hyde* the allegory of writing resolves into handwriting, handwritten texts, the material medium of Jekyll's and Hyde's shared identity, or duplicity: "Nor must I delay too long to bring my writing to an end," we read in the last paragraph of the story; "Should the throes of change take me in the act of writing it, Hyde will tear it in pieces" (371–72). So when Jekyll remarked earlier of the fictive envelope in which the forged letter from Mr. Hyde had supposedly arrived, "I burned it," he also named in a figure the implied fate of his bodily person. It, too, is a nonexistent or interminably deferred envelope, that has fallen from being into writing, where it suffers the "throes of change."

Letters call for envelopes, some outer conveyance to envelop their inner content. Spiritual messages require material vehicles, but the agents transporting those messages may not deliver them properly. As message-carrying agencies, in related but distinct ways, writing and allegory both operate according to the logic of the supplement.[18] Written texts can be misappropriated, altered, misdelivered, or misconstrued. At the intersection of allegory and

metamorphosis, the inevitable slippages sustained by the supplementary and vehicular status of writing are reified *in the form of
the daemonic*. The mythopoetic realm of the daemonic depicts intermediation and transformation within a complexly communicat-
ing cosmos. The daemonic status of writing is personified through
messenger figures who may either act as the herald—the representative signifier—for an Other, or assert independent agency. Structurally considered, the intermediary realm of the daemonic is this
very oscillation between majority and minority, primary and secondary status, autonomous and delegated action. Angel or devil, as
a figure of communication the daemon is a supplementary agent,
a personified message moving rapidly through space and across
borders: thus it is depicted as winged.[19] Consider Diotima's description of Eros as a daemon in Plato's *Symposium*: Eros is "a great
spirit, Socrates: the whole of the spiritual [τὸ δαιμόνιον] is between
divine and mortal . . . interpreting and transporting human things
to the gods and divine things to men; entreaties and sacrifices from
below, and ordinances and requitals from above: being midway
between, it makes each to supplement [συμπληροῖ] the other, so
that the whole is combined in one" (*P* §202e).[20]

My treatment of the daemonic closely follows Fletcher's (1964)
philological excavation and recovery of this ancient theological term
for allegory theory. "Daemons, as I shall define them, share this major
characteristic of allegorical agents, the fact that they compartmental-
ize function" (40). Fletcher brings the daemonic forward as a textual
and rhetorical form of "possession," that aspect of allegorical apparatus that exerts structural power over and so determines the possible
range of an agent's activity. In literature, "the increase of daemonic
control over the character amounts to an intensification of the allegory. It is striking that this progress in abstraction is accompanied by
an increased importance given to the name . . . to name a person is to
fix his function irrevocably" (49–50). The "supernatural" or metamorphic force of the daemonic is thus anti- or trans-organic: "Constriction
of meaning, when it is the limit put upon a personified force or power,
causes that personification to act somewhat mechanistically. The perfect allegorical agent is not a man possessed by a daemon, but a robot"
(55). The contemporary daemonic is thus clearly evident in the elabo-
ration of post-organic creatures such as cyborgs, but this note of on-
tological transgression is deeply rooted in traditional ideas of the
daemon: "Daemonic forces thus become participants is the cosmic
drama of man versus god, almost as if the daemons were the relationships, personified, of man to god. To the extent that he follows this
intermediary pattern, the allegorical agent is not quite human, and
not quite godlike, but shares something of both states" (61).

With regard to its allegorical function, the daemon typically bears a message with a moral content—good or evil whispering to the human soul. As transmitted by Platonic allegory, the mythic divinity Eros becomes the model for Socrates's daemon—a message-bearing demigod on the order of Hermes. In the *Phaedrus*, forced to advance Lysias's disgraceful thesis that one should prefer a "non-lover" to someone under the genuine sway of Eros, Socrates veils himself, ironically dramatizing his sense of shame with the implication that his sign of conscience is on the alert well before he explicitly mentions it: "When I was about to cross the stream, the spirit and the sign [τὸ δαιμόνιόν τε καὶ το εἰωθὸς σημεῖόν] that usually comes to me came—it always holds me back from something I am about to do—and I thought I heard a voice from it which forbade my going away before clearing my conscience, as if I had committed some sin against deity" (*P* §242b–c). Socrates's phrasing places the daemonic and the semiotic into apposition.

In his playfully lyrical daemonological tract *On the God of Socrates,* Apuleius develops the sense of the daemonic as a signification of the moral psyche: "The poets, from this multitude of demons, are accustomed, in a way by no means remote from the truth, to feign the Gods to be haters and lovers of certain men, and to give prosperity and promotion to some, and to oppose and afflict others. Hence, they are influenced by pity, moved by indignation, racked with vexation, elated with joy, and are subject to all the affections of the human mind; and are agitated by all the fluctuations of human thought, with similar commotions of the spirit and agitations of the feelings. All which storms and tempests are far alien from the tranquil state of the celestial Gods" (*GS* 360–61). As a buffer between the human and the divine, the "middle nature" of the daemonic is an allegorical defense of the divine from its mishandling by poetic visionaries who portray celestial gods as susceptible to human desires.[21] Such a vision of the daemonic is a certain response to monotheistic moral pressures. But when the divine is redefined as beyond affective values, that very exclusion produces an identification of the daemonic with human affectivity.

The daemonic is nothing if not equivocal. The ethereal and aerial realm of daemons is poised between heaven and earth; although immortal like the highest gods, daemons are affected like mortals, subject to passion. Daemons are "capable, just as we are, of being affected by all that soothes as well as all that moves the mind" (362). Both humans and daemons are moved by feelings: passionate daemons behave like mortal persons, passionate persons turn into daemons. Without dogmatic Platonic moralization, Apuleius has translated the Platonic daemonic into an affective psychology. Now comes the crucial turn in Apuleius's account: "According to a certain signification, the human soul, even when it is still situate in the body, is called a demon" (*GS* 363). And when Apuleius arrives at the "god" of Socrates in particular, he makes explicit the psychological connection between the daemonic and the moral imagination.[22] The daemonic according to Apuleius intersects with the uncanny according to psychoanalysis. The daemon is a "divine sign," the superego or parental letter in the unconscious, the script of the conscience. The allotted daemon is a magical double, reconceived here on the model of the myth of Er in the *Republic* as an impartial representative before a divine bar:

> Plato is of the opinion that a peculiar demon is allotted to every man, to be a witness and a guardian of his conduct in life, who, without being visible to any one, is always present, and is an overseer not only of his actions, but even of his thoughts. But when life is finished, and THE SOUL has to return *to its judges*, then the demon who has presided over it immediately seizes, and leads it as his charge to judgment. . . . The demon scrupulously takes part in all these matters, sees all things, understands all things, and dwells in the most profound recesses of the mind, in the place of conscience. (*GS* 365)

On the God of Socrates is thus a psychological rhapsody on the allotted daemon as moral signifier. With regard to Socrates and his *daimon,* Apuleius had just mentioned a passage from the *Phaedrus*: "Once, for example, when he was with Phaedrus, beyond the precincts of the city, under the covering of a shady tree, and at a distance from all onlookers, he perceived a sign which announced to him that he must not pass over the small stream of the river Ilissus, until he had appeased Love, who was indignant at his censure of him, by a recantation" (369). Apuleius, the ironic amorist of the *Golden Ass*, points to a moment when a daemonic sign, the advocate of Socrates's conscience, comes not to prosecute but to defend the powers of Eros.

However, the term d(a)emon—as its unstable orthography indicates—has become a discursive vehicle overloaded with incompatible tenors, complexly weighted with Western cultural freight, and sustaining wide changes in meaning over at least three millennia of currency (see Fletcher 1964, 41–48). The use of "demon" to mean "evil spirit" is "a Jewish application of the Greek word, anterior to Christianity" (*OED*). In Judeo-Christian culture, Eros is suppressed or infantilized and the daemonic splits off into angels as heralds of the divine and devils as agents of evil. Ambivalence is incorporated into the pagan idea of a daemon as a being situated between the human and the divine, whereas in Judeo-Christian usage, that positional ambiguity is polarized and an unbridgeable chasm set up between heaven and hell, good and evil. Discussing Augustine's pivotal role in the codification of Christian theology, Barkan notes that his treatment of demons is especially connected to ideas of metamorphosis. For Augustine, "the demonic explanation of metamorphosis is both satisfying and significant. It locates metamorphosis in that special realm where the pagan and Christian traditions intersect, that of the ancient gods who were permitted to survive as demons or fallen angels. . . . Demons are intrinsically metamorphic" (Barkan 1986, 99–100).

As such, the daemonic is also intrinsically allegorical: it personifies the supplementary status of allegorical meaning. Moreover, its structural role of cosmic intermediation parallels allegory's historical role of cultural intermediation, as between Christian moral authority and its problematic pagan inheritance. In the early nineteenth century, while participating in the Romantic demotion of neoclassical allegory relative to the aesthetics of the symbol, Goethe provided pagan allegory with some discursive shelter by resuscitating the term "daemonic" with its intermediary, aleatory, and mischievous nature intact: "It was not divine, for it seemed without reason; not human, for it had no understanding; not diabolical, for it was beneficent; not angelic, for it took pleasure in mischief. It resembled chance, in that it manifested no consequence; it was like Providence, for it pointed toward connection. All that restricts us seemed for it penetrable; it seemed to deal arbitrarily with the necessary elements of our existence; it contracted time and expanded space. It seemed to find pleasure only in the impossible and to reject the possible with contempt. To this entity, which seemed to intervene between all others, to separate them and yet to link them together, I gave the name daemonic, after the example of the ancients."[23]

Anticipating Goethe's Romantic reinscription of the pagan daemonic, Shakespeare's *A Midsummer Night's Dream* both reawakens and mocks the daemonic realm of metamorphic allegory. The relation between Oberon, the King of the Fairies, and Puck, his underling and prankster, parodies that of Zeus and Hermes, the Godfather and the Son/Messenger, as well as the paternalism for which they stand. But the more parodic the daemonic becomes, the more strongly it may be translated from mythic detachment into material significance. The manifest silliness of such characters gives them a kind of cover under which to

carry powerful and serious contents. Oberon and Puck have several
scenes where they expound the distinctions among daemonic orders. Puck declares, "yonder shines Aurora's harbinger; / At whose
approach, ghosts, wand'ring here and there, / Troop home to church-
yards: damnèd spirits all, / That in crossways and floods have
burial"; Oberon's cryptic reply, "But we are spirits of another sort"
(3.2.380–88), is perhaps not so cryptic, if by this remark Oberon
posits himself and Puck as spirits of the text, literary daemons.
The fairy realm emerges in Shakespeare's metamorphic farce as an
imaginary supplement needed to resolve the real human dilemmas.
In the allegorical construction of *A Midsummer Night's Dream* the
most profound level of cultural interpretation is to be found at the
extremities of the fairy nonsense.[24]

> *Puck*. How now, spirit! Whither wander you?
> *Fairy*. Over hill, over dale,
>   Thorough bush, thorough brier,
> Over park, over pale,
>   Thorough flood, thorough fire;
> I do wander everywhere,
>   Swifter than the moon's sphere . . .
> —*A Midsummer Night's Dream* (2.1.1–7)

"I do wander everywhere": the Fairy personifies pure
(mytho)poesis, the interminable movement of meaning through
contingent sequences of signs. By sounding the scale of nature, the
Fairy's song begins to orchestrate Shakespeare's comic vision of
prolific eros. But it also figures as ironic backdrop for Bottom's
mock-monstrous interlude, in that it alludes to another, peculiarly
unstable, "watery" figure of transformation, Proteus, with his virtue of passing elusively through long series of forms: "Hold him
struggling there, though he be violent to escape. / He will try it by
becoming all the many creatures / That move on the earth; and
then water, and divinely kindled fire" (*HO* 4.416–18). Conveyed
through this daemonic being, the phases of Proteus mirror the
metamorphic movements of allegory, the metaphoric carrying of
sense over and away from vehicle to vehicle.

The meta-writing by which literal signs are transposed into
literary figures is doubly daemonic. Tropes are occasions for semantic clash and overload, unstable and reversible relations, a
potential strife of agencies within the same scene. The tenor of a
figure may have predicated to it an infinite series of vehicles; but
any vehicle, once inducted, may overturn the original tenor. Figuration turns daemonic when the vehicle will not stay put but

overmasters the tenor, or when the tenor is already the vehicle for a previous tenor, to the detriment of the new vehicle. The play of figuration turns grave when signs and persons become interchangeable and the one proceeds to eliminate the other.[25] Reflecting on the trope of personification, Steven Knapp comments, "if personifications are animated through the intensification of metaphor (or more precisely, through the intensification of a metaphoric vehicle at the expense of its supposed 'tenor'), then mimetic agents may have a converse tendency to slide 'back' into metaphor (that is, the agent may turn out to be the vehicle of a previously unsuspected or forgotten tenor). The reversibility of personifications thus makes the boundary between rhetoric and agency less secure than it might have seemed."[26]

> *Quince.* Ay. Or else one must come in with a bush of thorns and a lantern, and say he comes to disfigure, or to present, the person of Moonshine. (3.1.51–3)

> * * *

> *Bottom.* Some man or other must present Wall; and let him have some plaster, or some loam, or some roughcast about him, to signify wall. (3.1.59–61)

> * * *

> *Wall.* In this same interlude it doth befall
> That I, one Snout by name, present a wall . . . .
> This loam, this roughcast, and this stone doth show
> That I am that same wall: the truth is so . . . .
> *Theseus.* Would you desire lime and hair to speak better?
> *Demetrius.* It is the wittiest partition that ever I heard
> discourse, my lord. (5.1.154–66)

In these passages, as if to underwrite the connection between the two devices, Shakespeare inserts a wry burlesque of allegorical personification into his pointed comedy of daemonic metamorphosis. Fixing themselves into a structure of emblematic props, so as to "disfigure the persons" of Wall and Moonshine, Bottom's ingenuous companions undergo comically grotesque mock-metamorphoses, reverse personifications in which clowns are transformed into ludicrous signifiers. Theseus and Demetrius, the play's own readers of these motley allegories, would interpellate the audience into their system of values with light ironic commentary, Theseus with a humorous personification, Demetrius with a pun. The larger point underscored by these passages is that the allegorical metamorph is a reverse or transposed personification, not the poetic animation of an abstraction but the fantastic fixation of a person within an alien structure of signs.[27]

In an allegorical personification or a personified abstraction, a scenic or inanimate tenor is joined to or replaced by a vehicle denoting some quality or property of an agent. To couple an abstract, inanimate tenor to an animate vehicle augments the tenor, compounds its connotative value by "bringing it to life."[28] But when a human agent is designated as the tenor for which a scenic vehicle is substituted, that meaning can be captured, trapped by the trope, "possessed" by the vehicle such that the tenor, the realm of the agent, as a result of the allegory, is dispossessed by and reduced to the arbitrariness of a signifier. The daemonic origin of the metamorph thus encodes the structural determination of the human subject. Myths of the daemon simply displace and repeat the catastrophic origin of the subject. If persons as social agents are constituted through and on the model of signifiers within sign systems (for instance, as tokens distributed within a kinship system), then there is no guaranteeing that some Other won't deploy them improperly, as metaphors, and thus exchange their literal identities for fictive figures, or simply rewrite them according to some other script. The human psyche is simultaneously set up and overturned by a rhetorical betrayal.

Thus myths of divine origin are supplemented by counter-myths of demonic corruption. In patriarchal epics, for instance, presumptuous females are variously portrayed as either the agent or the dupe of the daemonic. Placed next to Satan beside the Tree of Knowledge, Eve becomes an everlasting metonymy of the daemon. Yet the story that regards woman's creation in the first place as an afterthought, a secondary and belated performance, has already stigmatized the female as daemonic—a shifty, transformative supplement disrupting a prior, proper ratio. In Book 10 of *Paradise Lost,* when Milton's Satan takes credit for Adam's fall, he testifies as well to Eve's seduction with a *pharmakon,* an apple with a curse upon it:

> ". . . I found
> The new-created World, which fame in Heaven
> Long had foretold, a fabric wonderful,
> Of absolute perfection; therein Man,
> Placed in a paradise, by our exile
> Made happy. Him by fraud I have seduced
> From his Creator, and, the more to increase

Your wonder, with an apple! He, thereat
Offended—worth your laughter!—hath given up,
Both his beloved Man and all his World,
To Sin and Death a prey. . . ." (*PL* 10.480–90)

In *Paradise Lost,* Satan is the daemonic agent as "uninvited
guest," the "stranger in the house" of God's newest creation.[29] His
figure personifies the persuasive charms of allegorical displacement:
intruding upon the literal intentions of God's and Adam's previous
namings, Satan imposes the persuasive fictions ("you will be like
God") that Eve will accept as motives, corrupts literal ingenuous-
ness with figurative duplicity, and so dispossesses humanity of its
proper birthright. Eve believed a lie, but then, how was she to
know the difference between Satan's lie and God's truth without
tasting of the tree of knowledge? Just as allegorical figures disguise
their proper meanings, daemonic agents gravitate to scenes of oscillation between ignorance and knowledge. The questions of literal
belief and poetic faith produced by the "fluctuations" of allegorical
personifications are thoughtfully raised by Steven Knapp (1985):

> In one sense, the energy with which [personifications]
> shift from one mode of representation to another is the
> measure of their peculiar power. But such mutability,
> however pronounced in personifications, is a property that
> may spread, as if by contagion, to other, ostensibly more
> "literal" agents, as the example of Satan reveals. Not
> only does Satan, for all his psychological complexity,
> remain to some extent a theologically precise representa-
> tion of evil; but, just as the allegorical content of a
> personification can seem to dissipate, leaving a relatively
> opaque and independent agent, so Milton frequently al-
> lows psychology to lapse as Satan—suitably shrunken,
> enlarged, or otherwise transformed—freezes into em-
> blematic fixity. The result is sometimes a grotesque
> surprise, as in Satan's metamorphosis into a serpent.
> (59–60)

However, these interpretive questions are compounded with
regard to the reading of literary metamorphs. The interpretation of
Satan's character is complicated by the sanction Christian doctrine
provides to consider Satan somehow "literally real" in contrast for
instance to Milton's Sin and Death, which are never mistaken for
mimetic agents. But one can acknowledge the reality of evil without having to grant the literal or actual personhood of Satan. As a

catastrophically fallen angel, a daemon (not a human) to begin with, the figure of Satan is already a moralized trope. The interval between his expulsion from heaven and his metamorphosis into a serpent is drawn out sufficiently to enable him to include the New World in the orbit of his Fall. So Satan's metamorphosis proper does not inaugurate a metamorphic narrative, but terminates a demonic interlude with an emblem of judgment.[30] Satan's metamorphosis has the "emblematic fixity" Knapp observes because Milton has now detached his figure from the human action:

> His visage drawn he felt to sharp and spare,
> His arms clung to his ribs, his legs entwining
> Each other, till supplanted down he fell
> A monstrous serpent on his belly prone . . . .
> (*PL* 10.511–14)

As opposed to the figure of Satan, allegorical metamorphs like Lucius, Lamia, and Gregor, although they could not be more fictitious, are never frozen into emblematic fixity. This is itself a measure of their success as fictions. These narratives slip beyond the linear translations of dogmatic moralization to produce the "opacity" necessary for real characterization, for persuasive fictions of personhood. The metamorphic body is virtually ironic: a strong metamorph is cryptic, never transparent. At the least, for a literary metamorphosis to succeed, the metamorph must resist symbolical recuperation and remain opaque. Otherwise, the metamorphic defense collapses entirely, and the metamorph gets reabsorbed into some collective structure. Unless a metamorph gets up and walks away with the abstraction that would nail it down, it devolves into a moral personification of that abstraction.

Metamorphic allegories typically bear the mark of a daemonic supplement, the sign of an improper secondary. Stories of human metamorphosis trace a circuitous play of indetermination and intermediation between agents and terms positioned in proportions of proper to improper, primary to secondary—gods and humans, humans and beasts, masters and slaves, parents and children, males and females, literal and figurative meanings. A son's or a daughter's inscription can trace in the paradoxes of the filial position the fault lines that undermine central or primary terms. Kafka's fables amply demonstrate these structural dynamics. In his texts, traditional archetypes undergo a daemonic rupture from dogmatic significations. Allegorical types emerge in Kafka's text not merely as merciful clues to a hermetic signification. He positions them there and then operates upon them, or springs them open.[31]

The *Metamorphosis* is only the most obvious of Kafka's occasional reworkings of classical allegory. More than this once, Kafka doses mythemes with ironic deformations. With Kafka's parabolic version of Ulysses in "Silence of the Sirens" in mind, Benjamin comments: "Ulysses, after all, stands at the dividing line between myth and fairy tale. Reason and cunning have inserted tricks into myths; their forces cease to be invincible. Fairy stories are the traditional stories about victory over these forces, and fairy tales for dialecticians are what Kafka wrote when he went to work on legends. He inserted little tricks into them."[32] Hermes, too, the metamorphic master of the linguistic slip, is another allegorical agent who inserts "little tricks" into preexisting structures.[33] Kafka's heroes characteristically come to grief due to kinds of inscrutable interventions, but Benjamin identifies Kafka the writer with the Hermes who freewheels his way unscathed from episode to episode.[34] Like other daemonic tricksters—creatures of ecstatic flight that entrap the unwitting or outwit the entrapments of others—the Hermetic Kafka laughs: "he is an author who laughs with a profound joy, a joie de vivre, in spite of, or because of, his clownish declarations that he offers like a trap or a circus" (Deleuze and Guattari 1986, 41). The traps Kafka sets are those the ironic literary allegorist typically sets for over-zealous readers.[35]

Kafka's ironic daemonic often functions within the cosmos of imperial bureaucracy, the hierarchies constructed by the distribution and movement of powers through an unfathomable institutional apparatus.[36] Benjamin (1982) comments, "the world of offices and registries, of musty, shabby, dark rooms, is Kafka's world" (112). Kafkan bureaucracy burlesques the typology of the daemonic, as in his parable "Poseidon": "Poseidon sat at his desk, doing figures. The administration of all the waters gave him endless work."[37] In the figure of bureaucracy, mundane structure is amplified into an allegorical labyrinth. The bureaucratic cosmos domesticates the daemonic by making it the routine wielding of an Other's power over the mundane order. But the terms of Kafka's parody of daemonic types are already present in Apuleius's reworkings of Plato's myths.

Socrates's visionary palinode in the *Phaedrus* recounted the ranks of the "twelve great gods": "There are many blessed sights and many ways hither and thither within the heaven, along which the blessed gods go to and fro attending each to his own duties" (*P* §247a). In *On the God of Socrates*, Apuleius revises the Platonic daemonic: "being placed as messengers between the inhabitants of earth and those of heaven, they carry from the one to the other, prayers and bounties, supplications and assistance, being a kind of interpreters and message carriers for both. Through these same demons, as Plato says in his Symposium, all revelations, the various miracles of magicians, and all kind of presages, are carried on. For specially appointed individuals of this number, administer everything according to the province assigned to each" (*GS* 356–57). Apuleius's blatant parable of imperial government subverts to some extent Diotima's evocation of Eros as potent and venerable cosmic force, with the lesser figure of the generic daemon as an anonymous imperial functionary relegated to a specific "province" of the polytheistic bureau. Here the daemonic agent is doubled back, demoted once again to a strictly secondary role as a delegate of the imperturbable divinities it serves.

According to Fletcher (1964), "Kafka rewrote this mythology ironically in his parable, 'Couriers'" (44):

> They were offered the choice between becoming kings or the couriers of kings. The way children would, they all wanted to be couriers. Therefore there are only couriers who hurry about the world, shouting to each other— since there are no kings—messages that have become meaningless. They would like to put an end to this miserable life of theirs but they dare not because of their oaths of service. (Kafka 1958, 175)

If king and courier are read as father and son, then "Couriers" turns toward the family circle in the *Metamorphosis*. Gregor Samsa was once a courier, that is, a commercial traveler: "Oh God, he thought, what an exhausting job I've picked on! Traveling about day in, day out.... The devil take it all!" (*M* 9). So Gregor's profession bears an allegorical signature in the Hermetic attributes of travel and commerce. But Gregor is a mockery of Hermes, not a potent and aggressive operator, but an exhausted, exasperated victim of an irrevocable routine. In ludicrous, unintelligible explanation to the chief clerk when Gregor first breaks loose from his room, the metamorph says that such a life slips out of one's control: "Travelers are not popular, I know. People think they earn sacks of money and just have a good time.... And you know very well that the traveler, who is never seen in the office almost the whole year round, can so easily fall a victim to gossip and ill luck and unfounded complaints, which he mostly knows nothing about, except when he comes back exhausted from his rounds, and only then suffers in person from their evil consequences, which he can no longer trace back to the original causes" (37).

Within the family, Gregor's father is of course one of the "original causes" of Gregor's "evil consequence."[38] Whereas kings are immobile, Kafka's couriers race about, mercurially. Even the monstrous Gregor, when he is not hiding under the furniture, is impossibly crawling crisscross over the walls and ceiling. By becoming a courier, Gregor thought to possess the throne of the king. In this sense, Gregor's metamorphosis leads back at least to the father's catastrophe, "the collapse of his business five years earlier" (57).[39] Then it was that Gregor overtook the father's position: "almost overnight [he] had become a commercial traveler instead of a little clerk . . . his success was immediately translated [*verwandelt*] into good round coin" (58–59). Here is Gregor's first "translation," his *Verwandlung* from a low-paid pencil-pusher to a high-priced "agent" in his own right, whereby Gregor thinks to have usurped the father, in fact only to have inherited his debts. Thus Gregor's metamorphosis into an insect is *nachträglich*, an aftereffect signifying that the belated moment has come for the father to collect the debt the son took upon himself. The parasitic parent begins to emerge from his cocoon and reassert himself. Herr Samsa's new job is itself a parody of Gregor's former role. He too becomes a courier, in this instance, a messenger for a bank. As another parodic Hermes, the father enjoys a daemonic resurrection. He supplements and so supplants his abject, metamorphic son.

This discussion of writing as the daemonic can be summed up in the following theses. The metamorphic exile of the body is an allegory of writing, and the structural consequences of writing are reified in the form of the daemonic. The textual realm of the daemonic is an allegory of transformative communication. The comic or tragic ab-use and dis-figuration of the human body as represented in a metamorphosis conveys the poetic or duplicitous rhetoricity of language and the inescapable chain of translation. When signifiers construct the psyche, the foremost dispossessed property is the anterior body. As in language the signified is encrypted by the signifier, so in a metamorphosis the proper body is disfigured by figuration, derealized, and appears to fall away, either temporarily or permanently. The anterior body of the metamorph is bracketed, preserved as a moment in the metamorphic process, yet negated as a viable vehicle. Metamorphoses are allegorical tropes that turn on the notion of the given body (the proper name or literal term) as suspended form. Metamorphic stories reify the daemonic power of writing by making virtually deconstructive scenes that narrate the displacement or decomposition of prior determinations of bodily identity and psychological value. The trope of the *pharmakon* personifies writing itself as a daemonic power—a material substance taken within from without and transforming the self. From simple metaphors deviating from normal linguistic usage to full-blown imaginations of fabulous monsters, daemonic creatures are allegorical fictions that arise as exceptions to normal, natural, or mimetic production, exceptions that either underwrite or undermine the rule of the normality from which they deviate. The proper self of the metamorph is cast out of itself, fixed in some emblematic form, and forced to begin its wandering career as an outcast agent casting about for new scenes.

2. History of Metamorphic Allegory

From the classical epic to the modern scientific imagination, allegory is a literary mode that mediates the tensions of cultural transitions. Literary allegorizing operates on the cusp of world-views. Typically interceding between a problematic past and a present cultural desire, allegories take textual form as extended tropes that rewrite the significance of their historical pretexts. For instance, in the transition from archaic to classical Greek culture, the technology of writing that replaced oral transmission coincided with the development of allegorical rationalizations for mythic narratives.[1] The pre-Socratic philosophers introduced rational systemization into a body of mythic and legendary materials, and eventually the supplementary commentary was treated as more basic than the material explained.[2] So allegory was an interpretive system, a systematic method of recuperative reading, before it was a compositional technique.[3] These incursions of both writing and allegorical rewriting prefigure Plato's own literary campaign to displace the authority of epic poetry with a body of philosophical texts. Just as Plato's prescriptions for cultural renovation often took the form of allegorical banishments, contemporary visions of metamorphosis banish the organic body by imagining its translation into digital simulations, its technological conversion into protean data. This transformative survival of information at the expense of biological presence is the latest configuration of metamorphosis as an allegory of writing.

Narrative allegory folds literary structures and cultural trends together into textual tension. The interrelation of structure and history in allegory is both tense and tensed. Allegory declines the infinitive of structure into narrative, but that narrative often stages a quest to be reconnected to the infinite. Some allegories aim to abstract the narrative once more into the theological or doctrinal structure that informs it, the timeless moral or rational cosmos crossing through the temporal surface of the text. Other allegories differ from this dogmatic model by withholding the literary vehicle from symbolic collapse into an anterior structure of meaning. Rather, these ironic literary allegories challenge the authority of the pretext by drawing it into history and so marking its lapse into semantic mutability.

Allegories construct mobile historical frames. Some specific temporal cultural disjunction provides the warp across which the text weaves its episodes and images. De Man (1969) formulates allegory's diachronic axis along these lines: "in the world of allegory, time is the originary constitutive category. . . . It remains necessary, if there is to be allegory, that the allegorical sign refer to another sign that precedes it" (190). And de Man's essay refers implicitly to Benjamin's (1985) prior determination of the temporality of the German baroque *Trauerspiel,* in which "the word 'history' stands written on the countenance of nature in the characters of transcience. . . . The movement from history to nature . . . is the basis of allegory" (177, 182). In that movement, however, the historical frame is readily converted into a structural schema. When abstracted from concrete time, allegory gravitates to archetypes of disjunction, the fatality of structure, as in the myth of the Fall. Beyond history, the absolute temporality of allegory is the time it takes for the soul to fall into writing—no time at all. And yet the Fall—the paradigmatic allegorical event—is precisely a fall into time.

Within history, when emerging or competing ideologies need to subvert or preempt prior modes of authority, allegorical reading and writing mediate the tensions of such cultural contests. Allegory typically sets up a dialectic by which a present text reconfigures the significance of a pretext. For instance, allegorical revisionism figured prominently in Plato's philosophical fables of conversion or exile. Plato's aggressive stance toward Homer, Hesiod, and Pythagoras displays the agonistic character of literary allegory, in that it does not necessarily reinforce but often cancels or ontologically suspends the pretextual system embedded in the schemas it adapts.

Although the archaic sources of metamorphic myths are irrecoverable, the metamorphosis of human bodies by supernatural agencies is part of the fabric of the marvelous in epic poems as early as the saga of Gilgamesh. The classical origins of metamorphic stories are derived from epic transformations of mythic episodes, and further, from the transcription of oral narratives into written texts. Plato is crucial in the Western development of metamorphic allegory, for he rewrote the scripts of spiritual conversion he inherited, and in the process, provided textual blueprints for turning mythic accounts of human metamorphosis toward premeditated rhetorical and narrative effects. The Socratic deployment of metamorphosis as an erotic comedy of psychological development was then instrumental for the literary transition from the epic to the novel.

Plato's seminal treatments of metamorphosis can be traced in passages from the *Republic,* where the depiction of metamorphic divinities is explicitly censured, from the *Timaeus* and the *Phaedo,* where the metamorphosis of human beings merges with notions of metempsychosis to produce an allegorical rhetoric of moral judgment, and from the *Phaedrus,* where images of bodily metamorphosis become symbols of psychological development. In the *Phaedrus,* Socrates relates a fable about Eros and the growth of the soul's wings, explaining that the mania of erotic possession can be desirable, that certain erotic metamorphoses form part of a proper philosophical education.[4] From this Platonic myth of an immortal soul that loses and regains its divine wings, two routes opened out: an earnest avenue leading to the moralization of metamorphoses in Neoplatonic and Christian doctrine, and a rather skeptical but good-natured side street leading to mock-epic and ironic narratives of a first-person metamorph. Ovid and Apuleius will be the gates onto this shadier byway to ironic metamorphosis.

A literal Platonic condemnation of metamorphosis is evident in Book 2 of the *Republic,* when Socrates and his companions consider the education of the Guardians and criticize the traditional literary canon of Greek culture. It is stressed that Homer, Hesiod, and the tragic dramatists have been the makers of many false and pernicious tales. The greater the poem, the more detrimental its representations to impressionable minds, when divine gods are depicted as the authors of moral evils. Such stories, says Socrates, "have no place in our city, whether they purport to be allegories or not. Young minds are not able to discriminate between what is allegorical and what is literal" (*R* §378d). Literal images best suit the literal-minded. In addition, not only is the divine incapable of authoring evil, but also, because it is already in a state of perfection, any transformation it might undergo can only be for the worse. For that reason, Socrates proposes that the metamorphosis of a god is an impious notion, unworthy of representation:

> Do you think that god is a wizard? Do you think he would play insidious games with us, assuming one shape at one time and another at another? Would he actually change himself and pass from his own form into many forms? Or would he deceive us by sometimes only feigning such transformations? Or is god simple? In that case, he would be less likely than any other being to depart from his own true form.
>
> I shall need to think about that. . . .
>
> Then it is impossible for a god even to wish to change himself. Intrinsically good and beautiful, a god abides simply and forever in his own form.
>
> I think that is an unavoidable conclusion. (*R* §380c–381c)

With an eye toward ideological serviceability as well as theological veracity, Socrates criticizes poetic treatments of the metamorphosis of the divine. Clearly his objection is not to the notion of metamorphosis *per se* but to its application to gods that, in conformity with strict philosophical conceptuality, must be reconceived along logical rather than emotional lines. In Plato, as the divine is accommodated to a new set of principles, metamorphosis is reconceived as well. It is banished from the realm of the highest gods in Book 2 of the *Republic,* just as Poetry will be banished from the ideal state in Book 10.

In other Platonic dialogues, the trope of metamorphosis can represent both base and noble forms of intellectual and moral conduct. Images of human metamorphosis seem to serve two main purposes. One is the use of metamorphic allegory as a poetic vehicle for moral consequences and judgments. For instance, the *Timaeus* expounds the Laws of Destiny concerning the fate of the human soul after death: "And he that has lived his appointed time well shall return again to his abode in his native star, and shall gain a life that is blessed and congenial; but whoso has failed therein shall be changed into woman's nature at the second birth; and if, in that shape, he still refraineth not from wickedness he shall be changed every time, according to the nature of his wickedness, into some bestial form after the similitude of his own nature" (P §42b–c).[5] In the *Phaedo,* Socrates elaborates on these "similitudes," that is, the process of allegorical substitution by which wicked inner qualities determine bestial bodily reincarnations. But the comical framing of the following passage suggests that his auditors at the moment might be seen as the beneficiaries of some Socratic irony deployed at the expense of the credulous:

> "It is likely that those are not the souls of the good, but those of the base, which are compelled to flit about such places as a punishment for their former evil mode of life. And they flit about until through the desire of the corporeal which clings to them they are again imprisoned in a body. And they are likely to be imprisoned in natures which correspond to the practices of their former life."
>
> "What natures do you mean, Socrates?"
>
> "I mean, for example, that those who have indulged in gluttony and violence and drunkenness, and have taken no pains to avoid them, are likely to pass into the bodies of asses and other beasts of that sort. Do you not think so?"
>
> "Certainly that is very likely." (P §81d–e)[6]

Allegorical structures in the service of moral doctrines are founded on judgmental metaphors: for instance, "an unregenerate man is an ape," or "a willful woman is a serpent." If metamorphoses deployed as allegorical figures of judgment are to produce literal conviction, then the rhetorical nature of that ethical foundation must vanish, or be subsumed by an all-encompassing cosmic scheme. When moral allegories are elaborated from the level of the individual to that of the species, the idea of moral metamorphosis converges with (or reverts to) the theological doctrine of metempsychosis. Here, unlike those tales in which the metamorph returns to human form, the metamorphic judgment is transcendentalized and the metamorphic form is fixed beyond the limits of life. In a cosmic scheme of metamorphic reincarnation like Pythagorean doctrine, then, the soul is always already catastrophically fallen. Whether propounded ironically or in earnest, metamorphoses of this allegorical type are images of human catastrophe. The production of moral allegory appears to involve, or call forth, some form of catastrophe. A human metamorphosis can always be read as an image of the Fall.

Insofar as metamorphic narratives are composed as allegories of moral judgment, they are preceded by those judgments; that is, they are ideologically motivated set-pieces of theological rhetoric. Pythagoras had already refashioned canonical legends of Greek culture into a mystical mathematics. Mythic and epic metamorphoses could clearly be reinterpreted as allegorical masquerades conveying the tribulations of the immortal soul in a material world. These allegorical reconfigurations themselves invited Heraclitus's aphoristic as well as Plato's dialectical treatments.[7] Following upon these developments, Plato's dialogues invoke forms of allegorical rhetoric at times not to affirm them but in order to bring their logic to philosophical statement, to submit them to Socratic inquiry. In the passage cited above from the *Phaedo,* for instance, the judgmental functions of the metamorphic allegory may be suspended by dialogical context ("certainly that is very likely").[8]

The second main purpose of Plato's metamorphic images is as figures for intellectual development. A prime example occurs during one of Socrates's rhetorical tours-de-force, his second speech in the *Phaedrus,* also referred to as the palinode or "recantation," where he spins visions of the heavens and follows the circuit of the immortal soul into and out of mortal bodies. Here Plato turns the dynamics of daemonic intervention toward philosophic ends by paralleling "divine possession" to rhetorical power. In the *Phaedrus,* the medium of that transumption is the unhinged rhetoric of Socrates's second speech, as it is then anatomized in the ensuing dialogue. Applying multiple conversational frames, a network of intra- and intertextual allusion, and Socrates's ironic controls to the narration, Plato uses a metamorphic myth of the soul to articulate philosophical values for and so rewrite the realm of daemonic motivation, affective possession, from an unrationalized mythos to a philosophical datum. The conclusion of the *Phaedrus* subordinates the myth of the soul's descent into generation and potential return to its divine origin to larger and more concrete lessons on the use and abuse of rhetoric and on the dialectical method of argument in general.

The fall of the soul is the ground of possibility for another story, the one that the madness of philosophical eros produces a reunion of the human soul with the divine, and thus repairs that prior, catastrophic loss. There must have been a prior catastrophe for there to be (a need for) a philosophic conversion, a spiritual redemption. In the midst of the palinode, then, Socrates adapts some Pythagorean tales of metempsychosis and reincarnation to his argument, similar to but not identical with those previously noted in the *Timaeus* and the *Phaedo*.[9] The fate of earthbound souls and the proliferation of earthly forms are again explained as moral judgments placed at death upon departed souls:

> Now in all these states, whoever lives justly obtains a better lot, and whoever lives unjustly, a worse. For each soul returns to the place whence it came in ten thousand years; for it does not regain its wings before that time has elapsed, except the soul of him who has been a guileless philosopher or a philosophical lover; ... the rest, when they have finished their first life, receive judgment, and after the judgment some go to the places of correction under the earth and pay their penalty, while the others, made light and raised up into a heavenly place by justice, live in a manner worthy of the life they led in human form. But in the thousandth year both come to draw lots and choose their second life, each choosing whatever it wishes. Then a human soul may pass into the life of a beast, and a soul which was once human, may pass again into a man. (P §248e–249b)

Socrates then returns to the significance of the beauty of the human form into which the unwinged, fallen soul may settle or the reincarnated, upraised soul may return. The beauty of the human body is an echo of the divine beauty to which the philosopher has intellectual access. Now Socrates describes divine possession and the metamorphoses induced by metaphorical visions of the beloved. This "madness . . . causes him to be regarded as mad, who, when he sees the beauty on earth, remembering the true beauty, feels his wings growing. . . . This is, of all inspirations, the best and of the highest origin" (P §249d–e). The Platonic romance of the human soul is founded on this premise of "high origin," a premise that is also a trope for the philosophical construction of an abstract ideal as a formal cause. The way back to "true beauty" is through a detached meditation on physical beauty, through maintaining an erotic vision arrested and fixed by an allegorical perception, grasping a transferential vision that cancels the given body of the beautiful beloved. Suppressed as a libidinal object and raised up as a philosophical vehicle, the body of the beloved becomes a translucent symbol through which ideal beauty can shine. Possessed by such divine vision, says Socrates, the lover will enter into a series of essential changes, figured forth as bodily metamorphoses, a holy love madness:

> He who is newly initiated, who beheld many of those realities, when he sees a god-like face or form which is a good image of beauty, shudders at first, and something of the old awe comes over him, then, as he gazes, he reveres the beautiful one as a god, and if he did not fear to be thought stark mad, he would offer sacrifice to his beloved as to an idol or a god. And as he looks upon him, a reaction from his shuddering comes over him, with sweat and unwonted heat; for as the effluence of beauty enters him through the eyes, he is warmed; the effluence moistens the germ of the feathers, and as he grows warm, the parts from which the feathers grow, which were before hard and choked, and prevented the feathers from sprouting, become soft, and as the nourishment streams upon him, the quills of the feathers swell and begin to grow from the roots over all the form of the soul; for it was once all feathered. (P §251a–b)

Socrates recounts a process of spiritual metamorphosis, not a catastrophic fall but the redemptive growth of new wings where once before they had grown, only to drop away. The human soul's metamorphic recovery of wings is part of a fable idealizing erotic sublimation, in which the glorious, the delirious, and the silly are about equally mixed. The processes represented by such figures are not precisely "divine" but daemonic, that is, transcendental and erotic at the same time. They configure the union of eros and psyche through the poetic congress of sexual metaphor. The root metaphor of this Socratic metamorphosis is of a phallic insemination of winged seeds transferred from the vegetative to the avian to the linguistic field, as when Socrates says at the end of the *Phaedrus* that dialecticians plant and sow "in a fitting soul intelligent words . . . which are not fruitless, but yield seed from which there spring up in other minds other words" (*P* §276e–277a). The Platonic insemination of wisdom celebrates the fertility of the philosophic logos, in terms that analogize seeds, semen, and signs. Winged words are seeds transmitted not to the wind but directly to their bed in an aspiring soul. Properly planted and nurtured, they give birth to flowering, heaven-tending things.

However, the vehicle of this angelic vision of transcendent winged being at the end of the palinode is not only a bird on high. It is also a lowly sprout, just when it first breaks through the soil, its sepals fully spread, ready to thrust upward toward the sun. The Helmbold and Rabinowitz translation of this passage displaces the avian feathers in favor of the vegetative line of imagery reprised at the end of the dialogue: "Once he has received the emanation of beauty through his eyes, he grows warm, and through the perspiration that ensues, he irrigates the sprouting of his wing. When he is quite warm, the outer layers of the seedling unfurl—parts which by reason of their close-drawn rigidity had for a long time prevented anything from blossoming" (34–35). This earthier reading of the rebirth of the wings of the soul does not denigrate but subtilizes the dialogue. Apuleius had good reason to grasp Socrates as philosophic comedian as well as cosmic sage.[10] In the *Golden Ass,* Apuleius responds to the comic grotesquery of this passage, lampooning it in his description of Lucius's metamorphosis into an ass. While Lucius had hoped to be transformed into a bird, it is not, as in the *Phaedrus,* "the quills of the feathers [that] swell and begin to grow from the roots over all the form of the soul." Rather, "no little feathers appeared," but Lucius's asinine ears "shot up long and hairy" (*GA* 71). Read ironically as the literal depiction of a bodily metamorphosis, the affective and bodily commotions in the palinode of the *Phaedrus* are not far removed from typical Ovidian metamorphoses or from the scene of Lucius's transformation.

From the mystical mathematics of Pythagoras and Plato to the proto-science of Epicurus and Lucretius, the classical literature of metamorphic allegory is also connected with theological and philosophical impulses to renarrate mythic cosmologies. Angus Fletcher advances the idea of *kosmos* to describe a typical allegorical structure.[11] By interrelating two or more distinct realms of being or levels of meaning, the textual microcosm of a literary allegory prescribes the structure of the cosmos at large and also posits the presence of daemonic agencies capable of mediating among and interconnecting the levels at play. Reworking both mythic and rationalistic narratives of cosmogony such as Hesiod's *Theogony* and Lucretius's *De Rerum Natura*, Ovid's *Metamorphoses* narrates the creation and sorting out of the universe, the proliferation of species, the emergence of human beings in relation to supernatural agencies, the development of human intelligence and material culture, and the subsequent play of social transformations. In Ovid the trope of metamorphosis marks important moments of cultural origin. The tales mark natural objects—laurel tree, water-reed, amber, spider, Ionian sea, narcissus blossom—with the names and traces of human identities and desires. But they also imply that all cultural origins are catastrophic, which is to say, non–original, since they are already a turning away from something prior, already a disruption and alteration of original or natural structures. Ovid's origins alter as quickly as they originate. His account of the material creation moves quickly from morphogenesis, the origin of forms, to metamorphosis, the origin of transformations. The universal transition from chaos to order is perpetually confronted with an entropic pull back into chaos.

Bakhtin (1981) has addressed the proto-scientific complex of cosmogony and metamorphosis. For Bakhtin, Hesiod's cosmogonic metamorphoses exhibit duration and sequential stability. In mythic time, the crucial transformations are those that concern the origination of the abiding identities of matter and life and the shapes of abiding gods. Hesiod creates "a distinctive sequence of shifts in ages and generations (the myth of the five ages: Golden, Silver, Bronze, 'Trojan' or Heroic and Iron), an irreversible theogonic sequence of metamorphosis in nature, including the cyclical series of metamorphosis for grain and an analogical series of metamorphosis in the vine of the grape" (113). In the development from Hesiod to Ovid, however, Bakhtin traces a transformation in the temporal significance of metamorphosis. In Ovid,

> the general idea of metamorphosis has already become the private metamorphosis of individual, isolated beings and is already acquiring the characteristics of an external, miraculous transformation. The idea of representing the whole world of cosmogonic and historical process from the point of view of metamorphosis—beginning with the creation of the cosmos out of chaos and ending with the transformation of Caesar into a star—is retained. But this idea is now actualized through a selection of

metamorphoses taken from the whole of the mythological and literary tradition, of which separate instances
are superficially vivid but without connection to one
another. (114)

Bakhtin outlines developments in the meaning of metamorphosis that run parallel with the displacement of archaic Greek
and Roman cultural forms by classical and Hellenistic literature,
philosophy, and science. The opening book of Ovid's *Metamorphoses*
can be said to compress these cultural dynamics into the first 500
lines. In the shift from the sequential mythopoetic comprehensive-
ness of Hesiod to the fanciful and arbitrary juxtapositions of Ovid's
nonlinear narratives, Bakhtin locates a "disintegration" in the concept of metamorphosis, a gradual lapse from the cosmos to the
individual, from the body of nature in its beneficence and terror to
the human body in its processes and private obscenities. Indeed,
the metamorphosis of the individual bodies of persons is a tacit
reversal or alteration of cosmogonic morphogenesis, a demonstra-
tion that however potent its origin, no created form is absolutely
fixed or durable.

Stories of human metamorphoses narrate exchanges of form
and substance in which accounts must balance. The materialistic
economy of a metamorphic world forfeits creation *ex nihilo* in favor
of specific ratios of exchange between the old and the new. As Italo
Calvino has written concerning Ovid's *Metamorphoses,* "A law of
the greatest internal economy dominates this poem, which on the
surface is devoted to unbridled extravagance. It is the economy
proper to metamorphosis, which demands that the new forms should
recover the materials of the old ones as far as possible."[12] What
Calvino has described may be applied as well to the scriptive
economy of Ovid's poem, which is virtually a metamorphic recy-
cling of prior texts into newly imagined combinations. For Calvino,
the *Metamorphoses* possesses a structure of "universal contiguity"
that mimics the economies of the material world, amounting to a
poetic science. Ovid attempts "to endow this philosophy of nature
with a theoretical system, perhaps in competition with his remote
predecessor Lucretius" (159). However, Lucretius was not that
remote from Ovid; he died in 55 B.C., two generations before
Ovid went into exile in 8 A.D. with the *Metamorphoses* nearly complete.[13] Behind Ovid's metamorphic cosmogony, then, and contrib-
uting to some extent to the atomistic "disintegration" of his
metamorphoses, are Lucretius's Epicurean formulations of formal
genesis:

Now I'll describe how the chaotic motes,
The turbulent atoms, met, somehow to form
The basic order of the earth, the sky,
The deep, the courses of the sun and moon.
Never suppose the atoms had a plan,
Nor with a wise intelligence imposed
An order on themselves, nor in some pact
Agreed what movements each should generate.
No, it was all fortuitous . . . .
No sun with lavish light was visible then
Wheeling aloft, no planets, ocean, sky,
No earth, no air, no thing like things we know.
But a strange kind of turbulence, a swarm
Of first beginnings, whose discordances
Confused their intervals, connections, ways,
And weights and impacts, motions and collisions;
And so the battles raged, because these forms
Were so dissimilar, so various
They could not rest in harmony, nor combine
In any reciprocal movements. But at last
Some parts began to learn their separate ways—
Like elements joined with like, in some such way
As to effect disclosure—a visible universe
With parts arranged in order, as the earth
Was sundered from the lofty sky, as ocean
Spread with its waters kept in proper bounds,
As the pure fires of heaven knew their place. (L 5.416–48)

The contiguous structures and fluid narrative textures of the
Metamorphoses often echo Lucretius's overtly scientific narrative.
Lucretius's influence on Ovid is certainly as obvious and germane as
that of Pythagoras or Plato. But although Ovid retains the Lucretian
description of Chaos, especially in the powerful rhetoric of negation—"No sun . . . No earth"—Ovid's cosmogony proper eliminates
the atomistic minutiae of Lucretius's *clinamen* or primal swerve by
which the turbulent concourse of atoms suddenly bursts into form,
and reinstates what Lucretius had denied, a demiurge or "wise intelligence," the notion of a supreme agent responsible for initiating
the sorting. Still, if the atheistic Lucretius credited the visible creation to a random deviation or to the fertility of Chaos itself—the
intrinsically self-organizing nature of material substances—the credit
for Ovid's creation is undecided. Unlike Hesiod, whose cosmogonies
dwell insistently on the naming of the gods, Ovid will decline to fix

what agent, which god, brings about the primal sorting out of things: "Whatever god it was, who out of chaos / Brought order to the universe . . . , he molded earth / In the beginning, into a great globe" (*OH* 1.31–34). Ovid's cosmogony is essentially anonymous; like a pure myth, the created world itself has lost its first author's name, and so reveals its non-originality, its status as a cultural text.

As a syncretic poet, Ovid cribbed his creation myth from many sources. In addition to the Lucretian cosmogony, his mock-epical treatment of metamorphic origins also reworks Judaic, pre-Socratic, and Platonic accounts of genesis. Ovid was surely no philosophical dogmatist; nevertheless, many of his readers learned to see his tales through some form of Neoplatonic lens. "Within a couple of hundred lines, Ovid has created what will stand for centuries as the translation of Platonic cosmology" (Barkan 1986, 30):

> Before the ocean was, or earth, or heaven,
> Nature was all alike, a shapelessness,
> Chaos, so-called, all rude and lumpy matter,
> Nothing but bulk, inert, in whose confusion
> Discordant atoms warred: there was no sun
> To light the universe; there was no moon
> With slender silver crescents filling slowly;
> No earth hung balanced in surrounding air;
> No sea reached far along the fringe of shore.
> Land, to be sure, there was, and air, and ocean,
> But land on which no man could stand, and water
> No man could swim in, air no man could breathe,
> Air without light, substance forever changing,
> Forever at war: within a single body
> Heat fought with cold, wet fought with dry, the hard
> Fought with the soft, things having weight contended
> With weightless things.
>   Till God, or kindlier Nature,
> Settled all argument, and separated
> Heaven from earth, water from land, our air
> From the high stratosphere, a liberation
> So things evolved, and out of blind confusion
> Found each its place, bound in eternal order. (*OH* 1.5–26)

The first moments of this classical Western poetic cosmogony shift from a Lucretian to a Platonic cosmos by positing a discrete author whose fiat transforms chaos into order, turning an anarchic "single body" containing all things into a centered worldly scene containing the possibility of hierarchies of individuated forms.

But the myth of a demiurge, anonymous or not, responsible for the genesis of the cosmos also reinstates the notion of a perfect creator anterior to a belated creation that falls away from that perfection. Stories of daemonic human metamorphoses are inverted doubles of myths of divine genesis, and typically take the figure of a Fall. If in Genesis as seen through *Paradise Lost,* Satan's Fall precedes and determines the human Fall, in Ovid, humanity falls of its own weight. Once Ovid's creation sequence culminates with the original fabrication of humankind, it is followed immediately by the myth of Four Ages, adapting Hesiod's *Works and Days* to recount humanity's primal corruption and the form of divine judgment called down upon it. The notion of a declining creation captures the inherently catastrophic, "down-turning" or entropic impetus of metamorphosis. To some extent Bakhtin's perception of a "disintegration of mythological unity" in representations of human metamorphosis could be structurally motivated by the entropic dynamics of the topic itself.

Ovid's cosmogony does not institute the sequential stabilities Bakhtin ascribes to Hesiod. Rather, the inception of Ovid's text primes humanity for its own instantaneous metamorphoses. Ovidian humanity is constitutionally prone to transformations in which erotic innovations are always shadowed by entropic disasters. Ovid made human metamorphoses affecting and effective as literature by inscribing mythic metamorphs with the pathos of personal catastrophes. At first, when Daphne in flight from Apollo turns into the laurel tree, there is just a brief vestige of personhood to measure the meaning of her change: "The laurel, / Stirring, seemed to consent, to be saying *Yes*" (*OH* 1.566–67). But this lack of sustained self-affect in the metamorph modulates quickly as Ovid proceeds to Io. The Ovidian narrator has the metamorphic Io-as-heifer dwell in detail on her consciousness of bodily alienation and verbal aphasia, and use her hoof to reassert human identity by impressing her name in the sand. Similarly, in the next book, the metamorphic Actaeon-as-stag is narrated as fully and spectacularly conscious of his dismembering by his own dogs. When metamorphic subjectivity is left unwritten, the ironies of metamorphic stories remain repressed in favor of some particular ideal of transcendence or moral semantics. However, in skeptical or comedic literary treatments, by endowing the metamorph with signs of personhood, by bringing the metamorph forward in the first person, metamorphic ironies are made explicit and productive. Cosmogony becomes carnival.

The individualization of human metamorphosis marks the "disintegration" of epic forms, but also the first stirrings of the novel. In the dissemination of the legends about Socrates, Bakhtin

sees the formulation of a "prose hero" counter to the epic protagonist. The Socratic dialogues constitute Plato's seminal contribution
to the history of the novel (Bakhtin 1981, 24–25). Connecting
Socratic irony to Platonic metamorphosis, Bakhtin stipulates one
form of the ancient biography as *Platonic:*

> In the Platonic scheme there is also a moment of crisis
> and rebirth (the words of the oracle as a turning point in
> the course of Socrates's life). The specific nature of this
> "seeker's path" is all the more clearly revealed when
> contrasted with an analogous scheme: the course of the
> soul's ascent toward a perception of the Forms. . . . In
> such works the mythological and mystery-cult bases of
> the scheme are clearly in evidence. Such sources rein-
> force the kinship between this scheme and those "conver-
> sion stories" we discussed in the previous section.
> Socrates's life course, as it is revealed to us in the *Apol-*
> *ogy,* is a public and rhetorical expression of the same
> metamorphosis. Real biographical time is here almost
> entirely dissolved in the ideal (and even abstract) time of
> metamorphosis. (130–31)

Bakhtin's primary example of a "conversion story" is precisely
Apuleius's *Golden Ass,* where the metamorphic interlude can be
read as the prelude for Lucius's spiritual conversion to the cult of
Isis. Measuring the psychological import of metamorphosis relative
to Hesiod and Ovid, Bakhtin remarks that "In Apuleius, metamorphosis acquires [a]. . . personal, isolated, and quite openly magical
force. . . . Metamorphosis has become a vehicle for conceptualizing
and portraying personal, individual fate, a fate cut off from both
the cosmic and the historical whole" (114). But here Bakhtin slights
the concrete detail and intertextual resources of the *Golden Ass.*
Fergus Millar aptly notes how "Apuleius clothes his sequence of
fantastic episodes in a mass of vivid, concrete and realistic detail,
on physical objects, houses, social structure, economic relations, the
political framework of the local communities, and the wider political
framework of the empire."[14] And Winkler (1985) has shown how
Apuleius's novel mercilessly parodies contemporary literary styles,
especially the vogue in "quest-for-wisdom" narratives (251–75).
    Situating Apuleius's structures of motivation and time in re-
lation to Greek romances such as *Daphnis and Chloë,* Bakhtin
(1981) emphasizes Apuleius's enlargement of the factor of moral
choice and his grasp of the literary possibilities of developing the
fall of the metamorph beyond an irreparable fixation of moral guilt.

Nevertheless, he still reads the resolution of Lucius's transformation adventure on the model of the Cupid and Psyche story, in which metamorphosis is a fortunate fall preparing one for a spiritual conversion: "Thus the entire adventure sequence must be interpreted as *punishment* and *redemption*. . . . This entire sequence is grounded in *individual responsibility*" (118–19). Although Bakhtin's broad focus on metamorphic allegory as a preparation for the genre of the novel is very fine, his reduction of the *Golden Ass* to a moralistic fable is rather conventional. It also seems to draw his attention away from Apuleius's brilliant exposés of the sexual psychologies and political economics of late classical culture.

The prose narrative of the *Golden Ass* fashions an allegorical totality out of a simple romance plot: boy loves magic, boy loses body, boy loves Isis, boy regains body. But what Apuleius actually fashions is a parodic totality that dismantles its own allegorical dimensions as it constructs them. It is thus a *metamorphic* allegory, one likely to turn its dogmatic reader into an interpreting ass. Apuleius contributes to the development of the novel most profoundly as the author of an exemplary travesty of serious, established literary genres—philosophical allegory, knowledge-quest adventure, mystery-cult initiation tales, and metamorphic myths rewritten as cautionary parables.[15] Full of generous wit and wily narrative trickery, by turns Platonic, Isiac, Eleusinian, Stoic, Cynic, and Epicurean, the tales Apuleius tells manipulate for comic effect the economic and erotic ironies of the later Roman patriarchal imperium. Although the *Golden Ass* has often been read as an elaborate Neoplatonic allegory, this metamorphic comedy subverts whatever pieties may present themselves as the normative judgments of the text.[16] Apuleian metamorphoses are seriocomic, ironic, disruptive, transgressive not just in depiction but in intent. As a student of both Egyptian and Hellenic traditions, a connoisseur of the cultic and the occult, Apuleius had presumably studied a range of allegorical texts and readings. But the *Golden Ass* indicates that the source of the daemonic as well as the divine is allegorical: gods, monsters, and metamorphoses are rhetorical figures shaping and shaped by human desires. Apuleius's allusions indicate that his parody of the mythic daemonic in the service of a secular ideal derives from a reading of Plato.

The *Golden Ass* was completed in the mid-second century A.D. It is not definitively known whether it is the first or the last work of this polymath provincial, precursor of St. Augustine by two centuries, raised like Augustine in an African colony, who made his way in the Empire as a lawyer, rhetorician, writer, and story-teller.[17] William Adlington produced his classic English translation in 1566.[18]

"LUCIUS APULEIUS AFRICAN, an excellent follower of Plato his sect," Adlington begins his brief adulatory description of the Roman author, after offering a synopsis of the plot and a sketch of the moral allegory he took the narrative to convey, a spiritual sense that would surely defend him against any charge of translating merely licentious literature:

> The argument of the book is, how Lucius Apuleius, the author himself, traveled into Thessaly (being a region in Greece where all the women for the most be such wonderful witches, that they can transform men into the figure of brute beasts) where after he had continued a few days, by the mighty force of a violent confection he was changed into a miserable ass, and nothing might reduce him to his wonted shape but the eating of a rose, which, after the endurance of infinite sorrow, at length he obtained by prayer. Verily under the wrap of this transformation is taxed the life of mortal men, when as we suffer our minds so to be drowned in the sensual lusts of the flesh and the beastly pleasure thereof (which aptly may be called the violent confection of witches) that we lose wholly the use of reason and virtue, which properly should be in a man, and play the parts of brute and savage beasts. By like occasion we read how divers of the companions of Ulysses were turned by the marvelous power of Circe into swine. . . . (xvi–xvii)

Adlington brings Apuleius's erotic comedy forward to 16th-century English readers sheathed in the Neoplatonic version of metamorphic allegory. The metamorphic devolution of the erotic body is an edifying conceit symbolizing the moral devolution of the immortal soul.

But what manner of Platonist was Apuleius? As a "Pagan Middle Platonist," a second-century Latin writer, Apuleius's writings preceded the high Neoplatonism of the late Hellenic academy (cf. Gersh 1986, 1:220–27). Winkler (1985) suggests that "Apuleius's Platonism [is] more like the Skeptical version in Plutarch than like a fetal version of New Platonism" (252). By the fourth century, however, Augustine already viewed Apuleius in terms of a Neoplatonic tradition centered on Plotinus and postdating Apuleius's lifetime. Crediting Apuleius as an exemplary New Platonist, Augustine devoted several sections of the *City of God* to refutations of Apuleius's discussions of the daemonic in *On the God of Socrates*. In his exhaustive study, Gersh declares that "despite the citation of a number of different philosophical writers, it is beyond doubt that Apuleius sees his primary allegiance as being to the Platonic school" (1:220). However, A. D. Nock concludes that Apuleius was an earnest adherent of Isis: Book 11 of the *Golden Ass* strikes Nock as "the high-water mark of the piety which grew out of the mystery religions. . . . It cannot be supposed that his is a normal level of pagan religious emotion, but it should certainly be remembered that it is a level which it could and did reach."[19] Steven Heller rectifies this division of loyalties by arguing that the theoretical framework of the *Golden Ass* is "a Platonizing approach similar at least in general outline to Plutarch's in *de Iside et Osiride*."[20] Plutarch's Platonized version of Isis, says Heller, helped Apuleius to reconcile his Platonism with his Isiac faith.

Still, some of these views of Apuleius's intellectual and religious commitments come from identifying the author of the *Golden Ass* with the novel's hero, the author of *On the God of Socrates* with the various views expressed therein, in ways that may not be warranted. Some good-natured skepticism has been cast in Apuleius's direction. " 'Showman' may not be an overly complimentary term, but it is much closer to the truth of the matter than the appellation Apuleius himself would have preferred us to use— *philosophus Platonicus Madaurensis*, 'Platonic philosopher from Maudoros' " (Tatum 1979, 104). Tatum sees in Apuleius "a sophist in the Latin-speaking world" (110), a rhetorical virtuoso and oral performer, and makes the point that Apuleius's prose treatises are not philosophically methodical but popularizing in procedure. Winkler (1985) has argued, I think correctly, that as autobiography or sacred documentary the conclusion of the *Golden Ass* with its cultic ceremonies and spectacular epiphanies "is tainted evidence and cannot be used in any straightforward fashion as Isiac, or personal religious, data" (21). But Winkler brings to light an author "extraordinarily sensitive to distinctions of faith from fact and truth from conjecture" (21). Thus the texts of Apuleius should not be lumped together with those of mainstream Neoplatonists from Plotinus through Proclus.[21] Although Apuleius clearly owes debts to Plato, Plato owes a debt to Apuleius as well, for helping shore up against further ruin the skeptical and erotic trends in his text, and for carrying over some of the comic tonality of Socratic dialogue into the Western novel. Apuleius appears to grasp that Plato's narrative ironies wed rather than divorce eros and psyche, that erotic and moral ideas make reasonable claims on each other. Through Apuleius's influence in particular, Socrates's comic irony and the Platonic erotic are carried over from ancient to modern literature decently intact.

Apuleian irony notwithstanding, the device of metamorphosis has consistently called forth striking exegetical efforts by theologizing readers. In particular, metamorphoses confronted late pagan and early Christian attempts to contain and domesticate archaic myths and literary fictions with a specific problem. What is the exact nature of their witness? Should a metamorphic figure or episode be construed allegorically or literally? The element of the "miraculous" in the metamorphosis of a person into some other thing could be read either as a cryptic manifestation of the divine or as a literal testimony of some daemonic power (see Barkan 1986, 94–103). For instance, there were those who took Lucius's adventures as an ass in the *Golden Ass* to be autobiographical events in the life of the historical Lucius Apuleius.[22] In his sixteenth-century commentary on Ovid's *Metamorphoses,* George Sandys mentions some of these traditional disputes over the hermeneutics of metamorphosis: "But that a man can bee transformed into a beast, is utterly against the opinion of S. *Augustine;* who affirmes, that the Devil can create nothing being himself a Creature, nor change that shape but onely in shew, which God hath created. Allthough *Spondanus* with much fervor oppose him; alledging that place in *Aquinas,* how the angels, both good and evill, have a natural property and power to Metamorphize our bodies, going about to confirme it by sundry histories" (*OS* 653).

The pagan Neoplatonists of the third, fourth, and fifth centuries accommodated metamorphoses and other epic supernaturalisms within their own descriptions of a daemonic cosmos: "in the more complete Neoplatonic analysis of Homeric anthropomorphism that reaches us through Proclus, it becomes clear that much of what Homer says about the gods could be salvaged by imposing upon the Homeric myth the exegetical superstructure of a complex demonology" (Lamberton 1986, 98). But miraculous metamorphoses could not be smoothly accommodated to Christian doctrine either as literal "wonder" or divine emblem. They were too close to the pagan daemonic, and belonged not to God or Christ but to the order of "evil angels." For Christian dogma metamorphoses are usually signs of evil, demonic rather than daemonic occurrences.[23] Nevertheless, when Christian authors needed to moralize the metamorphoses at large in the pagan classics, their way had already been clearly mapped out by the allegorical schemata available in the usages of Neoplatonic exegesis.[24] On the literary side, this interpretive collaboration has meant that in Christian culture, metamorphoses have retained some power to disseminate polytheisms, or perhaps more importantly, to provide middle terms undercutting monotheistic moral dualisms.

The pagan Neoplatonists of the late Roman Empire could survey a long history of allegorical practices—Pythagorean, Judaic, Stoic—when they further developed such techniques to rectify perceived inconsistencies in Plato's attitudes toward poetry in particular and artistic mimesis in general. But the dogmatic wing of the Platonic academy in late antiquity did not read Plato's strictures on poetry, literature, and writing as ironic defenses of the very things they appeared to attack, by which dialectical treatment the pitfalls inherent in those activities achieved definition and so became amenable to discursive correction.[25] Rather, they typically took Socrates's condemnations of Homer and other poets and of Thoth's gift of writing to be in literal earnest, and so developed allegorical exegeses to "defend the values" of epic literature, while at the same time maintaining the spiritual authority of the letter of Plato's text. The Neoplatonic tradition as developed and systematized by Plotinus, Porphyry, and Proclus was a form of transcendentalism in direct opposition to the gathering Christian hegemony; it thus more or less turned into the thing it opposed.[26] From these sects, then, the early Church did not inherit the skeptical literary spirit of Plato. It did not pursue the Socratic line of ironic dialectic so much as duplicate and extend the Neoplatonic dogmatizing of Plato's myths and anthropomorphic rhetoric. Insofar as Neoplatonism developed in the mode of mystical theology rather than down the Socratic line of skeptical critique, it carried out a regressive cancellation of Platonic dialogue in favor of mythic monologue.

Neoplatonists often forgot that Plato's uses of myth were deliberately ironic in the midst of their allegorizing, that Platonic myth is "properly not mythos as eventful story, but mythos as paradigmatic story. . . . In their enigmatic imagery and statement we see the archetypal form which allegory takes. It is thus important to note that [Plato's myths] are the consequence of an ironic world view. A Platonic belief in the value of myth, though at first sight it seems transcendentalism, follows from a belief in the rightness of 'staying with it' " (Fletcher 1964, 232–33)—that is, of grasping and maintaining an ironic perspective.[27] As opposed to the Neoplatonic attitude, in the Socratic line of metamorphic allegory, narrative ironies undercut any ostensible monologism. Thus Socrates ironically deflates the manifest transcendentalism of his mock-Pythagorean palinode in the *Phaedrus* with the rhetorical comment, "the poetical expressions . . . I was forced to employ on account of Phaedrus" (*P* §257a). The figure of Socrates will be decisive for Apuleius's high development of metamorphic parody in the *Golden Ass*. In both the *Golden Ass* and the tale of Cupid and Psyche situated so profoundly in the midst of the ludicrous tale of the metamorphic Lucius, Apuleius turns the forms of Socratic metamorphosis to brilliant comic effect. Although his Psyche story anticipates the allegorizing trend of incipient Neoplatonism, the seriousness of its philosophical pretext is subsumed within the laughter of a parodic novel of erotic misadventures. Apuleius follows the Socratic trend of demythologizing the cosmos by humanizing the daemonic.

As opposed to Apuleius's ironic glosses on the Platonic myths, Neoplatonic allegory develops from a spiritual gloss on epic poetry and works to preserve the cultural authority of the epic as a literary adjunct to moral philosophy and theology. The epic tradition that runs circuitously through the Middle Ages to Dante and Milton becomes a complex discourse in which distinctions between poetry and philosophy, paganism and Christianity, literature and scripture, and author and reader, are often hard to fix. In particular, interpretive techniques for the moralization or defense of epic texts perfected by the pagan Platonists were handed along to the Church, and in Christian usages have affected both the composition and the reception of subsequent Western literatures. Lamberton (1986) demonstrates how the late classical Platonic academy developed "a vigorous and obtrusive interpretive tradition" (133) that imposed dogmatic Platonism upon Homer's texts, in particular translating metamorphic episodes in the *Odyssey* into allegorical scriptures bearing transcendental meanings. In the Hellenic intellectual world of late antiquity, Neoplatonic reading developed in tandem with Christian appropriations of the Old Testament. By the fifth century, both pagan and Christian authors such as Prudentius and Heliodorus were composing deliberately allegorical narratives for consumption by interpretive communities trained to expect metaphysical meanings to lie behind the physical images in literary as well as sacred texts.

Barkan (1986) locates alongside the moral allegoresis of metamorphosis a discrete scientific or "naturalist" trend: "we have two interlocking traditions, both very ancient: one, the Platonic tradition, of hidden mystic meanings approving the monstrosity of ancient fables but keeping their real meanings a secret; the other, going back to Homeric allegorizations, a 'scientific' tradition of entertaining the attractive frivolities of fables and researching in them the truths of nature and the cosmos" (113); in the medieval curriculum divided between the arts of the trivium and the sciences of the quadrivium, "pagan stories, and especially tales of metamorphosis, stand squarely between the two: their method of interpretation is rhetorical, but their field of reference is nature"

(117). Connected to the cosmogonic impetus in classical narratives of transformation, metamorphosis continues to be treated as a trope for universal material processes, especially for the uncanny deviations in those processes, singular monstrous creations: "the point of entry for metamorphosis is *monstruosae transformationes,* the bizarre tales that go back to the *mirabilia* of authorities like Pliny or, for that matter, Ovid's Pythagoras" (119); by the 12th century, as part of the humanist revival, "the goddess Natura herself is reborn from antiquity. . . . Nature enters the world of discourse as Myth" (120). Pagan metamorphic myths are recuperated as cryptic natural science:

> Metamorphosis, then, is joined with a guiding principle of twelfth-century Platonic cosmology: that the cosmic order consists in a *concordia discors.* Such a delicate balance is related to a metamorphic picture of the universe because transformation can either be a sign of peaceful flow, like the Pythagorean description of an elemental cycle (*Metamorphoses,* 15.244–51), or it can be a sign of the collapse of harmony in favor of discord, like the disastrous results of the Flood or Phaeton's ride. . . . So the myths demonstrate that nature is meaningful to human experience because of its metamorphic (i.e., anthropomorphic) origins, while metamorphic myths are made explicable through parallels to transformations in nature which are familiar to us from real experience. (Barkan 1986, 122–23)

An instance of Barkan's point would be that when Ovidian characters like Daphne, Syrinx, or Narcissus disappear into their metamorphoses—tree, reed, or flower—they can be taken to donate a human significance to nonhuman things. Classical metamorphoses of human beings may mean death, they can be death sentences, but they can also make the world meaningful by leaving human signatures, enduring and decipherable traces, that anthropomorphize the cosmos by turning nature into writing.

The English poetic tradition owes a great debt to Ovid's versifying of metamorphosis.[28] But the same tradition also owes a particular debt to Apuleius, as transmitted specifically by Adlington's 1566 translation and generally by the diffusion in Medieval and Renaissance culture of Apuleius's plots, motifs, and remarks on the daemonic.[29] "Mention of Apuleius today in the context of Shakespearean studies is likely to elicit among knowledgeable students a discerning nod towards *A Midsummer Night's Dream* and

the assification of Bottom, and not much else" (Tobin 1984, xi). But
Apuleius is a source for Shakespeare's imagery and incident equally
as important as Ovid. As Tobin documents in profuse detail,
Shakespeare was immersed in William Adlington's *Golden Asse*.[30]
Retrieving much of the wantonness and exuberance of Ovid's *Metamorphoses,* with the bonus of lyric and dramatic compression, and
adding some of the mordant comedy of Apuleius, *A Midsummer
Night's Dream* encapsulates fable within fable, playing the sublime
off the grotesque, Cupid and Psyche off the metamorphoses of an
ass. The Apuleian daemonic clearly places its marks on both *A
Midsummer Night's Dream* and Keats's *Lamia.*

From his various readings—for instance, the allegorical translations of Adlington, Chapman, and Sandys, as well as Shakespeare's
drama—Keats gathered that adaptations of metamorphic stories in
the Platonic dialogues, Neoplatonic interpretations of metamorphoses in Homer and Plato, the subsequent moralizations of metamorphosis in allegorical romance, and parodies of metamorphosis in
literary comedies, provided a sizable literary sphere in which a
poem like *Lamia* could take up its magical residence. Just as the
ironic mythopoeses of Plato's Socrates went beyond his legendary
precursors and allegorical sources in Pythagorean and Orphic cult,
and as Apuleius's comedies already outpaced the Neoplatonists who
wrote in the centuries that followed him, in *Lamia* Keats quite
transcends the moral codifications of his allegorical sources. In the
figure of Apollonius, Keats draws an uncannily apt portrait of the
patriarchal negativity inscribed within Neoplatonism.

As opposed to classical or Ovidian metamorphs, modern
metamorphs are more often figures of negation than of origin. Thus
they convey more readily the multiple ironies of human subjects
driven through alien signifiers, primordially inserted into collective
power structures, and overcome by arbitrary events before having
a chance to choose a preferable fate. While they retain their nominal or textual selfhood, Lamia the serpent, Gregor the monster-
beetle, and Sharikov the dog-man suffer fantastic constrictions
within some Other's moral scheme. They are not stable personifications but figures of exile, dispossessed agents tragicomically fleeing
in some manner from hierarchical powers and uncanny confine-
ments. Just as the metamorphic Lucius and his owners wandered
across the Hellenic economic landscape, in *A Midsummer Night's
Dream* Oberon and Titania lead footloose fairy entourages, and
there is machination between the two groups, to the ultimate result of dispossessing the Fairy Queen of her "changeling boy." In
the opening lines of Keats's *Lamia,* amidst echoes of Sandys's translation of Ovid, the hordes of Oberon momentarily reappear, displac-

ing the Nymphs and Satyrs from the "prosperous woods." In both of these texts, metamorphosis shadows ironic tales of migration and dispossession.

When modern literary metamorphs like Lamia, Dr. Jekyll, and Gregor Samsa disappear or die, they leave no redemptive traces, only a moral enigma and the corpse of the daemonic form.[31] Ironists of metamorphosis since Apuleius have often indicated that in the misprision of metaphysical metaphors, persons suffer in person the erasure meant for signs. Modern metamorphoses exploit more radically than their classical counterparts the thematics of linguistic dispossession. Matters of political determination implicit in Ovid and well-developed in the *Golden Ass* achieve further salience in modern metamorphic fictions. Bulgakov's *Heart of a Dog* is an allegorical satire on the social changes of the Soviet revolution, under the cover of a "scientific" medical transformation. García Márquez's *One Hundred Years of Solitude* matches its metamorphic business to episodes of Colombian social and political struggle. Both of these tales evoke and manipulate classical forms of metamorphosis to construct oblique allegories of cultural destruction.

The cultural inertia of unenlightened societies steers them toward catastrophic fates. *One Hundred Years of Solitude* reprises the forms of classical metamorphic epic to offer a tragicomically fatalistic allegory of cultural entropy. Gregory (1958) could have been discussing the saga of the Buendías when he commented that Ovid's *Metamorphoses* "was very nearly a mock epic. . . . Certain scenes in *The Metamorphoses* may be called less classical than violently baroque. The very theme of metamorphosis depended on violent and rapid transformations, distortions, if you will, of normal law and action" (xiv–xv). Janes has noted that *One Hundred Years of Solitude* is "mediated by a single epic voice," the narrator through which García Márquez transmits the parodic cosmogony of Macondo and updates the Day of Judgment with a vision of Macondo's entropic annihilation.[32]

Just as there is abundant energy and wit but no surcharge of outright comedy in Ovid's *Metamorphoses,* so there are ample sufferings to weigh against the pleasures of Macondo. Even when entirely parodic, the miraculous in García Márquez is not especially Apuleian, but partakes of the Ovidian sense that human metamorphoses are mostly dire, not beneficial, that they are primarily punishments or forced defenses and only intermittently desirable escapes. The author's tragicomic attitude toward metamorphosis shows when José Arcadio first meets a "languid little frog," a gypsy girl "in the crowd that was witnessing the sad spectacle of the man who had been turned into a snake for having disobeyed his parents" (*GM* 40, 39). Or we are told of "soft-skinned cetaceans that had the head and torso of a woman, causing the ruination of sailors with the charm of their extraordinary breasts" (19). These passages are at once parodies of moralistic fables and omens prefiguring the Buendía destiny. Most of all, of course, the dire metamorphosis feared by the Buendía line is the fatal stigma of incest: "they were afraid . . . of breeding iguanas. . . . An aunt of Úrsula's, married to an uncle of José Arcadio Buendía, had a son . . . with a cartilaginous tail in the shape of a corkscrew and with a small tuft of hair on the tip. A pig's tail" (28).

The mock cosmogony of Macondo relates the primal miswanderings of the Buendía line, a primitive genesis leading to a fatal fall: "Over [the Buendías] a fatal curse looms, harrying them down the generations: the threat of the birth of a child with a pig's tail as the result of violating the incest taboo. Atreus and Oedipus presiding, this is the plot device on which the novel turns, and the fulfillment of the curse ends the action of the novel" (Janes 1981, 50). The moment of fulfillment—the birth of the pig-baby—and final revelation—the decoding of Melquíades's parchments—releases the curse and everything else, when the last Aureliano discovers that he and Meme were fated to "seek each other through the most intricate labyrinths of blood until they would engender the mythological animal that was to bring the line to an end" (*GM* 382–83). Metamorphosis in *One Hundred Years of Solitude* is an fable of social entropy as the fatal dissipation of genetic as well as cultural information.

In the development of modern science and technology, the scene and control of physical transformations gradually shifts from a hermetic occult and an anthropomorphic Natura to a capable and culpable humanity. By the same token, agents wielding metamorphic powers shift from supernatural to human. Through science, human agents acquire literal technologies for the range of supernatural functions: for metamorphosis, modes of material transformation; for uncanny productivity, automation; for prophecy, electronic communication; and for daemonic flight, aeronautics and space travel. That is, through science, humanity confirms its daemonic status. In this regard, *A Midsummer Night's Dream* remains parodically premodern. Shakespeare invents an origin for Oberon's love potion—the juice of the flower "love-in-idleness"— that is purely Ovidian and mock-mythic. In *Lamia* as well, the lapsed novice apothecary John Keats revises classical forms of the Neoplatonic supernatural. Nevertheless, some critics have commented on the scientific edge of Keats's rhetoric, especially in this work.[33] Sperry (1973) sees Keats's familiarity with chemistry as a crucial element in *Lamia*'s caustic ironies. In chemical or pharma-

ceutical terms, the human Lamia beloved of Lycius is literally a
pharmakon or elixir, a "fiery distillation" (303) too potent for Lycius
to handle.[34] In more recent metamorphic fictions such as *Jekyll and
Hyde* and Calvino's tales, the machinery of transformation has been
thoroughly naturalized, made "scientific." The sciences of nature
now occupy the register of the daemonic vacated by the supernatural and operate its productive ambivalences.

For instance, Mikhail Bulgakov's *Heart of a Dog,* a striking
modern instance of the perennial interconnection of metamorphosis
and allegory, provides a marginally plausible medical technology as
the agency of a metamorphosis, within the larger frame of a political
allegory about the state of Soviet Russia in the mid-twenties. Under
the aegis of social "rejuvenation," the medical metamorphosis is a
trope for social revolution as the surgical crossing or neutralization
of socioeconomic classes. The device of a metamorphosis proves ideal
for Bulgakov's satiric purposes. The transformation of a dog into a
man is a bitingly cynical figure for the fate of the proletariat after
the Bolshevik revolution. "The sinister implications" of this revolutionary transformation, Lesley Milne points out, "emerge as Sharikov,
the dog-turned-man, incarnation of the lumpen-proletariat, learns to
manipulate denunciations and revolvers."[35]

Milne (1990) warns about the dangers of retrospective bias,
cautioning against excessively rigid or anachronistic allegorical
readings. To be precise, *Heart of a Dog* is an "NEP farce": "the
artistic key to the story lies not in any satirical 'allegory' but in its
theatricality and its NEP setting. The background is the housing
crisis" (65, 60). Milne reconstructs the specific topical environment
to which the satire is responding in the period of Bulgakov's composition—January–March 1925:

> The revolution had brought for Bulgakov defeat and dis-
> tress, but NEP was bringing life, lights, food, private
> publishing houses: somewhere to work, something to eat,
> somewhere to publish. In mid-1925 NEP was at its height.
> . . . In 1925 there was no reason for the 'bourgeois intel-
> lectual' in the Moscow street either to feel guilty about
> NEP or to foresee its end, when scepticism would be
> outlawed as a mode of thought and the Sharikovs would
> control the professors. It is the retrospective reading that
> gives a grim seethe of satire to the brilliantly ebullient
> humour in *Heart of a Dog.* (67–68)

Nevertheless, it is difficult to read *Heart of a Dog* today without
projecting upon Bulgakov a certain prescience about the imminent

demise of the New Economic Policy and the corollary suppression
of unauthorized artistic expressions: "by the end of 1925, anything
'satirical' was suspect, no matter how incidental the satire or how
humourless the reading. . . . On 7 May 1926 Bulgakov's flat was
subjected to a search and a typescript of [*Heart of a Dog*] was
confiscated" (Milne 1990, 60). It was not published in the Soviet
Union until 1987.

Previous interpretive attention has gone mainly to the character of Philip Philippovich Preobrazhensky, a surgeon with a thriv-
ing private practice providing surgical forms of sexual rejuvenation
to middle-aged Muscovites: "That initial premise, organ transplant
in connection with experiments on rejuvenation, was in the mid–
1920s a topical subject, much vulgarized by the popular press"
(Milne 1990, 62). Given the professor's similarity to Bulgakov's own
bourgeois background and medical training, Preobrazhensky has
generally been read as a straightforward mouthpiece espousing
Bulgakov's own antiproletarian views. Milne rightly underscores
Bulgakov's parodic treatment of the imperious professor, "the mask
of caricature" (62) that detaches the author to some degree from
this character. Nevertheless, "the focus of identification between
author and character . . . lies in Filipp Filippovich's positive attitude to the process of natural evolution and his rejection of his own
experiment in 'forcing nature.' This can obviously be read as an
allegory on the 'Russian experiment' in forcing a proletarian revolution in an industrially backward country" (63).

Within *Heart of a Dog,* however, the author's ambivalent position is equally well represented by the dog Sharik, a satire of the
bourgeois artist as free but threatened individual. Having thrown
over his own medical career for a literary one, Bulgakov had exposed himself that much more precariously to the political winds.
In the end, the victim of this tale is the dog, the *pharmakos* or
sacrificial offering, which will survive only as lobotomized. Thus
the element of Bulgakov's implicit identification with the dog's
metamorphic subjectivity is perhaps the deepest and most productive vein of the allegorical deposit. In fact, the dog-turned-man
known as Sharikov turns sinister due not to his canine but to his
human inheritance, the testicles and pituitary gland or "hypophysis" recovered from Klim Chugunkin, petty criminal, "a boor and a
swine" (*HD* 104). Preobrazhensky accomplishes the metamorphosis
through the surgical combination of the two species. In the name
of scientific progress, the Professor forces Sharik the free dog into
an unholy (daemonic) alliance with a man who represents the practical regressive inertia of the theoretically progressive masses.
Bulgakov uses metamorphic allegory to explore as well as enact the

conditions of freedom and constraint abroad in Soviet society at the time and place of his writing.

Like Sharik's transformation into Sharikov, the technological metamorphoses depicted in the various movie versions of "The Fly" concern the monstrous crossing of humanity with its own technological offspring. In the 1986 version, a scientific researcher attempting to perfect a teleportation device—a machine for the transmission of bodies—accidentally transforms himself into a monstrous composite of man and fly, and then of man/fly and machine.[36] Metamorphosis here results from a destructive noise breaking into the transmission circuit, the buzzing of an insect that scrambles the recoding of a decoded body. This cinematic science fiction offers an allegorical spectacle of the impossibility of transparent transmissions. Once again, a bodily metamorphosis is generated by a misreading, here, a scrambling of genetic texts.

On the basis of contemporary scientific paradigms, daemonic metamorphoses may now be read as fables of cybernetics.[37] From a cybernetic perspective, the daemon as messenger returns in the transmission and distortion of data, and metamorphosis is reconfigured in the universal medium of coded information. In Italo Calvino's *Cosmicomics* and *t zero*, cybernetic reinscriptions of physical and biological systems determine an ultimate relinquishing of organic models, and thus the end of metamorphosis based on biological bodies. Postmodern speculations cease to imagine metamorphosis as an alternation between or chimerical combination of discrete organic forms—ass, swine, snake, dog, or what have you. In a world of absolute simulation, there is no return trip, nowhere now for a reverse metamorphosis to revert. As Jean Baudrillard (1988) comments in *The Ecstasy of Communication*, "the body has been reduced to a division of surfaces, a proliferation of multiple objects wherein its finitude, its desirable representation, its seduc tion are lost. It is a metastatic body, a fractal body which can no longer hope for resurrection" (44).

That vision of cybernetic monstrosity is countered, however, by robotic theorists pursuing a cyborg technology in which the human mind will be downloaded into silicon circuits, as in the terminal vision of Hans Moravec's *Mind Children*.[38] The next phase of metamorphosis may be that which occurs when the organic body literally disappears altogether as a genetically specific configuration, whether human or otherwise, and is replaced by interchangeable generations of modular components. The organic body formed and transformed in the medium of earthbound hydrocarbon is thought to be disappearing with the advent of what O. B. Hardison, Jr., hails in *Disappearing Through the Skylight* as the "silicon creation," what Hardison's technological mentor Moravec envisions as the "postbiological world."[39]

The metamorphosis theme comes home to Hardison's discourse as a late variation on the Neoplatonic mortification of the living world and desire to escape the constraints of the generated creation. Hardison (1989) invokes the trope of metamorphosis to reinscribe it in a Pythagorean myth, reproducing a form of perception grounded in the hoariest of classical ideologies. The thought of the disappearance of the body takes the form of a sublime deliverance of the mind from the "carbon creation," and so merges with myths of the immortality and transcendence of the soul: "Perhaps the relation between carbon man and the silicon devices he is creating is like the relation between the caterpillar and the iridescent, winged creature that the caterpillar unconsciously prepares to become" (335).

Hardison's disappearing body is literally ecstatic, the technological fulfillment of theological images of spiritual metamorphosis. The imminent creation of immortal, extra-planetary silicon cyborgs is perhaps "the moment at which the spirit finally separates itself from an outmoded vehicle. Perhaps it is a moment that realizes the age-old dream of the mystics of rising beyond the prison of the flesh to behold a light so brilliant it is a kind of darkness" (347). Hardison compares his vision here to those of the aging Yeats, that sometime avatar of the classical Neoplatonic who, in verse at least, would renounce Circe's "honey of generation" and sail off to a spiritual Byzantium. So too Hardison envisions a cybernetic smithy to hammer the human spirit once and for all into cosmic machines, "shining constructs of silicon and gold and arsenic and germanium" that will "sail the spaces between worlds" (348). From this sublime perspective, as a weightless, sentient computer roving the galaxies, it is clear that "it was only the need to survive on a dangerous planet sculpted by gravity, covered with oxygen and nitrogen, and illuminated by a sun that led carbon creatures to grow feet for walking and ears for hearing and eyes for seeing. These are part of the dying animal to which carbon man is tied. . . . Silicon life will be immortal" (348).

The fate of the human body at this postmodern moment has to do with the continuing perfection of technologies capable of literalizing archaic tropes of transformation. There may be a "resurrection of the body" after all, but not for entropic humanity, for in the aftermath of this metamorphosis, intelligent machines will leave the earth far behind. Organic humanity will be the abandoned body of a transformation without return. Thus its enjoyment of this technological triumph will necessarily be vicarious, unless "a way to get our mind out of our brain" is perfected (Moravec 1988, 109).

In a section of *Mind Children* entitled "Transmigration," Moravec sketches the creation of a silicon creature by transfusion with and digital replication of a human personality:

> *You've just been wheeled into the operating room. A robot brain surgeon is in attendance. By your side is a computer waiting to become a human equivalent, lacking only a program to run. Your skull, but not your brain, is anesthetized. You are fully conscious. The robot surgeon opens your brain case and places a hand on the brain's surface. This unusual hand bristles with microscopic machinery, and a cable connects it to the mobile computer at your side. Instruments in the hand scan the first few millimeters of brain surface. . . .*
>
> *The surgeon's hand sinks a fraction of a millimeter deeper into your brain, instantly compensating its measurements and signals for the changed position. The process is repeated for the next layer, and soon a second simulation resides in the computer, communicating with the first and with the remaining original brain tissue. Layer after layer the brain is simulated, then excavated. Eventually your skull is empty, and the surgeon's hand rests deep in your brain stem. Though you have not lost consciousness, or even your train of thought, your mind has been removed from the brain and transferred to a machine. In a final, disorienting step the surgeon lifts out his hand. Your suddenly abandoned body goes into spasms and dies. For a moment you experience only quiet and dark. Then, once again, you can open your eyes. Your perspective has shifted. The computer simulation has been disconnected from the cable leading to the surgeon's hand and reconnected to a shiny new body of the style, color, and material of your choice. Your metamorphosis is complete. (109–10)*

In this last daemonic translation, humanity crosses over and into the medium of its own information sciences. One gives new birth to oneself from out of one's head, as Athena had sprung from the mind of Zeus, or Sin from the lust of Satan. Entropy and ecstasy combine in a metamorphic allegory of spiritual release from the mother of living matter. Yet the idea of a postbiological metamorphosis only makes technologically literal the sense in which all previous imaginations of bodily metamorphosis have also been allegories of writing.

3. Metamorphic Subjects

Allegory has often been criticized as a credulous, regressive literary mode, a vestige of unenlightened, superstitious times that preserves the prerogatives of exploded doctrines. The burden of superstition is that human beings are caught up in some hierarchical cosmos of adversarial powers and are liable to be put upon by those powers, and thus to lose their spiritual autonomy. By contrast, disabused of archaic taboos, the realistic hero increasingly moves in a world purged of daemonic obstacles. However, at present the value and possibility of absolute individual autonomy is under question, and the resurgence of literary interest in allegory has accompanied the progress of this critical skepticism. The autonomy of the ego championed by the realistic tradition is now thought to be unrealistic. The self cannot absolve itself from history; always already subjected to some collective discourse, the self is understood as a contingent ideological construction.[1] Transcoded into this structural idiom, metamorphic narratives allegorize the linguistic construction of the human psyche and its insertion into the ideological structures of the sociopolitical cosmos. In Althusser's (1971) formulation, "Ideology represents the imaginary relationship of individuals to their real conditions of existence" (162). As a kind of dream-work carried out at the level of an entire society and effecting a manifest inversion of latent social relations, ideology is itself an allegorical structure in need of analytical interpretation. Literary realism is therefore twice-removed from the real—an allegory of the bourgeois ideology of the subject, which is in turn a dark conceit masking the "real conditions of existence." If literary realism necessarily cloaks an ideological investment, then literary allegory is, ironically, more straightforward, because its manifest nonrealism declares its ideological nature and signals the need to decode its surface.[2]

In the working out of its own logic, the Enlightenment project that constructed the autonomous self has brought about the deconstruction of its own project, signaled by the re-emergence of a taste for the daemonic. Angus Fletcher's notion of "daemonic agency" in allegory returns in the deconstruction of the autonomous self, its subjection to specific positions within an overlapping network of collective structures. Where autonomy was, we now see

53

allonomy. Part of our interest in the allegorical tradition, then, is
the recognition that our structural destiny is already encoded there,
in the guise of the daemonic. At the same time, deconstructive
interpretation is itself allegorical in that it carries out a universal
retranslation of nominal spiritual presences into the matter of language. So if the daemonic cosmos of traditional allegory can now be
read as encoding some specific material structure, so too may the
discourse of structure be read as an allegory of the daemonic, as in
Lacan's (1977) formula that the Unconscious is "the discourse of
the Other" (172).[3] Linguistic structurality is now the psychic or
ideological operator taking daemonic possession of persons, thus
the defensiveness with which it is resisted. Thus, too, we can look
at the theory of allegory for insights into the poststructural theory
of the subject.

The literary-critical academy continues to be divided between
the humanist maintenance of the primacy of individual agency and
the poststructuralist dismantling of the subject into its collective
discourses. This persistent dispute over the competing claims of
self and system is a modern instance of the tensions between freedom and fixity, dynamic and static agency, metamorphic stories
have always dramatized. Images of metamorphic subjectivity are
profoundly ambivalent, fluctuating between capture and liberation,
structural sentence and personal escapade. Skulsky (1981) focuses
on the maintenance of identity in the midst of transformation: the
idea of metamorphosis "forces a confrontation with some or all of
a small cluster of concerns associated with the nature of personhood
and personal identity," and metamorphic texts proclaim "the autonomy of the mental" (6, 5). But Fletcher (1964) inflects these
abiding tensions in an opposite manner: "To be not a free agent,
but a fixed one . . . , I think, is the case with all allegorical agents,
and when an author is interested in what seem to be free metamorphoses and changes of state, he is in fact not showing his characters acting freely. He is showing them changing, presto, from one
facet of a destiny to another. . . . The chief metamorphic poet, Ovid,
is naturally turned to exegetical use in the *Ovide Moralisé,* since he
himself draws attention so often to the opposite of change, namely
fixity" (63–64). Fletcher's study anticipates the convergence of allegorical and poststructural agency by emphasizing what he elsewhere terms the "compartmentalization" and "segmented character"
of the daemonic agent, its circumscription within a collective hierarchical cosmos, such as Kafka's daemonic bureaucracies.

Yet the force of Fletcher's analysis of allegorical destiny depends on the counterstress of transformative change, that is, on the
possible mobility of desire in dialectical opposition to the status of

conceptual fixity. Massey (1976) approaches bodily metamorphoses as ironic figures of self-defense against collective constraints. Physical transformations into nonhuman kinds are forms of self-preservation, purchased at the expense of one's proper species. Metamorphic changes constellate the tension between autonomous persons and the structural impersonality of linguistic and moral codes. Refusing to identify with a communal body or with the given norms of a system, the metamorph attempts to escape the possession of language itself, the language of an Other. For Massey, metamorphs "are engaged in protecting themselves from the demands of public communication, from the requirement that they utter, and that they fit into a verbal social order by confessing to a name" (32). Metamorphosis plays out a dream logic undercutting imposed identities and asserting a nonverbal level of individual authenticity. Deleuze and Guattari (1986) carry the view of the metamorph as ecstatic, speechless renegade to an extreme: "to become animal is to participate in movement, to stake out the path of escape in all its positivity, to cross a threshold, to reach a continuum of intensities that are valuable only in themselves, to find a world of pure intensities where all forms come undone, as do all the significations, signifiers, and signifieds" (13). And yet these authors go on to remark that episodes of metamorphic flight in Kafka remain suspended and constrained by opposing forces: these metamorphoses appear to "oscillate between a schizo escape and an Oedipal impasse" (15).

It is clear at least that the subject of metamorphosis is bound up with the structure of the semiotic subject. Metamorphic allegory is an intersection or structural crossing-point between verbal tropes and human subjects, a reification of the transformative interplay between linguistic and psychological figures. Tales of metamorphosis may be read as stories of self-preservation in the midst of soul-destroying powers—a reading that descends from classical allegorizations of Odysseus's encounter with Circe—but they may be read with equal facility as mythopoetic expressions of the tropic determinations of the human psyche. Metamorphic episodes carry with them residual trappings of the mythic, the supernatural, or the daemonic, but in any guise they reflect the displacements and deformations of identity produced by commerce with material structures and cultural forces. The next section traces the epic inscription of affective transformation in the Proteus and Circe episodes of Homer and Ovid. The following sections of this chapter scale the cosmos of metamorphic allegory from the level of individual psychology to that of the communal dynamics of collective subjects— houses and states—in the *Golden Ass, One Hundred Years of Solitude,* and *Jekyll and Hyde.*

Transformations of Affect

Joel Fineman (1991) has remarked that structural psychoanalysis "is not simply the analysis of, but the extension and conclusion of the classical allegorical tradition from which it
derives—which is why psychoanalysis so readily assimilates the
great archetypes of allegorical imagery into its discourse: the labyrinths, the depths, the navels, the psychomachian hydraulics" (4);
he has in mind Lacan's "barring of the subject—the loss of being
that comes from re-presenting oneself in language as a meaning,"
which "makes the psyche a critical allegory of itself and is what
justifies psychoanalysis as the allegory of that allegory" (20). In
certain prestructural formulations of Anna and Sigmund Freud,
the self-divisions produced by the installation and displacement of
psychic signifiers are developed phenomenologically as "transformations of affect": "Love, longing, jealousy, mortification, pain and
mourning accompany sexual wishes," writes Anna Freud; "hatred,
anger, and rage accompany the impulses of aggression; if the instinctual demands with which they associated are to be warded off,
these affects must submit to all the various measures to which the
ego resorts in its efforts to master them, i.e., they must undergo a
metamorphosis."[4] The younger Freud may have been thinking of
her father's comment that as a result of repression, "the vanished
affect comes back in its transformed shape" (*"Der verschwundene
Affekt kommt in der Verwandlung . . . wieder"* (*SE* 14:157;
Gesammelte Werke 10:260). This psychoanalytical metaphor concerning the metamorphosis of affect can be usefully extended and
coupled to a structural redescription.

With the institution of a verbal psyche, human affectivity is
necessarily modulated through linguistic structures. Metamorphoses in literature can be read as allegories of these processes of
dynamic affect. It is a commonplace that the epic hero personifies
the ego—its developmental trials, its dragon-slaying exploits.
Odysseus self-bound to the mast as he sails past the Sirens is a
famous case in point of the epic dramatization of ego-mastery. Similarly, the device of a bodily metamorphosis may be considered within
this structure as a mythic or literary representation of the suppression and transformation of the affects connected to drives. "In repression," Freud notes in "The Unconscious," "a severance takes
place between the affect and the idea to which it belongs . . . each
then undergoes its separate vicissitudes" (*SE* 14:179). Just as repression splits the drive into a discontinuous composite of idea and
affect, metamorphosis severs the mental and the physical identity
of the metamorph. The conveying of erring souls into errant bodies

represents the punitive or defensive dislocation and wandering of signs and drives. In the same way, the notion of a reverse or restorative metamorphosis may represent some recovery of a prior propriety, a welcome or unwelcome return of the repressed, a homecoming in which the dynamized affect is discharged, either by reconnection to its original idea, or by displacement to an adequate substitute.

Imagining the undoing and possible recoupling of the connection between a physical form and a mental identity, metamorphoses plot the dispossession of a given subjective relation and the displacement of its terms. Extending this metaphor to its limit, metamorphosis becomes an allegory of the death drive—absolute en-tropy, the complete literalization of the figurative.[5] Like "*an instinct*," the metamorph—suspended by an allegorical narrative somewhere between the loss and the possible recovery of a proper body—may be said to represent "*an urge inherent in organic life to restore an earlier state of things* which the living entity has been obliged to abandon under the pressure of external disturbing forces" (*SE* 18:36).[6] The serpentine Lamia cries to Hermes from the crypt of her change, "When from this wreathed tomb shall I awake! / When move in a sweet body fit for life" (1.38–39). One way or another, the metamorph longs to die, altogether, or back into life.

In their large movements, literary metamorphoses reify the vicissitudes of repression. If in its uncanny imprisonment the metamorph discovers opportunities for experiences disbarred from the proper body, transformative wandering is equally marked by the duress of repression: dispossession, exile, and travail. The German term for "transformation" is *Wandlung,* from the verb *wandeln,* "to change," but with a secondary sense of locomotion, a changing of positions: "to amble," "to wander." "Metamorphosis" is *Verwandlung,* and the prefix *Ver-* puts a strong turn on the root meanings, for metamorphosis is a "mis-change," metamorphs "mis-wander." The thematic fields of metamorphic allegory are united in the figure of the metamorphic mis-wanderer as dis-possessed agent. Cast out of its proper body, the metamorph can personify the wanderings of signifiers, the change of meanings under metaphoric processes, the wandering of the components of drives under repression, the metempsychoses of the departed soul, the circulation of commodities, and the literal exile of materially displaced persons. In this account, the human psyche is a catastrophic creation, a scene of double dislodging, with the gradient always rolling away from naive origination, producing an inescapable surplus of loss. The repression of drives not only erases ideas from consciousness, but also dislodges and dislocates the affects bound to repressed ideas and dynamizes them into metamorphic forms. So metamorphic narratives are a primary language for the affective metamorphoses of persons. .

The transformations affects both endure and create are literally at play in the *Odyssey*. In Book 4, Menelaos recounts to Telemachos one of his homecoming adventures: how he languished in the doldrums on the island of Pharos, how he was given a plan by Eidothëe—the mischievous daughter of the divinatory sea god Proteus, "the unerring old man of the sea" (*HO* 4.349)—instructing him how to extort from Proteus the intelligence necessary to continue his journey. When Menelaos worries that "it is hard for a god to be subdued by a mortal man" (397), Eidothëe replies:

> "I shall tell you all the cunning of this old man.
> At first he will number the seals and go over them,
> But when he has counted them by fives and looked at
>   them all,
> He will lie in their midst like a shepherd amid flocks of
>   sheep.
> And when you first see him lying down to rest,
> At that very moment give heed to your strength and
>   might.
> Hold him struggling there, though he be violent to escape.
> He will try it by becoming all the many creatures
> That move on the earth; and then water, and divinely
>   kindled fire.
> But hold him firmly yourselves and constrain him the more.
> When at last he questions you with a speech as himself
> And is the way he was when you saw him resting,
> Then, hero, hold back your strength and release the old man,
> And ask him which one of the gods oppresses you,
> And about a return, how you may go on the fish-laden
>   ocean." (*HO* 4.410–24)

To read this episode as a psychoanalytical allegory is only to update the Neoplatonic practice of reading Homer as an author of theological allegories. Lamberton (1986) passes along Proclus's reading: "Proteus is an angelic mind . . . containing within himself the forms of all things that come to be and pass away . . . Eidothea is a demonic soul . . . joined to that divine intellect . . . seals are the mythoplasts' means of representing the flock of individual souls dependent on this particular divine 'procession' " (viii).[7] In my psychoanalytical version, Menelaos becomes the heroic ego, the surface voyager of conscious identity, Proteus the drive aspect or surface/depths of affective response. Human feeling is an ancient mariner or "old man of the sea," a deep structure cunning with the genetic wisdom of ages. But still, Proteus is gullible enough to be tricked by his daughter. Proteus has been subverted, "troped" by his daemonic daughter Eidothëe, enabling him to be duped and tamed by the hero. Through polytropic trickery and Homeric cunning, Menelaos (the heroic ego) masters Proteus (metamorphic affectivity), suspends and subjugates the demigod, marks its transformations, releasing it once its energies are spent or appropriately converted. Mastering Proteus, Menelaos produces the intelligence he needs to procure his own homecoming; otherwise the hero would have remained in the doldrums, spiritless, lacking a text.

Coming between Proteus and Menelaos, Eidothëe is the daemonic middle term or shifter, the pivot that doubles the relation. Once Proteus (the drive) has been doubled or double-crossed by Eidothëe (the idea), he turns into a metamorphic wanderer (the affect) oppressed by Menelaos (the ego). So in Homer's story of Proteus, metamorphosis as a parable of affect doubles metamorphosis as an allegory of writing and (mis)reading. Proteus "counts" his seals but misreads the counterfeit seal, Menelaos. Signifiers simply cannot be trusted eternally to duplicate the same significations. Without warning they turn into figures, either the previous figures that once constituted the signifiers, or new figures produced as the terms are given in new combinations. Proteus suffers the potential fate of any signification: he is trapped by a trope, metamorphosed by a metaphor.

Moreover, Eidothëe's advice to Menelaos amounts to a chiasmus crossing the human and the divine: you oppress Proteus the way the gods have oppressed you. Menelaos accomplishes this feat by mimicking the divine prerogative of metamorphic disguise.[8] In order to ambush the old man of the sea, Menelaos performs a mock metamorphosis, disguising himself beneath the sealskin. Proteus produces his own metamorphoses as a defense in an unsuccessful attempt to escape possession by the letter—the hero and his daemonic name, "son of Atreus." He ends up compelled to render Menelaos the script he demands. Menelaos describes his encounter with Proteus:

> "At full light the old man came from the sea and found
>   his seals
> Well nourished; he went over them all and counted their
>   number,
> And us he numbered first among the seals, nor did it
>   occur

> To his heart that there was a trick. Then he lay down
>   himself.
> But we rushed on him with a shout and threw our hands
> Around him. The old man did not forget his wily skill.
> First of all he became a lion with a mighty beard,
> And then a serpent, and a panther, and a great boar.
> Then he became watery water, and a lofty-leaved tree.
> But we held on firmly with an enduring heart,
> And when the old man of cunning skill was exhausted,
> He spoke out to me and questioned me with a speech:
> 'Which of the gods, son of Atreus, has devised plots for you
> That you catch me in ambush against my will? What do
>   you need?' " (*HO* 4.450–63)

And yet the deviser of this plot was no god, it was his daughter. Metamorphoses represent the transformation by exchange or inversion of prior relations between primary and secondary terms, here anthropomorphized as a father and his child. That which was previously subordinate asserts mastery, as Eidothëe puts one over on the old man, as the mortal Menelaos proceeds to reduce the immortal Proteus to the panorama of his scenic properties. Proteus captured and compelled by Menelaos represents in mythic literalness the production of metamorphic figures in the dynamic career of affective processes. An affective transformation, produced by a trope, initiates a (mytho)poesis, a narrative of errant scenic changes throughout which a thread of identity is loosely laced—the thread by which, for instance, the "unerring" Proteus remains the erring and errant Proteus as well. The wisdom of the dupe Proteus is that human feelings have their own orders of heroism and victimization.

The next metamorphic scene in the *Odyssey*, the Circe episode in Book 10, also plays on the transformation of affect. First, here is the working of Circe's spell in Homer, as Odysseus narrates it to the Phaeacians. Circe invites Odysseus's men into her halls on the otherwise deserted island of Aiaia, and bids them eat:

> "And she stirred into the food
> Woeful drugs that make one forget his fatherland wholly.
> But when she had given it and they had drunk, she at once
> Struck them with her wand and shut them up into sties.
> They had the heads of swine and the voice and the hair
> And the body, but the mind was steady as before.
> So they were penned in, weeping . . . ." (*HO* 10.235–41)

In the *Metamorphoses,* Ovid chooses to narrate the episode from the perspective of a supposed participant and survivor, one Macareus:

> "We took the cups she offered,
> And we were thirsty, and we drank them down,
> And then the cruel goddess touched our foreheads
> With her magic wand—I am ashamed to tell you,
> But I will tell—I had bristles sprouting on me,
> I could not speak, but only grunting sounds
> Came out instead of words, and my face bent over
> To see the ground. I felt my mouth grow harder,
> I had a snout instead of a nose, my neck
> Swelled with great muscles, and the hand which lifted
> The cup to my lips made footprints on the ground.
> They shut me in a pigsty with the others." (*OH* 14.276–86)

In this classic metamorphic tableau, Circe takes Odysseus's men into her halls, then takes them in further, tricks them with a drug. The patriarchal ratio of the epic is reversed, as a female overpowers and enslaves a male band. The daemonic agent Circe serves up a daemonic agent, a drug with the power to induce an exile from a "fatherland." Tricked and charmed, they are imprisoned within bodies of swine, as the swine are then penned within their sties. Accompanying these metamorphic processes are affective key-notes: in Homer's version, the weeping of the men, signifying horror at their transformation, mourning for their lost bodies, but also, their enduring consciousness, the maintenance of identity at the level of feelings. Ovid exploits the larger episode for the fantastic opulence of Circe's halls and the sensational aspects of the transformation proper, downplaying the theme of the heroic ego by shortening the account of Odysseus's rescue mission. Yet Ovid too strikes an affective keynote—"I am ashamed"—one that displaces that sign of affect from the metamorphosis proper to its narration, its "confession." Ovid's text is rendered ironic, modernized, by making the narrator a former metamorph. The narrator of the Circe episode within Ovid's narration is a victim, not a hero, and so has no epic authority, whereas in Homer's account, Odysseus's mastery is measured exactly by his ability to circumvent the shame of falling under Circe's spell.

Homer's Odysseus gives a long account of how Hermes enabled him to avoid Circe's transformation and rescue his men:

"And when I was about to go through the sacred glen
To come to the great house of Circe of the many drugs,
Hermes of the golden wand came across my path. . . .
'Well, I will release you from evil and rescue you.
Here, take this excellent drug to the halls of Circe
And enter; so it may ward off from your head the evil day.
I shall tell you all of Circe's pernicious wiles. . . .'
When he had said this, the god, the slayer of Argos, gave
          me the drug,
He had plucked out of the earth, and showed me its nature.
It was black at the root, but its flower was like milk.
The gods call it moly. . . ." (*HO* 10.275–305)

Thanks to the intervention of Hermes, Odysseus's *pharmakon* protects him from Circe's *pharmakon*, the Homeric hero wards off the
metamorphic power of a daemonic adversary and forces her to
restore human forms to his transformed companions. Circe

"went in their midst
And with another drug she rubbed each one of them.
The hair fell off their limbs that the baleful drug
The queenly Circe gave them before had made grow there.
They became men again, younger than they were before
And far more handsome and larger to behold.
They recognized me, and each one grasped my hands.
The longed-for weeping came on them all. The house about
Terribly resounded, and the goddess herself felt pity."
                                      (391–99)

     In Circe's restoration of Odysseus's men to human status, the
significant psychoanalytical detail is "the house resounded," a figure
that gathers and unifies the affective repercussions of the metamorphoses. Once the "minds" of the men are rejoined to their proper,
now enhanced, bodies, weeping comes over them. "Weeping" properly accompanies both the tragic and comic ends of affective transformation, first as a function of the grief of loss, last as a function
of the joy of recovery. Post-metamorphic weeping in the *Odyssey*
signifies two things at least: the release and discharge of a post-
poned, suspended affect, heightened by the deferral occasioned by
the metamorphic interlude itself; in addition, the patriarchal regu-
lation of masculine affect, Odysseus's discipline concerning *kairos*,
the proper and improper moments for self-display. As such this
episode glances forward to the familial and patriarchal climax of
the epic, the return to "the fatherland," when after a last episode

of delay Odysseus reveals himself to and reconnects himself with Laertes: Odysseus's "heart was aroused, and a piercing throb had already / Struck through his nostrils when he saw his dear father" (24.318–19).

Just as dynamic affects take on metamorphic figures, metamorphic fables trace the fates of outcast agents. Some trauma, judgment, or severing circumstance dissolves an original participation. The community of body and soul is sundered, as lovers and groups are sundered and cast out of proper scenes. Severed agents wander, during which disguise (substitute representation) and metamorphosis (qualitative transformation) are either inescapable circumstances or desperate survival tactics. Metamorphic wandering leads either to catastrophic conclusions as the outcasts encounter utter shipwreck or nightmares of endless repetition, or to comic resolutions, some recuperative episode of recognition, a reunion or homecoming, the construction of a new home, the reconstruction of a substitute home adequate to bind the heart. The irrecoverable proper bond between ideas and affects signifies but forever defers the naturalness of instinctual being. When eros proceeds from the unconscious memory of this loss, it figures its desire as the scenic recovery of a proper body.

Shame and Disappearance

A metamorphosis determines at once a monstrous exhibition and a total concealment of the self. The metamorph's ambivalence between spectacular display and complete effacement plays off the psychology of shame. Shame is to metamorphosis what melancholy is to Baroque allegory: the affective keynote.[9] Metamorphic fictions are often studies of inappropriateness and misappropriation, embarrassment and theft, because the trope of metamorphosis is particularly measured to feelings of shame produced by "misreading." Metamorphoses are typically generated by mistakes or inappropriate acts. In this the metamorphic mis-take mirrors, repeats and doubles, what Lacan (1977) terms "the *méconnaissances* that constitute the ego" (6). The misprision that displaces the fictional agent and reconfigures it as a metamorph is a symbolic repetition of a prior misprision, the fall into self-division that "constitutes the ego."

Metamorphoses underscore the slipperiness of human identity. Our egos are always poised for a pratfall, tripping over what looked like smooth ground. Bodily transformations produce a displacement of identity, a certain humiliation, as with Apuleius's Thelyphron or Shakespeare's Bottom present a literal "loss of face," a tragedy of sorts, but a mockery in which the element of shaming can pivot in either epic/tragic or comic/parodic directions. Depending on the valence of its presentation, a human metamorphosis can indicate either a shamefully mortifying or a shamelessly mischievous episode. Although the rhetoric of shame is especially prominent in metamorphic fictions—in *Jekyll and Hyde,* for instance, Jekyll repeats his "almost morbid sense of shame. . . . I laid aside restraint and plunged in shame" (*JH* 350–51)—the postures of moral response can always turn into matters for mockery, embarrassments that can easily be played for comedy.

A metamorphosis presents an improper spectacle, exposing to comic ridicule that which should be concealed. The scene and vehicle of this tragicomedy is at bottom the human genitalia, the pudenda, the *Schamteile.*[10] The penitential or inadvertent public exposure of private parts is an archetype of metamorphic judgment or metamorphic comedy. In the first anecdote of the *Golden Ass,* Lucius chances to hear a story about the unfortunate trip of "Socrates," who had been brought low in a strange town through the love magic of the witch Meroë and given up for dead. On the face of it, this "Socrates" represents the shame of impoverishment; the humiliation of dispossession; material, economic misfortune as a consequence of and a motive for scenic transformations. But his transformative reversal is sexual as well as economic, an unmanning by a daemonic female. When his old friend Aristomenes comes upon the pathetic, dispossessed Socrates, the latter fears to be recognized, to have his identity known in his circumstances: "he covered his face, which had long since begun to redden from shame, with his patched cloak, baring the rest of his body from his navel to his loins" (*AM* 15). In this comedy of embarrassment, Socrates's attempt to hide his blush leads only to further and more extreme exposure.

Like all the voluble confidence men and women since Satan, the shameless are eloquent. By contrast, metamorphs from Lucius to Gregor are aphasic. Like the contemplative melancholiac of Baroque allegory, the agent that has taken shame upon itself is silent. In Kafka's *Metamorphosis,* the verminous Gregor signifies an opaque state of shame. All the significant actions in the tale are turns on the exhibition and concealment of the metamorphic self. Even before anyone knows of Gregor's new condition, the chief clerk cries through the closed door: "I thought you were a quiet, dependable person, and now all at once you seem bent on making a disgraceful exhibition of yourself" (*M* 25). Gregor's transformation into an aphasic metamorph creates an uncanny enclosure within which the person disappears. Although for a while Gregor still knows he exists, he cannot finally convince anyone except an un-kempt charwoman of that fact. As Léon Wurmser has written, "Shame's aim is disappearance. This may be, most simply, in the form of hiding; most radically, in the form of dissolution (suicide); most mythically, in the form of a change into another shape, an animal or a stone."[11]

In the *Golden Ass* such metamorphic seriousness is dissolved in parodic laughter, as a series of gags are built on comic humili-ations and embarrassing mistakes. Lucius's metamorphosis proper is closely preceded by an elaborate practical joke, exposing him to ridicule and humiliation, all in fun of course. I will pass over the details of the "Festival of Laughter," to focus in on the effect of its climax on Lucius:

> As the great crowd poured out of the theatre, drowned in floods of mirth, every face was turned back for a last hilarious look at me.... I had been standing there as stiff and cold as stone, exactly as if I had been one of the marble columns that supported the roof.... Then my tears burst out once more, and I could not restrain my compulsive sobbing.... [Milo] tried to calm me by cheer-ful attempts at consolation, but I was now burning with such indignation at having been victimized in this in-sulting way that he could do nothing with me. (*GA* 60)

For the Festival of Laughter, an annual town rite, Lucius has the misfortune to be the butt of the joke; the town ceremoniously and gleefully makes an ass out of him. In response, at first he turns stone cold (immobilized, fixated by shame); when that ice thaws out he flows with tears (grief over his loss of face); then he starts to boil ("burn" with anger). Here Lucius's phases of feeling take Protean or fleeting, watery shapes, as icy shame heats into steamy indignation. These are in fact affective fore-tremors, credible pre-monitions of the incredible metamorphosis into an actual ass he will soon undergo.

Some of the embarrassing errors figuring in the comedy of the *Golden Ass* concern the mistaking of containers, a humorously thin disguise for the daemonic substitution of bodies. Lucius's actual transformation is a classic scene of comic misprision. The immedi-ate cause of his metamorphosis into an ass was that his lover, Fotis, mistook the *pharmakon*, the proper jar of magical ointment:

> Then my face swelled, my mouth widened, my nostrils dilated, my lips hung flabbily down, and my ears shot up

> long and hairy. The only consoling part of this miserable
> transformation was the enormous increase in the size of
> a certain organ of mine; because I was by this time finding
> it increasingly difficult to meet all Fotis's demands upon
> it. At last, hopelessly surveying myself all over, I was
> obliged to face the mortifying fact that I had been trans-
> formed not into a bird, but into a plain jackass. (GA 71)

As the result of his misconceived attempt to steal a magical secret,
in a sheer reversal and mortification of his personhood, Lucius is
dispossessed of his Roman physique for the body of an ass. Although Lucius retains his mind and his male member, materially
he is reduced from a free aristocratic agent to a slavish mute beast
of burden, a commodity to be stolen, abused, and discarded. And
Lucius no sooner suffers his metamorphosis than a roving band of
thieves knocks over Milo's house, where he had been a guest, lift-
ing Milo's goods and Lucius as well. The metamorphosis and the
theft are both of a piece: both represent a "mis-taking," a bit of
Hermetic embarrassment, a breakdown of personal boundaries
resulting in a certain redistribution of possessions.

Feelings of shame can be mobilized by the repression of pleasure in the senses, disbarments of erotic sensuality that extend to
vision and visual activity—looking and appearing, seeing and being seen.[12] Metamorphic myth tells a story of ocular shame when
Diana turns Actaeon into a stag for stumbling upon her at her
bath. His metamorphosis punishes his transgression, the guilt of
having looked at a forbidden sight. But that guilt is only a function
of the shame dynamic represented by Diana's inviolable space, her
"inner boundary."[13] The sacred concealment of a divine female from
profane male eyes, enforced with a metamorphic curse, is a mythic
expression of the gender topography of shame. By way of comparison, in the opening of Keats's Lamia, an invisible nymph hides
from a male god. As Keats has it, Hermes needs the uncanny Lamia's
assistance to render the nymph visible and thus possessable. Having bargained for Lamia's aid, Hermes "shames" the nymph, exposing her to his sight, to the (phallic) sight of himself, fixing her in
a visible posture, and so downing his prey. This parable treats the
way that shame dynamics mask the politics of gender identifications, the way that women tend to be identified with sensuality per
se, with the power to dismantle male spiritual resolve. Thus the
accusation of shame tends to fall or be deflected to the female
position. Shame motifs in metamorphic fictions generally mark a
trace of the dispossessed female in the text. A female metamorph
like Lamia is already a turning outside of the inside of metamor-

phic figures. When a metamorphosis eliminates the proper body, that repression can play out the script in which the invisibility of the feminine supplements a masculine identity.

Prior to his metamorphosis, Lucius's *curiositas* had been implicitly admonished by a statue of Diana in the courtyard of Byrrhaena.[14] Lucius's "deep blush" and "embarrassment" are especially noticeable when they meet in the street and she reminds him that his mother and she are "foster sisters, brought up together in the same house. . . . You must come to stay with me at once, and treat my house as your home" (*GA* 26). Although in deference to the proprieties of hospitality, Lucius declines her invitation—as a proper guest it would be discourteous of him to leave his host Milo—he soon visits her. In fact, Lucius's unwillingness to "treat her house as his home" is also in unstated, ironic deference to the incest taboo. Around this inviting mother-figure, Apuleius develops Lucius's "curiosity" as the manifest motive for his forthcoming metamorphosis.

Byrrhaena is Lucius's allotted daemon or good angel, giving him a sign intended to hold him back from erotic transgressions. Specifically, in the center of Byrrhaena's court is a statue of the goddess Diana in the act of transforming Actaeon into a stag. Byrrhaena thus admonishes Lucius with visions both of the forbidden goddess and of the metamorphic fixity visited as punishment upon the overly curious. Her warnings intervene just at the point of Lucius's fateful decisions to stay in Milo's house and to use sexual relations with the slave-girl Fotis to bargain his way to her mistress Pamphile's possessions, her magical, latently maternal, secrets of witchcraft. So relative to Pamphile, Byrrhaena is a "good witch," a bourgeois madonna trying to warn an errant son-figure not to pry any further into sexual magic:

> "My dearest Lucius . . . I swear by this goddess that I am very worried and afraid for you, and I want you to be forewarned far in advance, as if you were my own son. Be careful! I mean watch out carefully for the evil arts and criminal seductions of that woman Pamphile, who is the wife of that Milo you say is your host. She is considered to be a witch of the first order. . . . No sooner does she catch sight of some young man of attractive appearance than she is consumed by his charm and immediately directs her eye and her desire at him. . . . If any do not respond and become cheap in her eyes by their show of repugnance, she transforms them on the spot into rocks or sheep or any other sort of animal; some, however, she completely annihilates." (*AM* 67–69)

The Oedipal motifs of metamorphic allegory often coalesce in the figure of the witch, the female agent of daemonic possession. Both Diana and Pamphile represent that realm of the daemonic female in relation to which oedipal son-figures, whether peeping voyeuristically at chaste goddesses or defying the wishes of unchaste matrons, end up embarrassingly transformed. Lucius's misreading here is simply the refusal to read, his impetuous disregard of Byrrhaena's warning. Moreover, it is not Pamphile's but Lucius's lust that proves decisive: "far from being cautious of Pamphile, I yearned to turn myself over to an apprenticeship of that sort willingly and voluntarily, with all its high costs, and plunge right to the bottom of the pit with one quick leap" (*AM 69*). As matters quickly work out, Pamphile's maid Fotis, a socially improper but nonincestuous object for Lucius's desire, is herself in no mood for delaying sexual commerce with the noble but ingenuous youth. In general, human metamorphoses encode parental and filial sexual dynamics as a matter of course, perhaps as a necessary function of a filial mind's approach to the landscape of a parental body.

In metamorphic stories, then, the affective dynamics of shame are closely tied to the psychology of the incest prohibition. This cluster of concerns is emblematized in the Sphinx whose monstrous body confronts Oedipus with an image of his transgressive destiny. Another concatenation of shame, incest, cursing, matriarchy, and metamorphosis makes a prominent appearance in García Márquez's *One Hundred Years of Solitude*. To draw this complex out, I will focus briefly on two curses uttered by Úrsula, the matriarch of the Buendía family. Throughout the novel Úrsula is the hapless figure of proper repression and the primary, if ultimately unsuccessful, enforcer of the incest taboo. Úrsula's first curse occurs in an early passage detailing incidents leading up to the first incestuous crossing of the Buendía line during the 16th-century founding of the colony: "every time that Úrsula became exercised over her husband's mad ideas she would leap back over three hundred years of fate and curse the day that Sir Francis Drake had attacked Riohacha. . . . Actually they were joined till death by a bond that was more solid than love: a common prick of conscience. They were cousins" (*GM* 27–28).

As cousins, Úrsula and José Arcadio Buendía are simply siblings once removed. So Úrsula's first curse names incest as the original sin of the House, a definition proper to all persons and all houses constructed according to Oedipal blueprints. In dreams, as in Kafka, children are typically represented by insects; insects are connected to incest through association with the child.[15] In the second half of the novel, once her role in the House has been usurped by Fernanda, Úrsula curses a second time, and this curse is meta-morphic: the first curse, a prick of conscience over incest, turns now into the bite of an imaginary bug. As in Kafka's *Metamorphosis,* a daemonic (rhetorical) insect appears in the vicinity of an incestuous crossing:

> Úrsula ... felt irrepressible desires to let herself go ... putting her resignation aside and shitting on everything once and for all and drawing out of her heart the infinite stacks of bad words that she had been forced to swallow over a century of conformity.
> "Shit!" she shouted.
> Amaranta ... thought that she had been bitten by a scorpion.
> "Where is it?" she asked in alarm.
> "What?"
> "The bug!" Amaranta said.
> Úrsula put a finger on her heart.
> "Here," she said. (235–36)

Úrsula's first curse was on the circumstances that first crossed her family's line with that of her husband. She cursed because she felt stings of conscience, *Gewissensbisse,* the bite of the incest-bug. After her second curse, Úrsula borrows Amaranta's (metamorphic) misapprehension to give the curse a local habitation: inside the heart. The imaginary bug biting her heart is the curse on the line, the curse that keeps her ever-vigilant against "the shame of breeding iguanas." So Úrsula names and locates the incest curse: it is a parasite, a daemonic creature that has entered the blood of the line and lodged in the heart. But García Márquez means to signify something more by crossing Úrsula's curses with the incest plot. The "infinite stacks of bad words" that Úrsula could "draw out of her heart" also names the dysfunctions of the Logos. The curse of a deadly letter, the bad Word, has captured the flesh of the Buendías. In this novel, the Logos and its state apparatuses are corrupt: religion and politics that promise love and peace bring hatred and death instead. García Márquez turns the novel into a translucent protest against the tragic monstrosities of civil conflicts by using a comically curled vestige of metamorphosis—the incestuous "pig's tail"—to encode his text with the repercussions of state repression. So the incest motif covers another monstrosity, the pervasive virulence of the repressive state.[16]

In the second part of the novel, the curse on the house materializes as Fernanda herself, that is, as the Highland moral discourse

she personifies. Fernanda's allegorical emblem is her version of the
alchemical crucible, her gilded chamberpot, the occult scene where
shit is turned into gold. Because she is exogamous, Fernanda fits
ironically into the incest plot, but directly into the metamorphic
paradigms. As a cultural foreigner who is taken into the heart of
the House, she brings into Macondo not a literal but a spiritual
incest more monstrous than any previous of the Buendías' own
various copulations. Fernanda is implicated in the fulfillment of
the incest curse not through sex but through repression, for it was
Fernanda who out of shame banished Meme from the house and
then concealed the identity of Aureliano, Meme's child by Mauricio
Babilonia. By causing the last Buendía lovers to copulate in ignorance of their shared blood, Fernanda's shame sets up the metamorphic apocalypse of the Buendía line, the birth of the pig-tailed
baby. Repressing the authentic relations among persons and things,
Fernanda forces the family line onto its final, catastrophic course.
So Fernanda is pitted against Úrsula as a daemonic figure for the
descent of the bad Logos from the Highland into the flesh of the
House. She represents both a bitter parody of Christian theology
and an allegory for the corrupt, inappropriate repressions of the
political order.

> At night, after taps, they knocked doors down with their
> rifle butts, hauled suspects out of their beds, and took
> them on trips from which there was no return. The search
> for and extermination of the hoodlums, arsonists, and
> rebels of Decree No. 4 was still going on, but the military
> denied it even to the relatives of the victims who crowded
> the commandantes' offices in search of news. "You must
> have been dreaming," the officers insisted. "Nothing has
> happened in Macondo, nothing has ever happened, and
> nothing ever will happen. This is a happy town." (287)

Counter to Úrsula, Fernanda is the sign of corrupt repression,
the repression that does not prevent "monstrosity"—fundamentally,
the commission of incest—but rather shadows and promotes it by
closing up the house and so turning the line in upon itself. Fernanda
transforms the House by putting an end to healthy vulgar hospitality, casting out the undesirable elements, like a postrevolutionary
society turning its aggression in upon itself. The shamefulness of
Fernanda is a large figure for the shame of the state that terrorizes
its own citizens. But "incest" will breed its monsters, especially in
the national state crossing its own lines against itself, turning
against itself and its critics, its spiritual physicians, its writers.

The terrors of depraved regimes are fundamentally terrible inces-tuous solitudes, hysterical defenses enacted by the punitive state within the body politic.

The metamorphic apparatus of *One Hundred Years of Soli-tude* is a constant figural commentary on the literal state of politi-cal repression. García Márquez's choice and refining of the genre of "magical realism" is a totalized metamorphic figuration, an alle-gory of writing shadowed within the text by Melquíades's compre-hensive coding of Macondo's history within the prophetic parchments. As such, magical realism in García Márquez funda-mentally represents a defensive stance toward a repressive regime that writes its own demonic script by spiriting thoughts and per-sons entirely away, as with the disappearance of the three thou-sand striking banana-workers.[17] Thus the disappearance of Macondo altogether with the decoding of Melquíades's parchments is more than an absurdist, postmodern textual apocalypse; it is also a con-summate allegory for the death drive of repressive states, specifi-cally, for the problem of disappearance as political strategy or state policy. In political repression through "disappearance," the meta-morphic judgment turns entirely grave. Dissenting persons are misequated with erring drives and literally written off. This dire metaphor is the monstrous misapprehension by which the repres-sive state abuses its citizens. To assert as the author of a fantastic fiction the existence of something that could not exist is simply the reversed image of political repression, where those who exist one day, cease to be the next, for all one knows.

Through its turns on metamorphosis, *One Hundred Years of Solitude* joins a tradition of daemonic fictions where a metamor-phosis is the sign of a repression bringing about and operating through a disappearance. When human metamorphoses are imag-ined, it is generally certain that the prior body disappears. Dr. Jekyll wrote instructions into his will concerning the possibility of a "disappearance"; in the end, the metamorphic Gregor Samsa decided to "disappear." But when human metamorphs die *as* metamorphs, they often leave a material residue, the corpse of the daemonic form—the shriveled body of Hyde, the dessicated shell of Gregor. So when Macondo blows away without a trace except for the novel by which it is created, at one level it too leaves a material residue, the encoded history of Colombian political strife. At the same time, the disappearance of Macondo is a consummation of the metamorphic impetus of the text, and the metamorphic impetus is itself a figure for writing, for the death drive that shadows the eros of every metaphorical vehicle. The play of figuration turns grave when the vehicle is mis-taken, when the effect of reading is unrecuperated by poetic comprehension, and literal, univocal conviction prevents an appreciation of the irony of the trope. Allegorical ironists from Apuleius to Kafka and García Márquez have consistently turned tropes of metamorphosis against themselves, to bring to mind and expose to comic ridicule the rhetorical backside of moral and political tyrannies. With these authors, the charm of metamorphic irony is that it dissembles that seriousness so playfully.

Political Economy

The building, or warring, or migration of societies literally transforms the landscape. Cultures inscribe their given locales with marks of their identity and activities. The surface of the earth is successively marked, erased, written over by the masses passing over it. When foreign groups usurp indigenous or previously conquering peoples, the newly conquered must either submit to that control or suffer exile. The scenic body of the state will be changed to accord with the identity of its ruling agents. Taken literally at the level of the state, the metamorph's desire for the scenic recovery of a proper body can signify a political quest for the possession or recovery of a homeland.

> Upon a time, before the faery broods
> Drove Nymph and Satyr from the prosperous woods,
> Before King Oberon's bright diadem,
> Sceptre, and mantel, clasp'd with dewy gem,
> Frighted away the Dryads and the Fauns
> From rushes green, and brakes, and cowslip'd lawns ...
>   (1.1–6)

Lamia's opening veils with fairy-tale commonness the sterner historical stuff of racial conquests, theological rivalries, and ancient imperialisms. In a mock fable of political displacement, two mythical groups contest one mythical homeland, and in time prosperity changes hands, passing on to the owners of the land. Keats echoes the first book of Sandys's translation of Ovid's *Metamorphoses,* where Jove worries how, without destroying the human race, "Our Demi-gods, Nymphs, Sylvans, Satyres, Faunes, / Who haunt cleare Springs, high Mountaines, Woods and Lawnes" (*OS* 1.192–3), can avoid the contagion of human brutality. In Keats's revision of Sandys's Ovid for his own metamorphic poem, that potential violence is displaced from humankind and imputed to the parvenu Christian supernatural: "spirits of another sort," the English folklore "broods" of King Oberon usurp the fictive territories formerly occupied by the pagan nature spirits. In *Jekyll and Hyde*, the political thematics of metamorphosis concern territorial motives in a kind of spiritual colonialism. Jekyll's transformations into Hyde play out a corporeal dispute over what the legitimate distinction might be between two indigenous forces, either perceiving the other as alien and inflicting destructive transformations that the given body must passively suffer.

The landscape of metamorphic stories reifies the Western cultural text. Any given scene may be considered as either a permanent dwelling or a provisional one, as either a home or an inn. From scene to scene a road proceeds, the road along which Hermes moves, the road one must take in order to get from scene to scene, and homecomings are never quite certain. When one is homeless on the road, there is no secure rest, and no direction to follow, other than toward some accommodation, some place to stay. Depicted in motion over this landscape, Apuleius's Lucius as wandering metamorph is an allegory of writing, a mobile text rolling aimlessly if amiably along and away from its "original" occasion. Insofar as a figurative meaning is a guest in the house of another meaning, Lucius is also a walking allegory of allegory, before as well as after his metamorphosis. Milo's house is just the first of Lucius's many temporary residences. As a guest in Milo's house, Lucius already enjoys the status of a trope or transposed sign; thus he is already daemonically primed for his metamorphosis into asshood, that change being the trope of a trope, just another change of address in a series of displacements. Taken psychologically, the metamorphic Lucius is a shamed erotic drive, a wandering affect displaced from its proper body and its improper ideas. And taken economically, this metamorph is a person reductively transformed into a circulating commodity.

One point of Apuleius's comedies of metamorphic wandering is that on our earthly journey, we are all on the road all the time. As Lucretius had put it two centuries before Apuleius, "So one thing never ceases to arise / Out of another; life's a gift to no man / Only a loan to him" (*L* 3.968–690). That is, on our mortal road as well as in the structure of the languages that carry us along it, there are no homes, really, only inns. Thus we should be hospitable, proper guests. When we cling to the fiction of permanent dwellings, fictions that then secure the definition of exclusive property rights, we lose sight of our connections. Since claims of perpetual possession can not be realized, since they can only be written down as myths, political attempts to eternalize specific human identities are usually inappropriate acts leading to someone's embarrassment or dispossession.

Apuleius uses metamorphosis at times to poke fun at the local effects of Roman imperialism. The *Golden Ass* has numerous moments of lucid satire on the effects of colonial status. To be a conquered province, like the Greece under Roman dominion through which Lucius moves, is also to have been made an ass by some overbearing alien force. An ironic moral parable of economic defensiveness from the narrative of Lucius's metamorphic wanderings brings these dynamics to light. This Apuleian parable is a parody of metamorphosis as "migration": an outcast band wandering down a road is already a figuration of the metamorphic occasion. Lucius the ass has been staying in the stables at a country estate, when the people there learn that the owners have been killed. Fearing what conditions might be like under the new owners, the group decides to run off, loots the place, and sets out with Lucius also in tow. Having taken upon themselves this voluntary and culpable exile, they are on the road with all they now possess, defenseless against predators. They arrive at a town where they are warned against wolves on the further stretch of the road: "However, in their blind haste to shake off possible pursuers our rascally people disregarded this warning [and] . . . armed themselves as if for a pitched battle. . . . It only needed trumpet music to give the impression that we were an army on the march" (*GA* 182).

Lucius's group has both disregarded and respected the warning given them. They believe it enough to arm themselves, but not enough to overcome the impelling force of their guilty fears, their bad consciences and realistic anxieties over the sack of the farm from which they are fleeing. The group's very exile is defensive, and now it must proceed twice as defensively. The twist is that despite their flight, their defensive posture is now acute enough to be misinterpreted by an Other, another group of people, as a threat of aggression: "when we reached a small village, the inhabitants very naturally mistook us for a brigade of bandits. They were in such alarm that they unchained a pack of large mastiffs. . . . Posted on their roofs and on a small hill close by, the villagers pelted us with stones" (183). The terrified villagers misinterpret the metamorphic appearance of the terrified looters; here is another Apuleian "misreading" leading to comic mortification. More seriously, one reason why Apuleius speaks powerfully today is that he has grasped the ironies of economic defensiveness under imperial dominions. The episode just detailed especially strikes home in the context of modern geopolitical and geoeconomic conflicts. We have often been more endangered by our own defensive postures than by the potential aggressiveness of our neighbors or adversaries.[18]

When, as a result of the establishing of prices, commodities have acquired the form in which they are able
to enter circulation and gold has assumed its function as
money, the contradictions latent in the exchange of commodities are both exposed and resolved by circulation.
The real exchange of commodities, that is the social
metabolic process, constitutes a transformation in which
the dual nature of the commodity—commodity as use-
value and as exchange-value—manifests itself. But the
transformation of the commodity itself is, at the same
time, epitomised in certain forms of money. To describe
this transformation is to describe circulation.[19]

When Lucius turns into an ass, he turns into a commodity.
The wandering narrative told from within Lucius's metamorphosis
literally enacts the circulation of a commodity, or of a unit of currency for which a commodity has been exchanged. Enslaved within
his asshood, Lucius is always potentially transformable into cash,
and many of his owners just abandon him for cash. He passes from
hand to hand, a passive recipient of economic forces, a pawn of the
arbitrary Fortuna of the later Hellenic market, the overall Roman
economy. From this perspective, the character of Lucius does not
develop, it simply circulates, going in circles like the war-shattered
Colonel Aureliano Buendía of *One Hundred Years of Solitude,* who
killed his time crafting fishes out of gold that he exchanged "for
gold coins and then converted the coins into little fishes, and so on"
(*GM* 190).[20]

Apuleius's fiction secularizes the notion of metamorphosis by
modeling it on the malleability of gold and the magic of money, as
in Heraclitus's aphorism, "All things are exchanged for fire and fire
for all things, just as goods are exchanged for gold and gold for
goods" (cited in Cook 1980, 96). Just as bodies may be reductively
conceived as mere matter or pure scene, so in the medium of money,
all proper identities are repressed in favor of some universal currency without complex qualities. The metaphor of metamorphic
gold in the *Golden Ass* unites the spheres of public and private,
economic and psychological transformation. The episodic structure
of the narrative takes its cue from the circulation of commodities.
Apuleius seems to have grasped the metamorphic nature of economic relations and seen the potential for pointed parody in such
material. Money is daemonic. Money is, if not the root of all evil,
at least a powerful and precarious agent of material transformations. A common metaphor allows us to say "gold" to signify the

pure and priceless essence of the immaterial soul. Yet that very
metaphor reduces the spiritual to material conditions. Gold—the
currency of money—is to the soul of things as the metamorphic
body is to the proper identity; it transforms values, breaks down
spiritual proprieties. Money changes everything.

So, for instance, in the tale Lucius hears at the Mill-house
about the cuckolding of Barbarus, in order to corrupt the virtuous
wife Aretë and her faithful servant Myrmex, the adulterer
Philesietaerus thinks to himself: "Gold can smooth every rough
path and break down gates of steel. . . . He reinforced his gentle
pleas with a wedge that he reckoned would soon split this tough log
wide open: he showed Myrmex a handful of shining gold coins
straight from the mint" (GA 206–7). In this parable of moral reversal, the intervening daemon, the agent of corruption, is the rogue
Philesietaerus, who worms his way into the previously proper household of Barbarus. But the agency, the instrument with the power
to subvert the defenses of the household, is gold. The magic of
money, the daemonic power of economic colonialism of any description, is that the forces driving its circulation can overpower the
integrity of the forces aimed at withholding or denying its admission. At this level the daemonic circulation of gold becomes a figure
for the return of the repressed. Just as no physical defense is perfectly certain, so no psychological defense, no "spiritual virtue," is
perfectly certain against the introduction of a forbidden or unforeseen affective value, or the money to purchase the means to it.

The ultra-wealthy Dr. Jekyll discovers in his metamorphic
potion a device for reducing his body to a pure medium of exchange. This economic figure is elaborated through tropes of clothing, insofar as clothing or costuming may be metaphorically
exchanged for a metamorphic body: "I began to perceive more deeply
than it has ever yet been stated, the trembling immateriality, the
mist-like transience, of this seemingly so solid body in which we
walk attired. Certain agents I found to have the power to shake
and to pluck back that fleshly vestment, even as a wind might toss
the curtains of a pavilion" (JH 352). Jekyll's language evokes the
theological rhetoric of the pagan Neoplatonic tradition, as in On the
Cave of the Nymphs: "Moreover, the body surely is a cloak for the
soul around which it is wrapped, 'a wonder to see' whether you
consider it from the point of view of the composition of the composite entity or from that of the soul's bondage to the body" (Lamberton
1983, 29).[21] When the corpse of Hyde is discovered in Jekyll's private cabinet, "he was dressed in clothes far too large for him" (JH
336). For an affective economy, the clothes figure evokes the relation between public postures and private practices, the primary

moral identifications marked by pride and shame. A metamorphosis represents a travesty of identity, a di-vestment that sheds one identity while allowing for the donning or emergence of another.

Allegorical vehicles have traditionally been termed "veils" through which the meaning of the text is both obscured and revealed.[22] Similarly, clothes have a long history as tropes of trope, metaphors for metaphor:

> Cicero, *De Oratore*, III, xxxviii, 155, says that the metaphorical manner of speaking was engendered from necessity, found in the distress of poverty and embarrassment, but sought after for its grace. "Just as clothing was invented first to protect against the cold, and afterward was used for the decoration and refinement of the body, the *tropus* originated from deficiency and became commonly used when it was pleasing." (Nietzsche 1983, 122)

Like desire itself, according to this line of thought, clothing and metaphor are both cultural surpluses that derive from human lacks. Clothes and tropes are both defensive vehicles or "outsides" that either convey or supersede the "insides" they are originally intended to protect. In a complex or mixed clothes figure, Jekyll comments on his metamorphic license, "I was the first that could thus plod in the public eye with a load of genial respectability, and in a moment, like a schoolboy, strip off these lendings and spring headlong into the sea of liberty. But for me, in my impenetrable mantle"—that is, in the form of Hyde—"the safety was complete" (357). Becoming Mr. Hyde, Jekyll can both remove the hand-me-downs of social respectability and button up and protect his true ("naked") sensual identity. Mr. Hyde is indeed a protective "mantle" for Dr. Jekyll, but like any natural material he is not utterly "impenetrable." Rather, the metaphorical mantle ends up dismantling the man.

Structurally parallel to the clothes figure is the economic figure of the house, a primary vehicle for conveying corporeal, psychological, and political motives. Saposnik remarks that "the topography of *Jekyll and Hyde* may be seen as a study in symbolic location, a carefully worked out series of contrasts between exterior modes and interior realities."[23] Silverman (1983) notes that Stevenson's figures establish "a metaphoric relationship between architectural forms and their human inhabitants. As a consequence, the signifiers . . . provide a moral commentary as well as a physical description" (259). Metamorphic stories frequently load their

characters' dwellings with thematic content. Dr. Jekyll's obscurely
extended townhouse becomes a metaphor for his wandering mind,
while Gregor Samsa can hardly escape from his bedroom, cannot
escape at all from the family apartment. Because this device follows a typical oneiric pattern, such domestic analogues of the body
are ready figural vessels for ideological content.[24] Insofar as metamorphoses are preoccupied with the forms and fluctuations of the
body's boundaries, houses present obvious and immediate vehicles
for those preoccupations. The metamorphic house is an allegorical
cosmos often aligned with the scenic or subordinated body.

As a figure for the displaced, textual or (re)constructed body
or as a signifier of economic or social identity, the house measures
the status of gendered bodies with regard to possessive relations.
For instance, Apuleius places Lucius's arrival in Hypata and residence in Milo's and Pamphile's household in the extreme foreground.
It is a house tilted even further into metamorphic dynamics by
being "just outside the city walls" (*GA* 19). It is thus, so to speak,
an outcast house, a house that is outside of itself. Both a part of
and detached from the city, Milo's dwelling has a dubious or ambivalent status, an indeterminate existence appropriate for the
daemonic doings of its inhabitants. This scene already bears the
mark of its agents. Further, Lucius's adventures at Milo's house
are shot through with comic business derived from economic motifs. Milo himself is a miser and money-lender. Shortly after arriv-
ing at Milo's house, the comic hero visits the town market, where
he must haggle for a bargain: "though I was first asked two hundred drachmae a basket, eventually I beat a fishmonger down to
twenty" (22). A slapstick routine follows, which brilliantly shadows
the idea of metamorphosis as physical reduction, by compounding
the motifs of shame and money, embarrassment and theft.

Like Aristomenes's story of "Socrates," this episode also concerns a chance encounter with a long-lost friend and narrates a
reunion that turns for the worse. It seems that Lucius's old school-
chum, Pythias, has become the local Inspector-General of Markets.
Once Lucius informs Pythias that he had to "beat down" the
fishmonger's price, Apuleius takes that reduction motif and extends it to metamorphic absurdity. For in order to have Lucius
recompensed for his presumed mishandling by a fishmonger who
had nonetheless reduced the price, Pythias has Lucius's purchase
beaten to a pulp:

> He emptied the basket on the ground, ordering one of his
> constables to jump on the fish and squash them into
> paste on the pavement. Beaming moral satisfaction with

his own severity, Pythias advised me to go home. "All is well now, Lucius," he said cheerfully. "You need say no more. I am satisfied that the little wretch has been sufficiently humiliated." (*GA* 23)

This is a wonderful spoof of mistaken moral economies, civic justice gone haywire. Pythias robs Lucius of his fish, in exchange for his own official, representative delight in someone else's humiliation. A comic figure of arbitrary and brutal justice, Pythias squanders another's goods to purchase an abstract satisfaction in someone else's abasement.[25] Here the metamorphic intent of the main narrative is suggested by a reduction motif that is a figure for the repression of proper bodily forms. The mashing of the fish into a paste is an absurdly literal and material reduction in state and debasement in value, offered as an equivalent to and supposedly enacting the humiliation of the fishmonger, whose embarrassment is a figural or defensive, psychological reduction in affective state. The fishmonger's pride (his "high price") is reduced to his shame. But in the exchange between Pythias and the fishmonger, it is Lucius who is most affected and humiliated, and ironically, dispossessed of both his gold and his meal.

The most literal economic figure in *Jekyll and Hyde* is Jekyll's London mansion, setting forth in monumental spectacle the division in Jekyll's character. The "Story of the Door" opening the novel turns our attention immediately to the back-end of affairs, Hyde's door, the back passage opening onto the back alley, but connected to the main hall, Jekyll's ostensible public identity, by way of the examining room, Jekyll's private laboratory. Having severed his identity into a duplicable duplicity, Jekyll can exit alternately through the back and front doors of himself. So the double-doored house is a figure for Jekyll's "profound duplicity of life" (*JH* 350), an allegorical cosmos of public facades, private entrances, long hallways, and inner sancta. Anguish over that duplicity leads Jekyll to hope that his warring selves could be "housed in separate identities" (352). Jekyll will not see that the house itself, not what it houses, is the problem, a problem aggravated rather than resolved by the emergence of Mr. Hyde.

Mr. Utterson, Dr. Jekyll's lawyer and trustee, is the self-appointed detective who solves the enigma of Mr. Hyde.[26] One of the first things we learn about Mr. Utterson is that he "drank gin when he was alone, to mortify a taste for vintages" (*JH* 281), practicing an austere moral economy by taking the clear spirit over the ruddy wine his senses prefer. But in fact, Utterson exercises his most arduous self-restraint over his *curiositas*, his voyeuristic lust to see immediately and completely into others' inner affairs. "There sprang up and grew apace in the lawyer's mind," the unnamed narrator tells us, "a singularly strong, almost an inordinate, curiosity to behold the features of the real Mr. Hyde" (294). And later when Dr. Lanyon dies, seemingly from exposure to that same spectacle, the "real Mr. Hyde," and leaves Utterson a letter marked " 'not to be opened till the death or disappearance of Dr. Henry Jekyll,' " we are told how "a great curiosity came on the trustee, to disregard the prohibition and dive at once to the bottom of these mysteries; but professional honor and faith to his dead friend were stringent obligations; and the packet slept in the inmost corner of his private safe" (320).

In fact, the whole of Utterson's character can be taken as a moralized house figure representing "terror of the law" (307): as a banker of privacies, a self-effacing professional confidant, a man of impenetrable discretion, seemingly with no secrets of his own, he provides a secure vault for the secrets of others. Safely occupying his safe are the private possessions of high public figures. He is thus all the more the capable Victorian moralist, the impenetrable man of efficacious shame. But were he only a professional vault, Utterson's figure would signify only the vehicle and sign of another's possessions, he would be merely the "agent" of another's "will." However, Utterson is also significantly described as "a man of no scientific passions (except in the matter of conveyancing)" (292). That is, Utterson's professional passion runs to that aspect of civil and corporate law treating the transfer of titles of property. And as an expert in conveyancing, Utterson is a daemon, although hardly an archangel Gabriel. Rather, as a Hermes in disguise, Utterson is a free agent, opening and closing the vault (Utterson's Hermetic crypt) at his own discretion.

"When to open the vault?" is of course the worry of bourgeois moralists terrified of being swindled and unmanned. A simple reading of this story is that because Jekyll "opens his vault" and lets Mr. Hyde circulate, he perishes; because Utterson "keeps his vault shut," he triumphs. Jekyll's "transfers of title" to Hyde earn no surplus value, unless we take the pleasures Jekyll discovers as Hyde to be the interest on his investment; rather, Jekyll's transfers to Hyde are expenditures that bankrupt both the moral and the vital person. At first Jekyll makes Hyde the beneficiary of his will, but in the end Utterson takes Hyde's place and comes into a fortune. In a detail of the text suppressed by being given just prior to the reading of Lanyon's and Jekyll's sensational depositions, Utterson unsealed an envelope, "and several enclosures fell to the floor. The first was a will ... but in place of the name of Edward

Hyde, the lawyer, with indescribable amazement, read the name of Gabriel John Utterson" (338). With the resolution of the mystery of Hyde's identity, one last transfer of title occurs, the last judgment, Utterson's payoff, by which the "essence of Jekyll," the wealth and privileges of "title," are conveyed from the multi-titled Jekyll to Utterson.

Although Kaja Silverman's (1983) Barthesian criticism of *Jekyll and Hyde* is generally well-taken, she misses the mark slightly in the following comments on the thematics of the story in general and the character of Utterson in particular: "Christianity entertains so profound a mistrust of knowledge that it always treats epistemological ambition as a moral descent. . . . Utterson's reluctance to penetrate mysteries can only be understood in the context of this very negative attitude toward discovery" (277). To my mind, Utterson rather desires to penetrate mysteries, and is reluctant only to transgress confidences. Silverman makes Utterson out as morally squeamish, but his repression is expressed utterly in his discretion, in the fortress of character founded on an ideal of impenetrability. Silverman's depiction of Utterson seems related to her dismissive opinion of the ultimate resources of the story: "Stevenson's tale permits us to identify the voices which speak it, but not to disrupt their harmony. It enables us to scrutinize the symbolic order to which it belongs, but not to dislocate it from that order" (278).

In what it denies, this assessment is wrong. A more complex understanding of the subversion of allegorical coding in *Jekyll and Hyde* can be had by bearing in mind the economic climax, the jackpot at the end of the mystery. Utterson's payoff is as daemonic as the action that leads up to it. By slipping Utterson finally into Hyde's shoes, Stevenson deftly resolves the main, metamorphic action with a booby-trapped pot of gold. For since Hyde is actually Jekyll, and Utterson and Hyde are now equated, then Hyde is the eliminated middle term, and Utterson is now Jekyll. In fact, Jekyll's estate has been conveyed to Utterson, Utterson is now the economic metamorph. This event will displace Utterson entirely from the scene and order of his prior relationships, his former discourses. One wonders if his new life will flow calmly onward like his old.

4. Fabulous Monsters

Allegorical monsters are the genus of which literary metamorphs are a particular species. For Virgil the populating of the underworld with horrific anthropomorphisms is already an epic commonplace.[1] In Book VI of the *Aeneid*, Aeneas and the Cumaean Sibyl confront this subterranean gallery of hellish creatures:

> At the first threshold, on the jaws of Orcus,
> Grief and avenging Cares have set their couches,
> And pale Diseases dwell, and sad Old Age,
> Fear, evil-counselling Hunger, wretched Need,
> Forms terrible to see, and Death, and Toil,
> And Death's own brother, Sleep, and evil Joys,
> Fantasies of the mind, and deadly War,
> The Furies' iron chambers, Discord, raving,
> Her snaky hair entwined in bloody bands.[2]

In *Paradise Lost*, Satan encounters some of the same retinue around the abysmal throne of Chaos and his consort Night: "Rumor next, and Chance, / And Tumult and Confusion all embroiled, / And Discord with a thousand various mouths" (2.965–67). The descent from the level of natural generation into the nether world of allegorical monstrosity underscores one of Benjamin's (1985) most trenchant conclusions: "Evil as such ... exists only in allegory.... In the very fall of man the unity of guilt and signifying emerges as an abstraction. The allegorical has its existence in abstractions; as an abstraction, as a faculty of the spirit of language itself, it is at home in the Fall" (233–34). The allegorical monster as a creature of evil exists only in and through the abstraction of natural being into the forms of writing.

Metamorphic monsters such as insect-men and serpent-women are constructed when nonhuman vehicles couple with human tenors. Corngold (1988) has nicely sketched a process of monster-creation by reverse personification at the virtual rhetorical level, in relation to Kafka's *Metamorphosis*:

> If the metaphor ... is taken literally, it no longer functions as a vehicle but as a name.... If, now, the tenor—

83

> as in *The Metamorphosis*—is a human consciousness, the
> increasing literalization of the vehicle transforms the
> tenor into a monster. . . . *This genesis of monsters occurs*
> *independently of the nature of the vehicle.* The intent
> toward literalization of a metaphor linking a human
> consciousness and a material sensation produces a mon-
> ster in every instance. . . . The distortion of the metaphor
> in *The Metamorphosis* is inspired by a radical aesthetic
> intention, which proceeds by destruction and results in
> creation—of a monster, virtually nameless, existing as
> an opaque sign. (55–56)

Although Kafka's Gregor Samsa is at an ironic extreme on the
spectrum of metamorphic figures, he shares with other such fictions
an origin in a catastrophic miscreation produced by allegorical
intercourse. Daemonic creatures are regularly generated by the
copulation of personifications, as when "*Circe* was said to bee the
daughter of *Sol* and *Persis,* in that lust proceeds from heat and
moisture" (*OS* 654), or when Satan couples with his daughter Sin
to conceive the "execrable shape" of Death (*PL* 2.681). Metamorphic
monstrosity represents the uncanny productivity of linguistic reproduction, an illicit fornication in the basement brothel of the
verbal imagination always breeding new figures. The promiscuous
nature of metamorphic procreation can disrupt any discursive system. Metamorphic episodes consistently subvert the hierarchical
cosmos of traditional allegories just because they insert an unpredictable play into rational structures.

The Insect

Insects—moths, scarabs, bees—have long been powerful spiritual symbols. In the epic of Gilgamesh, having reached the place of
Utnapishtim the Faraway in quest of immortality, Gilgamesh is
informed, "There is no permanence. Do we build a house to stand
for ever, do we seal a contract to hold for all time? . . . It is only the
nymph of the dragon-fly who sheds her larva and sees the sun in
his glory."[3] In Utnapishtim's story of the Flood, once the waters
subside and sacrificial fires are rekindled, "When the gods smelled
the sweet savour, they gathered like flies over the sacrifice" (111).
But despite the archaic spiritual provenance of the insect, human
transformations into insects or insect-like creatures appear to be
relatively rare in archaic stories. Perhaps the most familiar one is
Ovid's version of Arachne's change into a spider.

Such stories seem to be more prevalent in our own time. Whereas Arachne is turned into a mere spider, in Kafka's *Metamorphosis* Gregor's monstrosity is to be not just an insect but a "monster cockroach," an insect of human size, an incest-bug.[4] In addition to the various movie versions of "The Fly," contemporary popular culture provides another form of insectoid monstrosity in the phenomenon of "transformers," minutely articulated plastic toys that metamorphose from man to machine to monster, and their animated counterparts on TV cartoon shows. The narratives of these segmented flying metamorphs derive ultimately from the long tradition and deformation of the allegorical daemonic—the endless warring of the forces of Good and Evil—but their imagery is drawn from the intersection of the anatomical features of insects, spacecraft, and microelectronic circuitry.

Curiously, however, the story of an insect-metamorphosis also occurs in the *Phaedrus,* when Socrates tells Phaedrus about the origin and function of the cicadas singing around them in the noonday heat:

> It is quite improper for a lover of the Muses never to have heard of such things. The story goes that these locusts were once men, before the birth of the Muses, and when the Muses were born and song appeared, some of the men were so overcome with delight that they sang and sang, forgetting food and drink, until at last unconsciously they died. From them the locust tribe afterwards arose, and they have this gift from the Muses, that from the time of their birth they need no sustenance, but sing continually, without food or drink, until they die, when they go to the Muses and report who honours each of them on earth. (*P* §259b–c)

Plato's parable of the cicadas traces the affective lines of the metamorphic daemonic. The locusts were once human, but were metamorphosed by an excess of rapture, at which sublime point the pleasure principle folded over onto the death drive. Their human forms were eliminated but their compulsively repeated song remained, and in that form, as singers, they were fixed. Now locusts are spies, outsiders nostalgically peering in on human affairs, and when they die, they become couriers, interceding with the Muses on behalf of human culture. The story of the locusts occurs as part of the long rhetorical post-mortem Socrates performs on the palinode and the other two speeches delivered previously in the dialogue. Thus it is all the more clearly a "fairy tale for dialecticians," an ironic deformation of a mythic etiology deployed for paradigmatic effects.[5]

But if the figure of the insect has a place within the literature of metamorphic allegory, the insect proper can be seen to represent the biological daemonic itself, the living register generally. The phenomenology of insects is the most apt natural analogue of the imagery of the daemonic. Insects come in both angelic and demonic anthropomorphic forms: the fluttering, ecstatic butterfly, the lethal wasp, the devout and philanthropic praying mantis, the evil, voracious weevil. Or else, like the mosquito or tick, they are "carriers," couriers of death and disease. With some exceptions, within the human scheme of things insects are uninvited guests, parasites that insinuate themselves into houses. These stealthy creepers cross over from the outside into the inside of the inside, and then crawl out of the woodwork, like the three lodgers whom Kafka conjures up in the third part of the *Metamorphosis*. In addition, many insects undergo a literal metamorphosis as part of their biological maturation. On one hand, in the use of the Greek term *psyche,* the name of the butterfly is fixed as a vehicle for the maturation of the soul. The metaphor of the diaphanous butterfly "clothes" the soul and then inscribes that essence with particular attributes (wings) and modes of development (metamorphoses). On the other hand, the word *larva* now signifying a transitional phase of insect metamorphosis derives from the Latin for "ghost" or "specter."[6]

Insects are nature's paradigm and parody of the winged soul as a metonymy of erotic functions. The final phase of their metamorphic maturation endows many insects with their wings and their genitals. Similarly, the primary metaphor for erotic philosophical metamorphosis in the *Phaedrus* is the nourishment of the wings of the soul (*P* §246e). Insects populate the human imagination most profoundly I think as winged figures, somehow both monstrous and blessed in their minuteness, absolute in their refusal of the human scale. The primary natural register of daemonic flight is found not in any bird but in the fly, the butterfly, the dragonfly, the bee, in their peerless ability to hover suspended between earth and sky, to find out the folds of flowers.[7] Attending to the hovering of an insect forces a shift of perspective, opens up another world with different orders of relationship. The winged figures and aerial daemons of the allegorical imagination are darkly connected to the magic of insects and the infinity of the tiny.

What manner of insect, then, does Gregor Samsa become? Like Plato's daemonic locusts, he loses all interest in food, but he is driven into ecstatic raptures by Grete's violin playing. Is Gregor an "imago"—"an insect in its final adult, sexually mature, and typically winged state"—or a "nymph"—the "larva of an insect (as a dragonfly or mayfly) with incomplete metamorphosis that differs from the imago esp. in size and in its incompletely developed wings and genitalia"?[8] Have Gregor's wings fallen off, or are they in the process of (re)emerging? "He especially enjoyed hanging suspended from the ceiling ... and in the almost blissful absorption induced by this suspension it could happen to his own surprise that he let go and fell plump on the floor" (*M* 69). Of course, Gregor must crawl to the ceiling, but through this routine he manages a rough parody of hovering, he recovers his aerial being, and he makes the metamorphic Fall into a game that shadows a birth fantasy, as if he were hatching out of a cocoon or dropping from a womb. Gregor's metamorphosis, his suspended form, gives him a sense of creaturely ease he had not known before, and a taste of prelapsarian power, the power of daemonic flight. Daemonic flight also marks Gregor's flight from the human condition, his progressive regression or death drive into a kind of intrauterine paradise or land of absolute incest.

The Basilisk

Deleuze and Guattari (1986) read metamorphosis in Kafka's animal tales as "stationary flight," an intermediate condition combining both resistance and fixity: "this escape doesn't consist in fleeing—quite the contrary. Flight is challenged when it is useless movement in space, a movement of false liberty; but in contrast, flight is affirmed when it is a stationary flight, a flight of intensity" (13). Unlike Gregor in the *Metamorphosis,* in Keats's *Lamia* the metamorphic heroine does attempt to flee her condition, both by magical transformation out of her serpentine condition and by literal transposition from Crete to Corinth. But her efforts prove to be futile, "a movement of false liberty," due to the destructive revelation rendered by her nemesis, Apollonius. Although Lamia's struggle for self-determination is inconclusive and erotically short-circuited, her daemonic flight does manage to reveal Apollonius as a monster in his own right.[9]

Lamia is ultimately the story of the creation and the catastrophe of Apollonius's conscience. His judgment on Lamia is a parable of the apocalypse attending not the omega but the alpha of patriarchal prerogative, Oedipalization and its fabulous monsters. *Lamia* dramatizes the psychological collusion between possessiveness and defensiveness, the processes and perversions of Oedipal subject-construction by which persons so often assume monstrous guises. In "Trophy and Triumph," Otto Fenichel writes:

> With the help of the superego the ego "participates" in the more powerful father's might, and the acquisition of the superego is the equivalent of the acquisition of a trophy. . . . All trophies are somehow personified "super-egos" [in] that they all have one thing in common with the superego: they both protect and threaten their possessor. As long as one keeps a trophy in one's house, one has the powerful being in the house, and compels it to protect one. But, just as behind the peaceful "participation" there always lurks the original intention of robbing, so is this protection always conditional too. (157)

These themes are first played out in mythic dress through the episode with Hermes and the invisible nymph. The nymph is a trophy, a prize Hermes desires to add to his collection. Compare Fenichel on the psychology of the collector: "I have acquired something by force or fraud that originally belonged to someone more powerful, but which is now a talisman for me, or which connects me magically with the previous possessor" (149). Hermes slinking past "his great summoner" Jove is essentially a son-figure intending to raid the Father's troves, a trial run for the patriarchal submission of the female to the status of property. Capturing the nymph, Hermes achieves a relative omnipotence, a disingenuous Oedipal victory.

Further changes are rung on the motif of the trophy in the story of Lamia and Lycius. Fenichel's topic of "Trophy and Triumph" is anticipated in Lycius's characterization of his motives for deciding to present Lamia to the world of Corinth:

> What mortal hath a prize, that other men
> May be confounded and abash'd withal,
> But lets it sometimes pace abroad majestical,
> And triumph, as in thee I should rejoice
> Amid the hoarse alarm of Corinth's voice. (2.57–61)

Fenichel defines triumph as "the disappearance of fear and inhibition as a result of the acquisition of the trophy" (159). At this point in Keats's story Lycius feels triumph right enough; he has forgotten entirely his fear and inhibition concerning his shadowy mentor Apollonius, "the ghost of folly" who now haunts only Lamia's dreams.

For Lycius, Lamia is his prize mare "pacing" him to triumph, carrying him "foremost in the envious race" (1.217). Of course, Lycius has misconstrued the situation. *He* is the prize that connects Lamia to Apollonius, the prize that Apollonius wants back.

Lamia herself apparently did not calculate sufficiently the power of the previous owner of her talisman, for in fact Lycius provides her no ultimate protection; rather, he manufactures their mutual downfall. Her magic is her only defense, a magic Lycius must cooperate with, "participate in," in order to remain effective. In a phrase, Lycius must remain inside the house, as Lamia knows she must, in order to maintain their magical defenses. The uninvited thought that buzzes into Lycius's head will thrust her out of the house—"you have dismiss'd me; and I go / From your breast houseless: ay, it must be so" (2.44–45)—as will be reenacted in earnest when the self-proclaimed "uninvited guest" Apollonius appears at the wedding feast to reclaim his prized possession (2.165). So Lamia foretells her own doom; as a metamorph in disguise, she has seen it all before. Apollonius, too, "look'd and look'd again" because he has uttered this curse before:

> Then Lamia breath'd death breath; the sophist's eye,
> Like a sharp spear, went through her utterly,
> Keen, cruel, perceant, stinging: she, as well
> As her weak hand could any meaning tell,
> Motion'd him to be silent; vainly so,
> He look'd and look'd again a level—No!
> "A Serpent!" (2.299–305)

Repetition links the principle of identity to the death drive.[10] Lamia and Apollonius are fatally drawn together by the repetition and reciprocation of their daemonic and Hermetic attributes. For instance, when the humanly reincarnated Lamia is set forth as "of sciential brain / To unperplex bliss from its neighbour pain" (1.191–92), her skill at unbinding is of a piece with Apollonius's notorious Newtonian ability to "Unweave a rainbow" (2.237). Garrett Stewart works through more of these details: "Lamia may have a demonic origin, but, in another inversion, the 'demon eyes' (2.289) now belong by accusation to Apollonius. One sign of the original serpent's womanly alter-ego was that, contrary to zoological fact, she possessed eyelids, whose 'lid-lashes' became 'all sear' (1.151) during her rebirth into full womanhood. In what seems like a reverse demonic metamorphosis at the end of the poem, the 'lashless eyelids' (2.288) have become a feature of Apollonius."[11] Here Keats underscores the gender distinction between the two in a way that humanizes Lamia while serpentizing Apollonius; she has a woman's eyes while his are reptilian. In addition, Apollonius is marked by the serpentine in the manner of his blighting of Lamia. If Lamia is a serpent disguised as a woman, Apollonius is a basilisk disguised as a man:

> Its name comes from the Greek and means "little king"; to the Elder Pliny (VIII, 33) it was a serpent bearing a bright spot in the shape of a crown on its head. . . . What remains constant about the Basilisk is the deadly effect of its stare and its venom. . . . The Basilisk dwelled in the desert; or, more accurately, it made the desert. Birds fell dead at its feet and the earth's fruits blackened and rotted; the water of the streams where it quenched its thirst remained poisoned for centuries. That its mere glance split rocks and burned grass has been attested by Pliny.[12]

Apollonius echoes the fabulous ferocity of the basilisk, a mythical serpent, when he annihilates its mythical counterpart the Lamia. Lamia's serpent form was all along a mark Apollonius had placed on her, a mark rendered decipherable only at the very end of the poem when Apollonius unleashes his "demon eyes" and reveals his daemonic and serpentine identity as well. The usurping agent transforming the wedding scene was also the usurper of her first or prior life. Thus, the climax of *Lamia* is also its unstated prologue. The Hermes episode is a "screen prologue." By adding it to the story transmitted by Philostratus and Burton, Keats stealthily displaces the "unhappily ever after" of Lamia's conclusion back "upon a time, before" the Hermes episode.

Compare the negativity of the basilisk to the "venomous eye" of *ressentiment:*

> The slave revolt in morality begins when *ressentiment* itself becomes creative and gives birth to values: the *ressentiment* of natures that are denied the true reaction, that of deeds, and compensate themselves with an imaginary revenge. While every noble morality develops from a triumphant affirmation of itself, slave morality from the outset says No to what is "outside," what is "different," what is "not itself"; and *this* No is its creative deed. This inversion of the value-positing eye—this *need* to direct one's view outward instead of back to oneself—is of the essence of *ressentiment*. (Nietzsche 1968, 472–73)

Apollonius's concluding banishment of Lamia is a piece of obsessive repetition and the reenactment of a prior scenario of repression.

His triumph is possible only because Lamia had been previously compromised, primed by a prior dispossessive metaphor. His negativity proclaims that his own identity is founded on spiteful reaction. Apollonius is a "little Apollo," a bringer of (b)light, the anti-Dionysian ascetic whose gaze derives its withering potency from the negativity of his sublimations, that is, from the drawing up of eros from the phallus to the eye, "like a sharp spear . . . keen, cruel, perceant, stinging." Apollonius is not so much a sophist as he is a shaman, a black magician of negativity, a devious sublimator transforming erotic desire into defensive aggression. Lamia comes forth as the displaced and victimized Python that the pythic Apollonian subject, as its founding act, casts forth from itself.

Keats's description of Lamia's metamorphosis indicates that her serpentine state is an earnest parody of the fabulous monsters of the Apocalypse:

> The colours all inflam'd throughout her train,
> She writh'd about, convuls'd with scarlet pain: . . .
> And, as the lava ravishes the mead,
> Spoilt all her silver mail and golden brede;
> Made gloom of all her frecklings, streaks and bars,
> Eclips'd her crescents, and lick'd up her stars. . . . (1.153–60)

Abominated by the resentful patriarch Apollonius, Lamia's figure echoes the great Mother "clothed with the sun, with the moon under her feet, and on her head a crown of twelve stars" (*Revelation* 12.1), hounded into the wilderness by "a great red dragon, with seven heads and ten horns, and seven diadems upon his heads. His tail swept down a third of the stars of heaven, and cast them to the earth" (12.3–4), the outcast woman who returns in chapter 17 "sitting on a scarlet beast which was full of blasphemous names, and it had seven heads and ten horns. The woman was arrayed in purple and scarlet, and bedecked with gold and jewels and pearls, holding in her hand a golden cup full of abominations and the impurities of her fornication; and on her forehead was written a name of mystery: 'Babylon the great, mother of harlots and of earth's abominations' " (17.3–5). In Keats's telling, Apollonius's stare shares with John of Patmos the resentful eye of this Revelation.

Life-in-Death

Part of the peculiarity surrounding the *Ancient Mariner* is Coleridge's critical role in demoting the notion of allegory for postromantic readers, effectively insulating his own greatest poetic text from serious or conscious scrutiny as a prime example of literary allegory. In his alterations for the *Sibylline Leaves* edition of 1817, roughly concurrent with his declarations in favor of the aesthetic symbol, Coleridge both appends an epigraph to and composes a gloss for the poem.[13] The seventeenth-century divine Thomas Burnet's epigraph, addressing the mystery of "invisible natures" abroad in the world, highlights the daemonic imagery that already gave the poem its Neoplatonic edge. The epigraph warns about the interpretive obscurity of daemonic agencies, and thus about the doubtful nature of allegorical reading. Burnet affirms such spiritual fantasia only when held in strict logical control: "we must be vigilant for truth and keep proportion, that we may distinguish the certain from the uncertain, day from night" (*ERW* 405).

As if to provide such a control, Coleridge now layers the entire poem with a running commentary, a canny stroke of textual simulation, which alludes to the bifurcated typography of traditional allegorical texts. But Coleridge's gloss does not perform like a traditional moral commentary. For instance, the gloss in Bunyan's *Pilgrim's Progress* closely doubles and reconfirms the agency of the personifications and reifications that populate the dream narrative, with comments like "Faithful *and* Talkative *enter discourse,*" or "*A Key in* Christians *bosom, called* Promise, *opens any Lock in* Doubting *Castle.*"[14] Coleridge's gloss often works in just the opposite direction, naturalizing images that are powerfully emblematic in the poem itself. For instance, the poem's lines, "And now the STORM-BLAST came, and he / Was tyrannous and strong" (406) project agency onto the storm, and thereby encourage its interpretation as a form of allegorical threshold, the point when the Mariner's own volition is suspended by some cosmic cross-purpose. But the gloss empties out that suggestion, matter-of-factly returning the storm to a mimetic register: "The ship driven by a storm toward the south pole." Coleridge's allegorical gloss avoids systematic allegoresis.

Relative to Bunyan's gloss in *Pilgrim's Progress,* Coleridge's is both more cryptic and more garrulous. Coleridge as self-annotator fills out his classical allusions with a commentary that responds to Burnet's epigraph. Whereas Burnet had asked about the nature of spirits, "who shall describe for us their families, their ranks, relationships, distinguishing features and functions? What do they do? Where do they live?" and then responded, "The human mind has always circled about knowledge of these things, but never attained it" (405)—Coleridge's gloss confidently affirms of the Mariner and his shipmates, "A Spirit had followed them; one of the invisible inhabitants of this planet, neither departed souls nor angels; concerning which the learned Jew, Josephus, and the Platonic

Constantinopolitan, Michael Psellus, may be consulted. They are very numerous, and there is no climate or element without one or more" (407). The gloss emphatically reminds the reader of this longer cultural background and supersedes the Mariner's own idiom of Christian piety by evoking the classical Neoplatonic cosmos.[15] So the body of Coleridge's gloss deflects the Christian moral with which it and the poem eventually conclude, by directing interpretive attention to the very Hellenistic cultural arena out of which Western literary allegory proceeds. The gloss specifies the *Ancient Mariner*'s position at the typological crux between the Neoplatonic cosmos and its revision within the Christian orders of the demonic and the angelic.

Complicating the cosmic machinery of the poem by supplementing the Christian supernatural with the pagan daemonic, Coleridge not only discourages monotheistic or univocal readings of the Mariner's voyage. In effect, by crossing the Judeo-Christian against the classical imageries, he also opens up the secular interpretive space within which the next great Western allegorical system, psychoanalysis, will emerge at the end of the nineteenth century. This is not to say that epic allegory from Dante to Milton did not also breed important effects from comparable combinations of the classical and the Christian. But in the *Divine Comedy* or *Paradise Lost*, classical pretexts and paraphernalia were evoked in order to be subsumed into the Christian cosmos. Coleridge's confessional anti-epic does not convincingly reconfirm any cosmos typically associated with a Biblical pretext. Rather, by playing both Neoplatonism and Christianity off each other it creates secular mental space, at the price of narrating the Mariner's transgression and ensuing anxiety. In this reading, then, shooting the Albatross is an emblem of the poem's own literary transgressions of the Christian moral dispensation.

The Polar Spirit begins its daemonic retribution for the death of the Albatross by stranding the Mariner's vessel in the doldrums—all this is stock moral supernaturalism. But Part III of the *Ancient Mariner* performs the crucial revision to conventional moral allegorization by which the poem confirms its literary rather than dogmatic function. In communication with the "sign" of guilt into which the dead Albatross has been converted, the first gloss to Part III explains that "The ancient Mariner beholdeth a sign in the element afar off." "Beholding a sign" constitutes the next episode as an allegory of active textuality, reading and writing, for the interpretation of this "sign" is the very point of the poem. At first the Mariner misreads it, taking it to signify a natural event—a returning wind bringing someone to their rescue. But this vessel moves

"Without a breeze, without a tide"—not by the causalities of the
natural order but on the slippery surface of the signifier. The uncanny approach of the skeleton ship is an emblem of allegorical
structure, conveying to the Mariner the message that his route
back to Nature has been foreclosed.

> Are those *her* ribs through which the Sun
> Did peer, as through a grate?
> And is that Woman all her crew?
> Is that a DEATH? and are there two?
> Is DEATH that woman's mate?
>
> *Her* lips were red, *her* looks were free,
> Her locks were yellow as gold:
> Her skin was white as leprosy,
> The Night-mare LIFE-IN-DEATH was she,
> Who thicks man's blood with cold. (*ERW* 408)

The allegorical personification of Death is conventional, and
Coleridge's 1817 version deletes his prior attempt to body it forth.
Its presence within the vessel is now simply declared. Coleridge
grants a few lines to describing the other figure, but still in a
cursory and stock Gothic way. The most significant detail is its
name. The pronunciation of the name Life-in-Death marks the
textual arrival of the "sign in the element" foretold (after the poetic
fact) by the gloss. But unlike "Death," this complex sign has no
conventional moral purchase; rather, it immediately scrambles standard moral schemas. How then does the Mariner or the Mariner's
bard know its name? Into what allegory does it fit? To what other
text does this episode allude?
    A major pretext is not far to seek. A daemonic duo, one of
whose members is Death, prominently appears toward the end of
Book II of *Paradise Lost* in the figures of Sin and Death, Milton's
supreme deployment of sublime personification.[16] Several details of
Coleridge's text confirm the plausibility of this connection. As the
skeleton ship emerges on the horizon:

> At first it seemed a little speck,
> And then it seemed a mist,
> It moved and moved, and took at last
> A certain shape, I wist.
>
> A speck, a mist, a shape, I wist!
> And still it neared and neared.... (407)

The poem's double pronunciation of the visually blank term "shape" echoes Milton's description of the Gates of Hell: "Before the gates there sat / On either side a formidable Shape" (*PL* 2.648–49). Sin and Death, as well as the skeleton ship that conveys the figure of Life-in-Death, are all allegorical "shapes" in that they are visual reifications of moral abstractions. In contrast to Coleridge's minimal descriptions, Milton's personifications are filled out in epic detail. Sin receives a fairly definite and monstrous visual figure, relative to the strategically amorphous rendering of Death that prompted Coleridge to praise the figure for its "substitution of a sublime feeling of the unimaginable for a mere image":

> The other shape,
> If shape it might be called that shape had none
> Distinguishable in member, joint, or limb,
> Or substance might be called that shadow seemed,
> For each seemed either; black it stood as night ...
> (2.666–70)[17]

However, in Milton, Satan's confrontation with Death is subordinated to his long conversation with Sin, who explains to her father-lover that Death is their own monstrous offspring. Milton's figural schema here reifies the Biblical passage, "When lust hath conceived, it bringeth forth sin; and sin, when it is finished, bringeth forth death" (James 1.15), and so this allegory remains within the Christian hermeneutic enclosure, if not, as many eighteenth-century readers complained, within the bounds of epic decorum. But Coleridge's appropriation deflects its pretext, most powerfully by renaming the figure of Sin, a transparent moral signifier, as Life-in-Death, an opaque oxymoron. Another passage from Sin's dialogue with Satan may indicate the route by which Coleridge reconfigured his Miltonic pretext. Upon the birth of Sin from out of Satan's head, "amazement seized / All th' host of heav'n; back they recoiled afraid / At first, and called me Sin, and for a sign / Portentous held me" (2.758–61). Milton's line divulges the evil pun that proclaims the fallenness of language, the sin embedded in the sign.

The sinfulness of signifiers is their infidelity, the equivocal way they slide from level to level, system to system. Among Satan's minions, Sin is immediately taken as a sign, just as the Ancient Mariner tries to interpret the "shape" on his horizon. But when the Mariner's "sign" unfolds its script, the sign of Sin is transformed into the signifier "LIFE-IN-DEATH." Milton's Sin is thus precipitated into the medium of allegorical reinscription, and so stripped of its conventional universality and its doctrinal efficacy. The fabulous monster Life-in-Death does not reinforce a Christian hermeneutics; rather, it embodies the allegorical transmutability of any moral lexicon. In particular, Coleridge's trope of Milton's Sin renders sin itself as "unimaginable," replacing conventional moral essentialism with a free-floating signifier of modern anxiety. In this reading, what Coleridge has rendered into literary allegory is a moment of uncanny confrontation between the paranoid modern subject and the arbitrary imperatives of psycholinguistic structurality. Transcoded into a psychoanalytical idiom, the sign "LIFE-IN-DEATH" portends the eclipse of eros by the death drive, the grip of which within the text is dramatized when the Mariner's shipmates "drop down dead" and he is then forced to repeat his tale.

So theological forms give way to psychological structures. In other words, you get from allegory only another allegory, another text whose truth does not coincide with its signs. This is why Benjamin (1985) concludes his study of the *Trauerspiel*, "Allegory goes away empty-handed" (233). Allegory's perennial theme—"the unity of guilt and signifying," or the sin embedded in the sign—proclaims the fallenness of any system of meaning, and thus the futility of any quest for an eternal verity. "Evil as such," Benjamin continues, which Baroque allegory "cherished as enduring profundity, exists only in allegory, is nothing other than allegory, and means something different from what it is. It means precisely the non-existence of what it presents" (233).[18] What Coleridge's Life-in-Death reveals is that Sin as well as Satan, all abstract moral fallenness, "exist only in allegory." They are no less fatal for possessing structural rather than substantial being. And the structural fatality of allegory is continuously regenerated because it operates at the historical threshold of collective discursive transformations.

Sharikov

Mikhail Bulgakov's *Heart of a Dog* occurs at the threshold of a modern political revolution, in response to a major social experiment dictated by a science of history. In the *Ancient Mariner* and *Lamia* the device of fabulous monstrosity reached back to late classical and Christian forms of patriarchal dogma, and the Romantic poets tried with some success to subvert the traditional moralizations of their sources. The daemonic creature of *Heart of a Dog* is more closely circumscribed by the tradition of scientific monsters initiated with Mary Shelley's *Frankenstein,* in which the semblance of a human being is pieced together from nonliving or nonhuman components.[19] As opposed to metamorphic romances in which human beings are transformed into nonhuman forms and then regain their original shape, both Keats's Lamia and the dog-man Sharikov are anthropomorphic metamorphs whose stories climax in reversals that negate their suppositious human forms.

At the beginning of *Heart of a Dog,* a nameless hound into whose articulate mind the reader is immediately plunged sets up a howl over the treatment it has been receiving from the Soviet economic regime in Moscow in the winter of 1925. To stop its rooting through a garbage heap, the cook of a People's Cafeteria has just thrown boiling water over the dog, scalding it across one side of its body. Besides, in this winter of discontent there is no place left for a stray animal to run. The dog resigns itself to extinction: *"I've tasted everything, but I've made peace with my fate, and if I'm whining now, it's only because of the pain and the cold—because my spirit hasn't yet gone out of my body. . . . A dog is hard to kill, his spirit clings to life"* (*HD* 2). The dying dog is an allegorical sheath for the author in his representative situation as threatened artist, its howling the spirit of individual witness under attack by the communal authorities.

Suddenly the pitiful dog at death's door is fully inserted into human society with the additions of an outer narrator shifting into and out of the dog's thoughts and of human characters who give the beast a name, Sharik. A practiced critic of human character, Sharik can easily distinguish from the rabble of his usual tormentors the gentleman walking toward him with a package of Cracow sausage. As Sharik makes a last dying effort to beg some food, "the blizzard clattered over his head like gunshots, and swept up the huge letters on a canvas placard, IS REJUVENATION POSSIBLE?" (6). Preobrazhensky tosses him pieces of sausage and whistles for the mutt to follow him home to his spacious medical offices and residence in the Kalabukhov House on Obukhov Lane. A wealthy epicure and opera buff who incessantly hums choruses of "Aida," the professor is also the target of constant harassment from Comrade Shvonder and the house management committee. Sharik thus stumbles into a scene from the Moscow housing crisis, or more widely, the ongoing Soviet dismantling of the pre-Revolutionary bourgeoisie. Philip Philippovich is an eloquent comic mouthpiece for the outraged professional classes beleaguered by the petty details of enforced social transformation.[20]

Sharik, rapidly recuperating and luxuriating under the care of the doctor's household, is no longer the suffering anarchist hero, but the individualistic artist securing a form of private economic shelter from a bourgeois patron. The materially rejuvenated Sharik

smugly reflects on the restoration of his fur, and in his slavish
canine gratitude apotheosizes Preobrazhensky, content to worship
his human godhead and remain the chained and collared lap-dog
of the haute bourgeoisie. But the good doctor has an ulterior motive
for his ostensible altruism. In fact, Sharik has been pampered and
fattened up in order to serve as guinea pig for an experimental
operation in human rejuvenation, testing the efficacy of particular
organ transplants. Even when Sharik is out cold under the anes-
thesia, the narrator's perspective tends to his position, as in the
following quote through the epithet "the bitten one"—the professor's
medical protégé, Dr. Bormenthal: "The instrument flashed in the
bitten one's hands as if he were a sleight-of-hand artist. . . . Short,
moist threads whirled and jumped in the hands of the professor
and his assistant" (52).

    Chapter 5 of *Heart of a Dog* is rendered in the form of Dr.
Bormenthal's notebook, into which he logs the stages of Sharik's
post-operative recovery after the procedure carried out on December 23, 1924. Literary narrations of metamorphic changes are typically instantaneous and powerfully compressed. But Sharik's
transformation from dog to man proceeds in slow motion over the
period of a week and a half, as the astounded physicians observe,
and the maid, in obligatory fashion, faints:

> *December 29*. Sudden shedding of fur on forehead
> and sides of body. . . . First bark in the evening (8:15).
> Sharp change of timbre and lowering of tone noted. In-
> stead of "wow-wow" sound, bark consists of syllables,
> "a-o," remotely reminiscent of moan.
> *December 30*. Falling out of hair assumes character
> of progressive general depilation. . . . growth (lengthen-
> ing) of bones. . . .
> *December 1*. (*Crossed out, corrected*) *January 1, 1925*.
> Photographed this morning. . . . At 3 P.M. (*in large let-
> ters*) he laughed, causing the maid Zina to faint. . . .
> *January 2*. Photographed, smiling, by flash. Got out
> of bed and remained confidently on hind legs half an
> hour. Almost my height. . . . In the presence of myself
> and Zina, the dog (if, indeed, one may use this designa-
> tion) swore obscenely at Prof. Preobrazhensky.
> *January 6*. (*Partly in pencil, partly in violet ink*)
> Today, after his tail dropped off, he enunciated with
> utmost clarity the word "saloon." The recording machine
> is working. The devil knows what is going on. (57–58)

Bormenthal's "the devil knows" provides an appropriate daemonic flourish to underscore the emergence of "the creature," this composite daemonic dog/man. In line with the long tradition of metamorphic allegories, these research scientists trace this unforeseen creation to a mistake, an embarrassing swerve in the subject: "a change of hypophysis produces, not rejuvenation, but complete humanization" (60). In the first flush of this realization, Bormenthal gets carried away by the thought of this monumental advance in medical technology. Like Victor Frankenstein while at work on his monster, Bormenthal has dreams of scientific glory. As the co-creator of what seems at first to be a productive metamorphosis, Bormenthal here is the victorious revolutionary whose heroic operation has not only rejuvenated but also transformed the social body.

But that feeling is short-lived. Bormenthal's log records that the professor fainted and fell ill on January 2nd, and that he himself came down with influenza two weeks later. While the two of them recuperate, the creature begins to exhibit its characteristic dog/man behaviors: eating, defecating, scratching, laughing, swearing, smoking, jumping, and yammering. Unsettling indications of the creature's incorrigiblity send the professor in search of the human donor's records, and Preobrazhensky soon throws cold water on Bormenthal's revolutionary enthusiasm. The details on Klim Grigorievich Chugunkin are not heartening. Into the dog Sharik have gone the testes and hypophysis of a small-time hood and drunken balalaika player who died in a bar brawl "struck with a knife in the heart" (64). So the operative "mistake" is compounded by the preliminary mistake of omitting to evaluate the predilections of the organ donor. The dog as mangy anarchist critic has been tricked by science and transmogrified with a man whose untranscended commonness only compounds the instincts of the canine body donor. In other words, Bulgakov's monster is produced by the copulation of personifications for "artist" (the dog Sharik) and for "proletariat" (the man Klim Chugunkin). "We are before a new organism," Bormenthal concludes his case history, "requiring a new and separate series of observations" (65).

As the professor's household attempts to accommodate the new organism, the texture of the comic narration turns intensely theatrical. By having a dog turn into a man, rather than, for instance, a man turn into a dog, Bulgakov can more easily exploit the essential theatricality of the daemonic spectacle. As Victor Frankenstein and his articulate monster had quarreled, so the professor and his creature square off within the close confines of the apartment, squabbling like fathers and sons. The political note of class struggle suddenly modulates into its familial subtext: the Communist revolution is a vulgar metamorphosis within the house of the state, like the emergence into puberty of an awkward, shiftless, and demanding teenager hurling threats under its parents' roof and receiving exasperated reprimands in return.

The monster's politics are not those of the reverent dog Sharik. An adolescent suffering an identity crisis, the creature wants to be all grown up. It demands identity papers, exclaiming to Preobrazhensky, "You know it yourself, a man is strictly forbidden to exist without documents" (72). So the anthropomorphic metamorph exacts of his creator a textual affidavit of its human status. The daemonic creature insists on its literary constitution, its insertion into the symbolic order. In Althusser's idiom, this ideological creature is driven by an absolute desire to interpellate itself into the state apparatus. By ingratiating itself with the professor's nemeses Shvonder and his comrades, Sharikov secures a document bearing a state title: "director of the sub-section for purging the city of Moscow of stray animals (cats, etc.) of the Moscow Communal Property Administration" (110).

The creature chooses itself a name: Polygraph Polygraphovich Sharikov. Milne goes into detail on the comic topical aspects of this allegorical denomination and also speculates on its semantic resources. "Polygraph" does not denote what may first occur to American readers, a lie detector:

> A 'polygraph' is a copying pad and 'polygraphy' relates to all the technical aspects of the production of printed works. 'Polygraphy' can also be a . . . miscellany of various writings and a kind of cipher or secret writing. A 'polygraph' . . . is either 'one who knows polygraphy' or 'an author of many works about various subjects and sciences'. . . . The name Poligraf, as 'voluminous author', might then be read as a satire on the attempt to create a new 'proletarian' literature. The satirical reference thus moves away from the historical experiment of the 'Bolshevik revolution' to the cultural experiment of the creation of a new literature. (66)

The name "Polygraph" inscribes this daemonic metamorph into an allegory of writing and also draws out further the sense of the dog Sharik as sheath for the writer. Bulgakov burlesques his own social function in the satirical form of this revolutionary simulation. Writing as a cultural agency is also undergoing the adverse effects of a metamorphic cross-breeding between literature and class politics. Bulgakov's allegory would seem to imply that these two realms could in fact, and should, be separated.

As a traditional allegorical composition, *Heart of a Dog* provides the reader with an episode spelling out the obvious moral of the fable. The professor decides that the only solution for his problems is to do away with his creation. According to Preobrazhensky, "science" has foolishly forced itself upon "nature" and now society suffers the disastrous offspring of this misalliance. Despite the triumph at the material level represented by the fortuitous metamorphosis of a dog into a man, this unlucky experiment fails at the spiritual level to transform the human soul, to produce in the daemon Polygraph even the "heart of a dog": "The whole horror," the professor informs Bormenthal, "is that his heart is no longer a dog's heart, but a human one. And the vilest you could find!" (105). Bulgakov has Preobrazhensky tap directly into the conservative resources of the metamorphic fantasy—its residual maintenance of a form of the soul standing apart from physical transformations, essentially detached from material considerations. The disastrous metamorphosis of this dog supplied with human organs is intended to confirm the impossibility of the instantaneous transformation of "human nature."

The denouement, a bourgeois wish-fulfillment eliminating the victory of the Soviet proletariat, moves swiftly, playing out one more comic resource of the metamorphic fantasy. Polygraph picks up a typist and informs the household that the girlfriend will be moving in, but this scheme is exploded when she is taken aside and informed of Sharikov's origins. The vindictive creature then informs on the Professor to the military authorities, denouncing his creator as counterrevolutionary. When the monster of ingratitude is confronted on this score, "some demon seemed to take possession of Polygraph Polygraphovich" (117). Sharikov flips off the professor and waves a gun at Bormenthal. Its number up, the creature is disarmed and anesthetized, and the medical men proceed to dismantle their experiment before it can couple and multiply. First the textual evidence is annihilated, when Bormenthal burns the experimental logbook. Then behind closed doors, the creature goes once more under the knife.

So P. P. Sharikov disappears, as the dog Sharik undergoes a reverse metamorphosis, seemingly setting matters at peace once again. Is this restoration an allegorical redemption? In the *Odyssey*, after Circe restores Odysseus's companions from their transformation into swine, they emerge better than ever, "younger than they were before / And far more handsome" (*HO* 10.395-96). But in the *Golden Ass*, Lucius's recovery of his human body and final transformation into a priest of Isis is at best an ironic redemption, arguably a last demotion of his personality. So too, Sharik is not restored whole. In terms of the retrospective allegory I have been spinning about the dog as a vehicle for the role of the author, the quietly ominous end of this tale foretells the coming amnesia of Soviet literature, as the narrator returns inside the canine subject only to find a delirious beast with the fight finally crushed out of it: "The superior being, the dignified benefactor of dogs, sat in his armchair, and the dog Sharik lay sprawled on the rug near the leather sofa. . . . I've been so lucky, so lucky, he thought, dozing off. Just incredibly lucky. I'm set for life in this apartment" (122). There would seem to be an oblique moral here as well about the domestication and corruption of the "polygraphs," a literary intelligentsia unable to preserve its own independence from "superior beings" willing to feed it on their scraps. Once the state succeeds in disposing of Preobrazhensky, this cozy dog could be back out on the cold street.

Qfwfq

In metamorphic allegory, monstrosity is not the exception but the rule. The unforeseen experimental deviation by which Polygraph P. Sharikov is created underscores the wandering or random nature of metamorphic processes, the operation of chance that can disrupt any systematic expectations. In our own time, science has accommodated itself to statistical probabilities rather than absolute values. Recent theorists of science have renewed interest in the physics of Lucretius's *De Rerum Natura,* especially its theory of the *clinamen atomorum* or "swerve of the atoms."[21] It bears remembering that Lucretius expounded his scientific cosmos in the wider context of the Epicurean campaign to eliminate the realm of divine causality from authoritative human accounts of the world. Positing a random or stochastic function within all material processes, Lucretius's *clinamen* sets out an atomistic theory of metamorphic origin and development:

> I'd have you know
> That while these particles come mostly down,
> Straight down of their own weight through void, at times—
> No one knows when or where—they swerve a little,
> Not much, but just enough for us to say
> They change direction. Were this not the case,
> All things would fall straight down, like drops of rain,

Through utter void, no birth-shock would emerge
Out of collision, nothing be created. (*L* 2.216–24)

Lucretius's program in *De Rerum Natura* resonates with classical
structures of metamorphic allegory and anticipates key terms in
poststructuralist theory and chaos science. The introduction of
chance and randomness into the processes of the cosmos anticipates the stochastic play of probabilities central to the methods of
quantum mechanics and information theory, in which material
objects are analytically or virtually transformed into quanta of
energy and bits of data.[22] By the same token, through this recovery
of the random *clinamen,* modern physics and informatics fall into
line with primary structures in ancient metamorphic texts—accounts of cosmogony, morphogenesis, unpredictable deviations, and
productive transformations. Although Ovid's cosmogony deviates
from Lucretius's account by invoking an anonymous demiurge as
universal origin, the *clinamen* returns in Ovid's *Metamorphoses* as
episodic metamorphosis itself, the playful, often turbulent cascade
of tales in which persons unpredictably take radical physical
swerves.

In its textual dimension, the *clinamen* is a kind of generative
trope. The atoms swerve like verbal figures displaced from semantic rectitude. And it is as a linguistic as much as a physical trope
that the *clinamen* has been resurrected for contemporary theoretical deployment. As an allegory of writing, the *clinamen* is a second-
order figure for the generation of narrative texts out of random
linguistic combinations. In "The Form of Space," Italo Calvino lit-
eralizes the literary allegory of the clinamen with the personification of three Lucretian atoms as a love triangle falling through the
void and randomly swerving into moments of jealous confrontation.
As this tale of atomistic eros ends, the form space takes is a written page: "so we pursued each other, Lieutenant Fenimore and I,
hiding behind the loops of the *l*'s, especially the *l*'s of the word
'parallel' " (*CC* 123).

Scientific reversions to mythic or anthropomorphic metaphors
are not new phenomena. But the heuristic facility of traditional
mythic and literary formations seems to have been reinvigorated
by chaos science. Dynamical systems theory has re-energized the
tropes of metamorphic allegory. In the literature of chaos science,
common discursive figures have reworked ancient themes of monstrous origin and transformative creation. "The irregular side of
nature, the discontinuous and erratic side—these have been puzzles
to science, or worse, monstrosities."[23] Daemonic creatures are typically intermediaries positioned at the borders between realms, for

instance, the winged cherub with a flaming sword placed at the gates of Eden to guard the tree of life, or the various hounds of Hell like Cerberus, or Milton's Sin and Death. The mathematically-computed "dragons of chaos" are discovered in the Mandelbrot set, clustering in the complex plane along the fractal boundary between functions that resolve either at zero or at infinity: "The greatest diversity flourishes in the border zone, where many cultures and customs are apt to mingle. This tangled region harbors a fantastic, baroque coterie of dragons, sea horses, and other strange creatures, contrasting sharply with the simplicity of the single mathematical expression responsible for the myriad forms that live in the zone."[24]

The metamorphic daemonic shadows the popular rhetoric of chaos science as it depicts the nonlinearity of the material world, the turbulent fluidities of physical substances and biological bodies. In fractal geometry, daemonic figures are evoked by the virtuality and kaleidoscopic shiftiness of ideal constructions like the Mandelbrot set. When the literary thematics of mythic cosmogonies and daemonic metamorphoses are compared with the emerging thematics of the chaos sciences, three areas of overlap come into view: (1) bifurcation scenarios, (2) boundary functions, and (3) phase transitions. Metamorphic stories may be said to capture in anthropomorphic narratives these material dynamics of reflexive folding, irregularity, and formal flux. The bifurcation scenarios that emerge within systems shifting from order to chaos echo processes of "doubling" familiar to students of the uncanny. Transformation narratives are regularly produced by the uncanny doubling or bifurcation of an individual character. Boundary functions—as illustrated in spectacular fashion by the computer graphing of nonlinear equations, such as the "self-squared dragons" of the Mandelbrot set—set up daemonic rhythms of intermediation, of crossing and recrossing a material threshold.

Plotted by boundary functions, phase transitions—as in transformations between solids and fluids, or within fluids from laminar to turbulent flow—underscore the tentativeness of given appearances, the ways that material states oscillate in time.[25] The uncanny fiction or ironic myth of a bodily metamorphosis could be said to echo or enact such a phase transition. For instance, in Kafka's *Metamorphosis,* on the morning of Gregor's change, the chief clerk remarks from outside the door of Gregor's room: "You amaze me, you amaze me. I thought you were a quiet, dependable person" (*M* 25). But prompted by Kafka's ironic pressure, Gregor has shifted bodily phase. Suddenly the docile, dutiful, and predictable Gregor has become recalcitrant and incomprehensible. As the sign of the transition from his former to his current and terminal phase, Gregor's bedroom door centers Kafka's narration. It has become the complex boundary and cross-over point separating two distinct and obscurely related realms of existence—the domestic and the daemonic spheres. Gregor as monstrous insect feeding off his family is the metamorph as parasite, the irruption of chaotic noise into the Samsa family's redundant transmissions.

Classical metamorphoses often present an erotic biological allegory. Beneficial mutations introduce a kind of productive noise into the channel of generation. But modern metamorphs emphasize the point that metamorphic origins are inherently catastrophic or apocalyptic. In Calvino's *Cosmicomics* together with the first two parts of *t zero,* cybernetic redescriptions of physical and biological systems determine a relinquishing of organic models. The interrelated short fictions united by a male-gendered narrator that calls itself Qfwfq plot an ironic movement through which the biological creation is ultimately liquidated in favor of intelligent machines. From chapter to chapter, while his gender remains unchanged, Qfwfq's species swerve as he assumes variously real and imaginary forms associated with particular moments of cosmological or evolutionary time.[26] For instance, in the first chapter of *Cosmicomics,* "The Distance of the Moon," Qfwfq is human, but after the model of mythological humanity in contact with celestial bodies, as in the myth of Endymion. In the next chapter, "At Daybreak," Qfwfq and his companions take the shape of nebular particles at the moment of the coalescence of the solar system. In "The Aquatic Uncle," Qfwfq is a frog who loses his fiancé to his great uncle N'ba N'ga, an unreconstructed fish who lures the amphibian Lll back into the primeval sea. In "The Spiral," a tale connecting the morphogenesis of the first sea-shell to the evolutionary emergence of eyes, Qfwfq begins as a blind and amorphous mollusk, who suddenly experiences jealousy over one particular watery female vibration: "It was then that I began to secrete calcareous matter" (*CC* 145). Part of the fun reading these stories for the first time is deciphering the momentary genus of the narrator.

One critic has determined the sense of Qfwfq's transformations under the figure of Proteus, the metamorphic sea-god who turns through a round of bodily and material forms: "Qfwfq is himself the continuity, the undifferentiated Protean urge that endures as long as matter endures."[27] Although ostensibly in the service of "Protean matter" rather than Platonic spirit, Fontana concludes his essay with an allegorical flourish that is positively Neoplatonic: "like Proteus in Bk. IV of *The Odyssey,* Qfwfq is a seer who sees into the past and who can help us on our homeward journey to Lacedaemon. . . . What Qfwfq tells us is as useful as what Proteus tells Menelaus, for it enables us to find our way home—to see matter not as Pharos, our prison, but as Lacedaemon, our home" (153). The materialist Fontana reverts to standard Homeric tropes from the Neoplatonic tradition of allegorical exegesis, producing something like a Calvino moralisé, an uplifting saga of evolution- ary optimism leading to the ultimate heaven/haven of life's reinte- gration into matter. But given Calvino's cybernetic frame of reference, to orient Qfwfq's allegorical figure toward the epic pre- text of Proteus is unduly anachronistic.[28]

Qfwfq is clearly an anthropomorphic operator, but his meta- morphoses take earnest physical or organic shapes only to the extent that one grants embodiment to what is at best a narrative shifter in textual space. In fact, Calvino presents Qfwfq's metamorphoses from tale to tale as "cosmic comics" because they are illusions pro- duced by animation, cartoon concatenations of still frames produc- ing the fiction of evolutionary movement.[29] The tales Qfwfq tells are meta-mythical fantasies prompting an allegorical conscious- ness of the ways that fictional narratives elicit and shape a reader's desires. Stories of metamorphosis typically force this interpretive issue. The dramatization of a bodily metamorphosis urges the reader to turn that literal impossibility into thematic sense. Thus I want to propose a better allegorical pretext than Proteus for the figure of Qfwfq. This metamorphic monster is not an epic but a scientific daemon: its proper pretext is not the Homeric Proteus but a figure such as Maxwell's Demon.[30] Qfwfq is a postmodern literary parody of a heuristic fiction. His metamorphic shifting enacts various tech- nologically-extended modes of scientific subjectivity. From the stel- lar dust and the duration of a galaxy's rotation to the lives and loves of an organic cell, Qfwfq occupies the masculinized subject- positions constructed by scientific explanations of physical, cosmo- logical, and biological phenomena.

When the topic of cybernetics recurs in Part Two of *t zero,* it significantly coincides with the lapse of Qfwfq's narration. Qfwfq's cybernetic apocalypse is a kind of last judgment passed on the organic creation celebrated in many of his previous tales. "Priscilla," the final and most complex Qfwfq story, opens with a cluster of epigraphs mapping out the biological sequence composed by its three sections—Mitosis, Meiosis, Death. All the previous tales' epigraphs are unattributed and are clearly Calvino's own synopses of sources in cosmology, physics, and biology. "Priscilla" is the first and only tale to present a complex epigraph composed of attributed quotations. The first quote, from Georges Bataille's *L'Erotisme,* offers an existential meditation on the erotic modalities of mitosis, the process of self-division by which single cells reproduce themselves.

The second epigraph, from the entry on "Gene" in the *Encyclopedia Britannica,* treats meiosis, the process by which male and female sex cells prepare to combine in the reproduction of multicellular organisms: "two homologous filaments, during their synapsis with one another, are apt to break, at identical points, and to become joined up again with their corresponding pieces interchanged, a process called *crossing-over.* Thus a given gene of paternal origin may in the mature cell find itself in the same chromosome with some other gene of maternal origin, instead of with its former associate gene" (*TZ* 56).

Meiosis is also as it happens the name of a rhetorical figure, a form of understatement: "the representation of a thing as less than it actually is in order to compel greater esteem for it." In fact, reproductive biology is replete with cellular events with the name and shape of rhetorical figures. During meiosis, as just described, the process of crossing-over is called chiasma, a cross-shaped configuration of paired chromosomes visible in the diplotene of meiotic prophase. In meiotic reproduction, parallel parcels of genetic material pass through a configuration akin to the rhetorical scheme of chiasmus, the inversion of the syntactic elements of parallel phrases. As a palindrome, the name *Qfwfq* is itself chiastic, a reflexive stucture or *inversio,* a self-inverting allegorical nomination. More broadly, if the fantastic metamorphoses of myth and literature are in some sense allegories of writing, the structures of writing and rhetorical construction are themselves parallel to those of reproductive transformations. The proverbial correlation of metamorphosis and the erotic has more than a merely thematic harmony. It also suggests that mythopoetic imaginations have access to forms of information about biological structures. Metamorphic cosmogonies in which an unformed or chaotic primal substance suddenly divides in two would be shadowy projections of primal cellular bifurcations.

Calvino concludes these epigraphs with an excerpt from Bossuet's *Sermon sur la mort,* then with a quotation from volume 5 of John von Neumann's *Theory of Automata:* "In what follows, all automata for whose construction the facility A will be used are going to share with A this property. All of them will have a place for an instruction I, that is, a place where such an instruction can be inserted. . . . It is quite clear that the instruction I is roughly effecting the function of a gene. It is also clear that the copying mechanism B performs the fundamental act of reproduction, the duplication of the genetic material, which is clearly the fundamental operation in the multiplication of living cells" (*TZ* 57–58). These cybernetic ruminations hint that the next metamorphosis, when automated or animated machines take upon themselves the tasks involved in their own reproduction, development, and evolution, will also be the death of humanity. Yet the final epigraph is a passage from Galileo in praise of mortality and changeability over eternal purity.

In "Mitosis," the first section of "Priscilla" following the epigraphs, the ever-voluble Qfwfq is a generic cell developing to point of mitosis and in that movement, "dying of love" (*TZ* 59).[31] Qfwfq experiences his cellular growth toward the moment of reproductive division as an aching sense of fullness that grows into a consuming desire for self-expression. Qfwfq remarks, chiastically, that "this movement of desire remained basically a desire for movement" (67). But since for this Qfwfq there is nowhere to move, "I was moved to express. . . . As language, I had all those specks or twigs called chromosomes, and therefore all I had to do was repeat those specks or twigs and I was repeating myself" (68). Calvino's tale explicitly presents the metamorphic scenario as an allegory of writing. The very possibility of linguistic iteration not only underwrites Qfwfq's narration of reproduction, the transformative doubling of mitosis, but also produces the lack through which Qfwfq comes to desire. Like a cosmogonic demiurge, as it were, this Qfwfq is moved by desire to declare "I am I." That predicative duplication by self-nomination creates the primal phase of cellular division, the prophase, in which the chromosomes are condensed from the resting form and split into paired chromatids.

Qfwfq's current saga is multiply metamorphic, for the entire process of mitosis is not completed in a single gesture, but depends upon a series of cytoplasmic reconfigurations. The second is the mitotic anaphase, in which the chromosomes begin to be distributed along the poles of the spindle: "I was seized with a need to stretch to my full width. . . . the nucleus had so to speak dissolved and the little sticks were poised there halfway along this shaft of tense and fitful fibers, but without scattering, turning upon themselves all together like a merry-go-round" (69). The next phase of this exquisitely prolonged metamorphosis is the mitotic metaphase, in which the chromosomes become arranged on the metaphase plate, the equatorial plane of the spindle: "from this state of chaotic congestion I tended to pass, in a vain search for relief, to a more balanced and neat congestion. . . . the redoubling which first concerned the individual twigs now involved the nucleus as a whole" (70).

Qfwfq's protracted transformations move inexorably to the final phase of mitosis, the telophase, in which the spindle disappears, two new nuclei—both with a full set of chromosomes—appear, and the cytoplasm is bisected between them: "I seemed to have two equal bodies, one on one side and one on the other, joined by a bottle-neck that was becoming finer and finer until it was only a thread [mitosis, from the Greek *mitos,* a thread] and at that instant I was for the first time aware of plurality" (72). In this sublime moment of "birth-death" or mitotic apocalypse, Qfwfq has a revelation of the Other, a prophetic vision of his future life in the world of plurality. He foresees his fall into gender and his opposite number coming toward him, to complement and heal the movement of self-division just completed: "I saw who was coming forward toward me from the void of the elsewhere, the other time, the otherwise with first and last name address red coat little black boots bangs freckles: Priscilla Langwood, chez Madame Lebras, cent-quatre-vingt-treize Rue Vaugirard, Paris quinzième" (74).

The next section, "Meiosis," does not unpack the intracellular phases of meiosis into vivid individual episodes of transformative subjectivity, for Qfwfq is now no longer a protozoan but a metazoan, a multicellular organism. Qfwfq does not experience meiosis from within the process, rather it occurs as an object within but separate from the narrator's awareness. Qfwfq now meditates from a generalized metazoan perspective on the dilemmas of identity in a world of organic complexity and sexual reproduction. The problem Qfwfq feels is that of the "void that remains in the midst of even the most successful couple" (81). For reproduction through sexual coupling is a fall away from the virtual immortality and self-sufficient self-presence of single-celled being. Between two parents there remains a void, a void reproduced within their offspring, within their very chromosomes: "Separation, the impossibility of meeting, has been in us from the very beginning. We were born not from a fusion but from a juxtaposition of distinct bodies" (81).

Qfwfq's theme throughout "Meiosis" might be called the rancor of the parents visited upon the children. The genetic compromises and choices brought about by parental sexual differentiation is preserved in the genes of the children: "in each cell . . . the contradictory orders of father and mother continue arguing" (82). At this point Qfwfq evokes the processes of the meiotic prophase—synapsis and chiasma—preparatory to the copulation of egg and sperm: "The desire to copulate outside myself now leads me to copulate within myself, at the depths of the extreme roots of the matter I'm made of, . . . and so the forty-six filaments that an obscure and secret cell bears in the nucleus are knotted two by two" (83).

Qfwfq thus looks deeply into the void that opens up before the gaze that considers human identity to reside in the stuff of the chromosomes rather than in the discourses of a subject. Qfwfq's comic ruminations are delightfully just that, the mock-paranoid discourses of a mock-subject ruminating on an infinite but suppositious void. According to Qfwfq, we briefly exist when the generational waves of biogenetic desire crest in the act of sexual union. But when Qfwfq finally takes Priscilla in coital embrace, we realize that we may have mistaken the species of the narrator and his partner. The metazoan lovers undergo a last metamorphosis: "oh how sweet those sunsets in the oasis you remember when they loosen the burden from the packsaddle and the caravan scatters and we camels feel suddenly light and you break into a run and I trot after you, overtaking you in the grove of palm trees" (86).

The final section, "Death," synthesizes the first two by contrasting protozoan to metazoan mortality. With the individual divisions of gendered reproduction, "the play of crossing messages has invaded the world" (90). Unlike the identical offspring produced by mitosis, sexual reproduction produces genetically unique individuals. By that same stroke, it creates the unavoidable death of all that has been individuated. Sex and death, eros and the death drive, are mutually constitutive developments, and both embrace within the genetic script of each cell of a sexual/mortal organism. Portraying this evolutionary vector as the "victory" of death-bound metazoans over the immortality of the single-celled creation, Qfwfq points out the further, faintly ominous horizon, rising beyond the limits of organic life:

> above us stretches another roof, the hull of words we secrete constantly. As soon as we are out of the primordial matter, we are bound in a connective tissue that fills the hiatus between our discontinuities, between our deaths and births, a collection of signs, articulated sounds, ideograms, morphemes, numbers, punched cards, magnetic tapes, tattoos, a system of communication that includes social relations, kinship, institutions, merchandise, advertising posters, napalm bombs, namely everything that is language, in the broad sense. (91)

The "broad sense" here is the one that cybernetics applies to language as a metaphor for the coding by which any system, structure, or process governs and reproduces itself. Qfwfq's vision of the cybernetic horizon is a striking scientific allegory. The cosmological vision of a sky full of signs is, in mythopoetic terms, a late variation of the daemonic horizons sketched by Socrates in the *Symposium* and elaborated by Apuleius in *On the God of Socrates*. Calvino's Qfwfq enacts another stage in the translation of the classical daemonic as an allegory of communication into cybernetics as the scientific technology of that allegory.

In "Mitosis," Qfwfq's duplicative self-expression opened up the realm of genetics to "linguistic" or cybernetic explanation. Here in "Death," cybernetics threatens to overtake the sexual functions of the biological creation and return them to primeval forms of sexless, infinite replication. Qfwfq's apocalyptic alarmism concerns the need to conduct cybernetic technology away from mitotic self-replication (the pathological mode of the computer virus) and toward the model of gendered reproduction. If machines are taking over the world, then it is critical that they take over the forms of sexuality and thus mortality as well: "There is no time to lose," Qfwfq intones, "I must understand the mechanism, find the place where we can get to work and stop this uncontrolled process, press the buttons that guide the passage to the following phase: that of the machines that reproduce themselves through crossed male and female messages, forcing new machines to be born and the old machines to die" (92).

The concluding paragraph of "Priscilla" nicely turns Qfwfq's critical reader into an immortalizing machine, remultiplying this metamorphic narrator in the form of his most native element, "a net of words where a written I and a written Priscilla meet and multiply into other words and other thoughts" (92). Qfwfq's ultimate transformation is a *Liebestod* proclaiming an infinite semiosis within a cybernetic afterlife, as science transmutes the forms of writing into metamorphic software programs. Coding apparatuses replace the organic body with the weightlessness of information but maintain the erotic gambit, the drives to couple and to die:

> The circuit of vital information that runs from the nucleic acids to writing is prolonged in the punched tapes of the automata, children of other automata: generations of machines, perhaps better than we, will go on living and speaking lives and words that were also ours; and translated into electronic instructions, the word "I" and the word "Priscilla" will meet again. (92)

5. The Gender of Metamorphosis

Barkan (1986) remarks that "the whole world of metamorphosis—both Ovid's poem and its tradition—is a world where female emotions, themselves associated with change, are given special prominence" (14). Metamorphic allegories in patriarchal culture are bound up with representations of the feminine, primarily because of the ideological status of the female as daemonic supplement, her systemic assignment to an ambivalently secondary position. Barkan has drafted a kind of metamorphic credo: "a belief in *das ewig Weibliche,* in an anti-heroic upside-down world of flux characterized by a reaction against the masculine-dominated world of stability" (18). Were a credo called for, this echo of Goethe would be good enough. However, literary tropes of metamorphosis are not especially amenable to the terms of spiritual conviction. Rather, bodily metamorphosis are stories written over the dialectic of gender and ideological processes of subject construction. These material and psychological subtexts are the foundation of all mythic action.

Literature tends to the mythic as the moth tends to the flame, it may be, because the mythic is a continuous flirtation with calamity. Typical metamorphoses in Stevenson, Kafka, or García Márquez as in Homer or Apuleius turn on the convergence of a literary character with a mythic catastrophe. Female figures of metamorphosis imposed upon by patriarchal allegory oscillate from the passivity of victimized virgins to the malevolence of vindictive nymphs. For instance, at one point Gilgamesh reproaches the goddess Ishtar over the fate of her lovers: "You have loved the shepherd of the flock. . . . You struck and turned him into a wolf; now his own herd-boys chase him away, his own hounds worry his flanks. And did you not love Ishullanu. . . . He was changed to a blind mole deep in the earth" (Sandars 1985, 86–87). The Sumerian Ishtar's treatment of the shepherd anticipates the Greco-Roman Diana's punishment of Actaeon—his transformation into a stag torn to bits by his hunting dogs. Such stories capture perennial male terror at the threat of female procreative powers. Patriarchal moral allegory has been a longstanding instrument for the cultural containment of the daemonic female. So it is especially important to distinguish the ironic byways of metamorphic allegory from the earnest misogyny of dogmatic interpretive traditions.

The Apuleian Psyche

The *Golden Ass* is a crucial exception to the patriarchal rule. Through ironic anecdotes portraying the sexual and the spiritual powers of females and female figures, Apuleius skewers male awe before the female mysteries and the driving paternal need both to mock and scapegoat witches and to idealize and revere protective maternal figures. His narrators depict a series of self-willed, often dominant females, who are both thoroughly parodic and deadly serious: from Fotis the serving-maid and commando of love, to Pamphile the jealous witch and Byrrhaena the wealthy, maternal socialite, from the nameless old woman in the bandit's cave who tells the story of Cupid and Psyche, to the epiphany of Queen Isis, Lucius's demanding and expensive savior. With Isis the ironies of the female daemonic are extended to goddess worship under Roman patriarchy and drawn to a head in the collusions between religious identity and capital, spiritual and economic value, that subvert the Isiac pieties of the last episode of Lucius's story.[1]

Witches are among the rhetorical monsters posited by the supposed shame of female being. Lacking the same, women are furious monsters who use their daemonic and metamorphic powers to steal the phallus. Apuleius's comically outrageous witches participate in the daemonic paradigms of the metamorphic business: break-ins, thefts, transfers of possession. Meroë, the witch who possesses Aristomenes's companion "Socrates," introduces the first of a series of such episodes, where improper agents, material or mystical thieves, enter and overtake the houses or the bodies of others. At the climax of the episode with Socrates, Meroë "thrust her hand . . . deep into my poor friend's body, groped about inside and at length pulled out the heart" (*GA* 12). After Meroë ransacks Aristomenes's room and Socrates's body, the former "lay prostrate on the floor, naked, cold, and clammy with loathsome urine. 'A new-born child must feel like this,' I said to myself" (12). Aristomenes's speculation interprets his terrible vision of heart-stealing, in that "a new-born child" beckons directly to the "heart" just delivered out of Socrates's body, and so redefines Aristomenes's vision as a distorted, cross-gendered representation or male view of the gore of procreation, when the new-born child emerges from the open wound in the mother's womb.

More generally, Apuleius weaves the metamorphic threads of his narrative out of extreme attitudes toward the female mysteries. The root of Lucius's metamorphic career is his lust to be privy to female and maternal powers. The most literal vehicle of human metamorphosis in our experience is in fact the procreative female body, the mother's pregnant body as seen by the child. Is this not in fact the landscape where most imaginations of daemonic metamorphosis take place? In his depictions of daemonic females, is Apuleius truly deriding the feminine, or mocking the (rhetorically feminine) realm of bodily or generated being, or is he mocking the mockery that has been made of women? Whose is the bad conscience here? In the *Phaedrus*, Socrates's daemon withheld him from a transgression, prevented his crossing the stream before he had recanted his blasphemy against Eros. But in the *Golden Ass*, having forfeited his good angel, "Socrates" dies of the uncanny wounds dispensed the night before by Meroë, when he tries to cross a stream. At this moment, Aristomenes inherits his fate: "With a conscience as bad as any murderer's, I abandoned my business, my home, my wife, my children, and exiled myself to Aetolia" (*GA* 17).[2] In Apuleius the comedy of metamorphosis cuts across the board.

Considered from the standpoint of gender ideology, the tale of Cupid and Psyche represents the good conscience at the allegorical heart of the *Golden Ass*. Read against the pretext of the *Phaedrus*, the tale of Cupid and Psyche is the palinode of the *Golden Ass*. That is, with Psyche's tale Apuleius ironically atones for the relentless travesties perpetrated in the rest of the text. The tale is not strictly speaking a metamorphic story. But within the *Golden Ass*, it is an allegorical romance situated in the midst of a metamorphic farce.[3] It is also a seminal document in the history of Western allegoresis. "The most beautiful allegory ever composed," according to Coleridge, "the Tale of Cupid and Psyche, tho' composed by an heathen, was subsequent to the general spread of Christianity, and written by one of those philosophers who attempted to Christianize a sort of Oriental and Egyptian Platonism enough to set it up against Christianity."[4] Whereas Apuleius's "Christianizing" intentions are doubtful, a Neoplatonized reading of the tale had already been established by the late-classical Christian author, Fulgentius: "The city in which Psyche dwells is the world; the king and queen are God and matter; Psyche is the soul: her sisters are the flesh and the free-will. . . . Venus, *i.e.* lust, envies her, and sends Cupido, *i.e.* desire, to destroy her; but as there is desire of good as well as of evil, Cupid falls in love with her" (*AW* 90).

Thomas Taylor's Introduction to his 1795 edition, *The Fable of Cupid and Psyche*, the probable source for Coleridge's subsequent remarks, expounds the tale as a pure Neoplatonic allegory:

> The following beautiful fable . . . was designed to represent the lapse of the human soul from the intelligible world to the earth. . . . When Psyche is represented as

descending from the summit of a lofty mountain into a
beautiful valley, this signifies the descent of the soul from
the intelligible world into a mundane condition of being,
but yet without abandoning its establishment in the
heavens. . . . In this beautiful palace she is attacked by
the machinations of her two sisters. . . . Their stratagems
at length take effect, and Psyche beholds and falls in
love with Love; that is to say, the rational part, through
the incentives of phantasy and the vegetable power, becomes united with impure or terrene desire. . . . In consequence of this illicit perception Cupid, or *pure desire,*
flies away, and Psyche, or soul, is precipitated to earth.
(Raine and Harper 1969, 429–31)

For a more recent example of unhinged allegoresis, there is
Neumann's (1971) extensive archetypal exegesis in which the Tale
allegorizes a specifically feminine psychological development. In
this reading, for instance, Psyche's duplicitous sisters "represent
projections of the suppressed or totally unconscious matriarchal
tendencies of Psyche herself, whose irruption produces a conflict
within her. Psychologically speaking, the sisters are Psyche's
'shadow' aspect, but their plurality shows that they reach down
into transpersonal strata" of the collective unconscious (73). Clearly,
many readers of the Tale have chosen to forget its virtual attach-
ment to the rest of the *Golden Ass,* and so to ignore the ways that
Apuleius has nuanced its allegorical dimensions precisely by positioning it within a novelistic carnivalization of religious credulities.

   As in the novel at large, significant allusions to Plato are
clearly evident. Coleridge (1936) goes on to say in his comments on
allegory, "The Cupid and Psyche of, or found in, Apuleius, is a
phaenomenon. It is the Platonic mode of accounting for the fall of
man" (33). The *Phaedrus* and "Cupid and Psyche" are most obviously connected by the figure of Cupid—the daemonic Eros. In
Plato, the presence of Eros's disfavor is foretold by Socrates's *daimon,*
who visits him with a saving sense of shame. In Apuleius, Cupid
is presented as a mighty daemon vulnerable enough to desire to be
wounded when the human Psyche shamelessly, heroically exposes
him to the light. Psyche in particular may be discovered in positions similar to those taken by Socrates in the *Phaedrus.* In Plato's
dialogue, having received the daemonic admonition from his
signifier-god, Socrates resolves, "before suffering any punishment
for speaking ill of Love, I will try to atone by my recantation, with
my head bare this time, not, as before, covered through shame"
(*P* §243b).[5] Psyche also goes from veiled darkness to the light, as

the result of unwarranted censures she literally wounds the god of Love, and she must also perform a methodical penance. However, these occasions do not necessarily confirm a Neoplatonic reading.

It is clear at least that Apuleius delights in spoofing the allegorical mode, enjoys the license for verbal heightening allowed to literary adaptations of fairy stories. But more to the point are the relations between his text and its context in the *Golden Ass*. Most critics agree with Bakhtin (1981) that "the inserted novella about Cupid and Psyche . . . turns out to be a parallel semantic variant of the basic plot" (111). That is, Psyche's story doubles Lucius's story, and seems to offer an interpretation, if not *the* interpretation, of Lucius's story. By inserting an obvious master key to Lucius's story in the midst of that story, Apuleius can subdue (or mock) the allegorical reading of Lucius's narrative, preserve the realistic, unromantic quality of its landscape and incidents, and so keep a sharper edge on the material and economic ironies of life in Lucius's Roman colonial landscape. Apuleius's lords and slaves, misers and bandits, various roving merchants and con men, arrogant centurions and oppressed peasantry, are played for critical and comic effects. Although Apuleius's characters possess consistently emblematic names—Aristomenes suggests the Greek for "heroic strength," Meroë suggests *merum,* "strong wine," and so forth—their intent is more satiric than allegoric.[6] The contrast with its picaresque narrative context serves to highlight the allegorical nature of the Tale of Cupid and Psyche.

The story of Psyche gives the story of Lucius an allegorical psyche. It is, so to speak, the metaphorical soul of the metonymic body of the text. As such, the Psyche story tends to float in detachment from the body to which it has been connected. In fact, Apuleius spoofs the positioning of the Psyche story within Lucius's tale *in* Lucius's tale. He provides a comic exemplum of the Psyche story by having the bandits devise the following punishment for the insubordinate ass Lucius and maiden Charite: "slit his throat in the morning, and then clean out all the guts. Strip the girl—whom he preferred to our company—and sew her up inside his belly" (*AM* 1:369, 371). The Cupid and Psyche story is the most detachable tale, the longest and most distinct in tone, within the *Golden Ass.* Its obvious detachability is itself an allegory for the detachability of any allegorical reading from the text being interpreted. The positioning of this tale within the body of another's tale is one more Apuleian parody of the allegorical structure of body/soul relations.

By placing this fairy tale within the carcass of the larger text, Apuleius invites the reader to overstep the economic and material dimensions of the larger story in favor of a myth of spiritual redemption. Is this invitation of a piece with other dubious opportunities and bad bargains throughout the novel? Like the floating away of Socrates's palinode from its context in the *Phaedrus,* the floating away of Apuleius's Cupid and Psyche story from its context within the story of Lucius has produced the subindustries of Neoplatonizing commentary reviewed above, which proceed as if Apuleius's borrowed-tale-within-a-borrowed-tale were the mythic *arché* itself. The most significant connection between the *Phaedrus* and the *Golden Ass* may be that they both contain detachable middles, seemingly separable logoi within logoi, that recant or atone for their context. An irony shared by both works would be that to detach that middle from its body is to misread the whole text. For if the Cupid and Psyche story is indeed a tale of redemption, it is an earthly fable of erotic redemptions ironically counterpoised to Lucius's earthy narrative of erotic catastrophes.

When the tale of Cupid and Psyche is detached from the story of Lucius, the first thing to be suppressed is the identity of its narrator within the *Golden Ass,* a "most suspicious old female" (Pound 1929, 16), the bandits' aged cook. By placing her in an outlaw, subterranean refuge, I take it that Apuleius alludes to the figure and fate of Hecate, the outcast Mother-goddess. The Cupid and Psyche story is literally an old wife's tale. Winkler (1985) comments on this nameless crone, "the robbers she saves and protects insult her: 'you cadaver on the edge of death, life's prime obscenity, unique reject of Hell.' The superlatives in this sentence *(extremum, primum, solum)* are transferable epithets that might be applied, say, to Isis, 'first offspring of the ages, highest of divinities, queen of the dead, first of the heavenly powers' " (54–55). If at the end of Lucius's story, the goddess Isis is publicly celebrated, in the margins of the Cupid and Psyche story, Apuleius appears to be invoking the matriarchate in the triple Goddess and her phallic consort, although in the saturnalian mode of invocation by obscenity and insult. The crone is Hecate, who tells a story of the aging "nymph" Venus and the ripe maiden Psyche, who battle over the same beloved, the daemonic god of love.

With a glance forward to *A Midsummer Night's Dream,* one could say that Cupid is the "changeling boy" of this tale, the phallic talisman on its way beyond the mother's as well as the father's sphere. For her part, at first the beautiful Psyche is an untouchable beloved, an unpossessable prize, and so has become the passive victim of others' detached adoration. But as Venus sees it, the transfer of her honors to Psyche makes Psyche an outlaw, a subversive and blasphemer, a thief of divine names. Venus orders her son Cupid to humble Psyche through an erotic misalliance. When the mystery of the identity of Psyche's dark lover is eventually solved, we learn that Cupid has in fact not submitted to a secondary status as Venus's messenger and flunky. Although Venus had delegated him as the agent of her desires, he asserts his own. Cupid's transformation from passive vehicle to active agent sets into motion the chiastic reversal that centers the Tale of Cupid and Psyche; just as the daemon desires to participate in the human, the human desires to know the daemonic.

As noted, the Cupid and Psyche story is not literally a metamorphic allegory, but thematically, as a fable of exogamy, it connects to the main line of metamorphic fictions: "Metamorphosis is a figure for all the fears and necessities of exogamy, and so stories of metamorphosis are stories of pursuit, of travel, of unfamiliar and alien loves" (Barkan 1986, 14). Psyche, ripe for sexual knowledge, does not go looking for love, Love comes for her and carries her off to a dark marriage. At this stage in the tale, Cupid completely possesses Psyche but swears her to a pact of ignorance. And although Psyche knows neither the name nor the appearance of her lover, Cupid demands that she conceal her ignorance, issuing a threat that proves to be false: " 'your womb, still a child's, bears another child for us, who will be a god if you guard our secret in silence, but a mortal if you profane it' " (*AM* 1:273).

Meanwhile, Psyche's jealous and unhappily married sisters, having witnessed the opulence of Psyche's palace, think to themselves: "Indeed, are we, the older, surrendered as slaves to foreign husbands and banished from home and country too, to live like exiles far from our parents; while she, the youngest, the last product of our mother's weary womb, has acquired all that wealth and a god for a husband?" (1:267).[7] Psyche's sisters come forth as sophistical hypocrites who attempt to dispossess the soul of its marriage to the goods of eros, by inventing a story of fabulous monstrosity. The wicked sisters reprise Plato's Lysias in the *Phaedrus,* the mercenary sophist who, with the disingenuous intention of possessing the beloved by usurping the true lover, defames Love with hypocritical lies. In this light, the tale of Cupid and Psyche is a parable about the abuse of moral allegory for purposes of domination and theft. In order to possess the Eros they have been denied, her sisters come to Psyche and say:

> "We now know the truth, you see, and since of course we share your pain and plight, we cannot conceal it from you. It is a monstrous snake gliding with many-knotted coils, its bloody neck oozing noxious poison and its deep maw gaping wide, that sleeps beside you hidden in the

night. . . . Are you willing to listen to your sisters in their
concern for your dear safety and avoid death and live
with us free from peril? Or do you prefer to be buried in
the bowels of a ferocious beast?" (*AM* 1:283)

Because Cupid has demanded ignorance of Psyche, she cannot
know that this rhetorical monster is a lie. Her sisters succeed in
putting her up to the task of killing the demonic snake. But to kill
the thing, she must see it. At the very point that the innocent
Psyche acts to preserve herself, her innocence is lost and her ignorance turns into knowledge. Violating Cupid's solemn commandment, Psyche "brought out the lamp, seized the razor, and in her
boldness changed her sex. But as soon as the bed's mysteries were
illumined as the lamp was brought near, she beheld that wild creature who is the gentlest and sweetest beast of all, Cupid himself,
the beautiful god beautifully sleeping. At the sight of him even the
light of the lamp quickened in joy, and the razor repented its sac-
rilegious sharpness" (*AM* 1:289, 291). Like the biblical Fall, the
moment of Psyche's enlightenment is also the moment of total
reversal. Psyche "changed her sex"; that is to say, she daemonically
transforms herself from a passive beloved to an active lover. Scorched
by a drop from Psyche's lamp, Cupid finds himself the object of *her*
knowing gaze. In this scenario of gender reversal, he becomes a
beloved, a passive victim, and so departs the scene.[8] The wounded
Cupid retreats heavenward: " 'I know only too well that I acted
thoughtlessly, and now look at the result! Cupid, the famous ar-
cher, wounds himself with one of his own arrows and marries a girl
who mistakes him for a monster. . . . Your punishment will simply
be that I'll fly away from you.' He soared up into the air and was
gone" (*GA* 119).
     Like Socrates's fledgling philosopher possessed by divine
madness and yearning for wings she does not yet fully possess,
"Psyche lay flat upon the ground and watched her husband's flight
as far as her sight enabled her, tormenting her soul with the most
piteous lamentations" (*AM* 1:295, 297). This moment is what
Coleridge saw in the tale of Cupid and Psyche as "the Platonic
mode of accounting for the fall of man." As in the Eden myth as
well, the discrepancy between a moral commandment and an act of
disobedience produces an expulsion from a paradise, sealed by the
flight of a daemon. In the holy love madness on which Plato's myth
of the fall turns, the beloved becomes the vehicle of a divine reminiscence that the soul has in fact suffered a fall from a higher
existence, a knowledge the lover spiritually possesses only by for-
going physical possession of the beloved: "when he sees the beauty

on earth, remembering the true beauty, [he] feels his wings growing and longs to stretch them for an upward flight, but cannot do
so, and, like a bird, gazes upward and neglects the things below"
(*P* §249d).

The revelation Psyche stumbles upon in her mistaken curiosity leads to her outcasting and exile. Parallel to the long metamorphic interlude in Lucius's tale, Psyche's wanderings lead inevitably
to a confrontation with Venus, as Lucius will be led to a dream of
Queen Isis. But unlike Adam's and Eve's enduring pain or Lucius's
enduring folly, in Psyche's case her transgression itself is redemptive, because it brings its own light. This Fall *is* fortunate: the
human soul must see eros for herself, must overcome as well as
acknowledge the prohibitions of another's shame. As Apuleius tells
it, the full story of Psyche's fall climaxes with a reversal of that
reversal. It redeems the curse of Eve, in terms that revise as well
as reprise Plato's myth of the soul in the *Phaedrus*.[9] Psyche's last
trial, a journey to the Underworld to fetch a box of Proserpine's
beauty and return it to Venus unopened, ends by seconding and
resolving her whole story. Psyche's climax may also present the
resolution of a conflict for which Eve can only endlessly atone. For
Psyche does not disown her past acts; rather, she repeats her first
transgression.

Echoing Fotis in the main narrative by misappropriating a
magical box, with the same sort of inquisitiveness that had dire
metamorphic consequences for Actaeon and his comic avatar, Lucius,
once again Psyche looks upon a forbidden sight. Although by doing
so she falls unconscious and momentarily fails in her appointed
labor, the repetition of her transgressive curiosity represents her
achieved daemonic identity. The very doubling of transgression
produces the reunion of eros and psyche.[10] Just as Cupid had left
upon her first transgression, upon her second, Cupid returns. So
Psyche's failure is in fact an ironic emblem of her self-possession.
In the Socratic mode of self-inquiry, Psyche's enduring mind takes
responsibility for and suffers the consequences of its own unwillingness to remain ignorant, and so draws a god to its protection.
This is no Neoplatonic fable of moral admonition, it is rather an
allegory of Socratic gnosis. Cupid's belated return denotes an erotic
redemption through self-knowledge, the earned reunion of an erotic
drive, erotic affect reunited with a proper desire, and thus a state
of "divine possession."

Psyche—the incorrigibility of the human soul in love with
Love—goes Eve one better and turns her serpent into a spouse. In
the conclusion, commanding Venus to accept Psyche as a daughter-
in-law, Jove raises Psyche up to heaven, placing her on an even

level with Cupid. But the true climax of Psyche's story is the return of Eros, the recovery of the necessarily once-repressed, the resolution of the human need to wound Cupid in order to know him. Next to the comic resolution of Cupid and Psyche in sacred marriage and their divine offspring Voluptas, the ascetic Isiac redemption of Lucius at the end of the *Golden Ass* seems especially ludicrous. I suspect that it was this vision of comic erotic redemption, rather than any so-called "Christianizing of Oriental and Egyptian Platonism," that moved Coleridge to proclaim this story the "most beautiful allegory ever composed."

Circe's Metamorphoses

We have seen that moral allegories based on human metamorphoses cannot be stabilized. This is because such allegorical readings are semantic transformations that repeat without repealing the metamorphic gesture, and so double rather than eliminate the daemonic device or material vehicle that they would overcome. For instance, the Neoplatonic moralization of the *Odyssey* presents the hero's physical endurance of his long homecoming as a trope for the soul's ultimate transcendence of the body and the physical world. Odysseus's wanderings are taken to allegorize the perilous passage of the immortal soul upon the sea of life. In turn, Circe becomes the emblem of the fall of the soul into earthly generation, the sorceress who succeeds in placing metamorphic charms on Odysseus's men, but who must cry to Odysseus, "You have in your breast some mind that is not to be charmed" (*HO* 10.329). Neoplatonic interpretive authority intends to fix Circe's meaning within a patriarchal moral cosmology and so contain the legendary potency of the procreative female. But it succeeds in this intention only by appropriating and doubling Circe's metamorphic gesture, that is, by authorizing a spiritual allegory that turns every human female into a moral peril or metamorphic witch.

The Neoplatonic reading of Odysseus's encounter with Circe has long been a touchstone for interpretive discussion, from the late classical academy of Plotinus and Porphyry to the English literary Renaissance—in George Chapman's translation of Homer (1611–15) and George Sandys's 1632 translation and commentary, *Ovid's Metamorphosis*. In Porphyry's reading of the Circe story, "the entire episode, read as an allegory, becomes a substitute for the exhausted myth of the *nekyia*" (Lamberton 1986, 119). Skulsky (1981) comments that "Allegorizers from antiquity on have claimed that the shapes of Circe's victims are simply emblems of their moral condition" (16), and goes on to cite "the ancient moralization of the text whose Christian curator and advocate is the twelfth-century Archbishop Eustathius," author of *Ad Odysseam:* "The phrase 'like pigs,' says Eustathius, 'corroborates the allegorical reading we advanced a little earlier, to the effect that those who succumb to Circe, the type of pleasure, have not literally become pigs, but "like" (that is, as if they were) pigs, because their way of life is swinish' " (20). Chapman neoplatonized Homer in his translation, while Sandys supplied his more literal rendering with lengthy neoplatonizing commentaries.

Sandys offers the following conclusion to his commentary on the Circe episode, as retold in Book 14 of Ovid's *Metamorphoses:*

> So the fortitude and wisedome of *Ulisses,* preserves him in the midst of vices against their strongest invasions, when some of his Companions are devoured by the *Cyclops,* some destroyed by the *Laestrigonians,* and others converted into beasts by *Circe:* their head strong appetites, which revolt from the soveraignty of reason (by which wee are onely like unto God, and armed against our depraved affections) nor ever returne into their Country (from whence the soule deriveth her caelestiall originall) unlesse disinchanted, and cleansed from their former impurity. For as *Circes* rod, waved over their heads from the right side to the left: presents those false and sinister perswasions of pleasure, which so much deformes them: so the reversion thereof, by discipline, and a view of their owne deformity, restores them to their former beauties. (*OS* 654)

Douglas Bush notes that Sandys's allegorical commentary on the fourteenth book of the *Metamorphoses* "expounds fully, and in a Platonic strain, the age-old conception . . . of Odysseus (the rational and celestial soul) protected from Circe (sensuality) by the magic herb moly (temperance)" (*OS* xii). Kathleen Raine has described "the essentials of Neoplatonism" as the "perpetual cycle of the descent and return of souls between an eternal and a temporal world, and the journey through life, under the symbol of a crossing of the sea. Of this journey, the voyage of Odysseus, his dangers and adventures, his departure and his homecoming to Ithaca, is the type and symbol" (1:75). In its Neoplatonic allegorization, the *Odyssey* turns into the most sublime of metamorphic romances. The wanderings of Odysseus are taken to shadow the soul's loss of transcendental status, the descent of the immortal soul into agonistic relation with the fluid, chaotic conditions of the body, "wrapping souls in an alien tunic of flesh."[11] The Circe story is then read as a microcosm of Odysseus's wanderings as a whole, a discrete fable tracing the grave difficulty of a "temperate" bodily existence when the offspring of "heat" and "moisture" apply their lures, the reduction to bestiality, the possibility of redemption therefrom, the return to one's better self, the return to the origin.

Lamberton (1986) remarks that once the figure of Circe is read "as the symbol of the cycle of metensomatosis [reincarnation], to which 'the thinking man'... Odysseus is immune,... the myths of Plato begin to be visible behind this hero who is liberated from reincarnation by the possession of reason" (41–42). But what Lamberton and other commentators have left unremarked, and what cannot be laid wholly at Plato's or Homer's door, is the virulent moralization of the gender subtext embedded in this story in particular and this line of patriarchal rhetoric in general, a destructive troping of the feminine beyond anything in Apuleius's texts. In sharp contrast to Apuleius's Psyche, the Neoplatonic Circe is an epitome of a classical patriarchal judgment rendered as a universal *mythos* and certified with Homer's and Plato's cultural authority. To allegorize Circe as the witch who presides over the fallen Earth, to imagine the Earth as an oceanic terrestrial sink or imprisoning womb into which Circe sucks unwary souls, is clearly to depreciate the female and the maternal body, relative to an immaterial male essence. With the Neoplatonic Circe, the notion of allegory as "defense" reconnects the literary/spiritual to the sexual/political arena, and Neoplatonic allegorization reveals its ideological project. For in this reading, the metamorphic condition, generated life itself, is the Hell over which Circe presides. What virile souls must flee is feminine being, possession by female powers over body and Earth.

As Book 14 of *Ovid's Metamorphosis* opens, the story of Glaucus, Scylla, and Circe is already in progress. Briefly, Glaucus had once been a mortal fisherman; some magic grasses turned him into a merman, an immortal sea-god. When the Nereid Scylla spurned his love, he turned to the witch Circe for magical aid. Circe desired Glaucus, but Glaucus spurned her in favor of Scylla. In revenge, Circe drugged the pool in which Scylla went bathing. When Scylla waded in waist-deep, the lower half of her body turned into monstrous hounds. Scylla thus became the vindictive bane of passers-by who, teamed up with Charybdis, posed a threat to Odysseus and his men. Like the Lamiae of legend and in Keats's poem, Scylla is a daemonized female transformed into a fabulous monster through erotic misfortune. Sandys's discussion of this episode goes as follows:

> *Scylla* represents a Virgin; who as long as chast in thought, and in body unspotted, appeares of an excellent beauty, attracting all eyes upon her. . . . But once polluted with the sorceries of *Circe;* that is, having rendred her maiden honour to bee deflowred by bewitching pleasure, she is transformed to an horrid monster. And not so only, but endeavours to shipwracke others (such is the envy of infamous women) upon those ruining rocks, and make them share in the same calamities. That the upper part of her body, is feigned to retaine a humane figure, and the lower to be bestiall; intimates how man, a divine creature, endued with wisdome and intelligence . . . can never so degenerate into a beast, as when he giveth himselfe over to the lowe delights of those baser parts of the body, Dogs and Wolves, the blind & salvage fury of concupiscence. (*OS* 645)

However, one must remark, in Ovid's text, Scylla had attempted to evade Glaucus's advances—Sandys's own translation reads, "Coy *Scylla* flies" (13.966)—preserving her virginity and forcing him to resort to Circean wiles, and was innocently bathing herself by the sea when she was overtaken by Circe's jealous revenge. Sandys's Puritanism is obviously not Ovidian, but offers another reminder that it is easy to deflect the trope of metamorphosis into cautionary moralism. Sandys's bending of the letter of his base text in pursuit of a consistent moralization duplicates similar contortions by the pagan Neoplatonists over a millennium earlier.

Collating the Puritan Sandys's Ovidian version with the Plotinian Porphyry's Homeric version, one obtains a useful synopsis of the puritan version of Neoplatonic dogmatism in the allegorical moralization of metamorphosis. There is "no doubt that Porphyry considered Homer a visionary allegorist and the episodes of the *Odyssey* screens for a transcendent meaning" (Lamberton 1983, 9). In a fragment of Porphyry's writing preserved in a text of Stobaeus, he remarks:

> What Homer writes about Circe contains an amazing view of things that concern the soul. He says:
> Their heads and voices, their bristles and their bodies were those of pigs, but their minds were solid, as before. [Od. 10. 239–40]
> Clearly this myth is a riddle concealing what Pythagoras and Plato have said about the soul: that it is indestructible by nature and eternal, but not immune to experi-

ence and change, and that it undergoes change and transfer into other types of bodies when it goes through what
we call "destruction" or "death." . . . The soul, remembering the good and repelled by shameful and illicit pleasures, is able to prevail and watch itself carefully and
take care lest through inattention it be reborn as a beast
and fall in love with a body badly suited for virtue. . . .
Homer, for his part, calls the cyclical progress and rotation of metensomatosis "Circe," making her a child of the
sun, which is constantly linking destruction with birth
and birth back again with destruction and stringing them
together. . . . We are no longer talking about a myth or a
poem but about truth and a description of things as they
are. The claim is that those who are taken over and
dominated by the appetitive part of the soul, blossoming
forth at the moment of transformation and rebirth, enter
the bodies of asses and animals of that sort. . . . Hermes
with his golden staff—in reality, reason (ὁ λόγος)—meets
the soul and clearly points the way to the good. He either
bars the soul's way and prevents its reaching the witch's
brew or, if it drinks, watches over it and keeps it as long
as possible in a human form. (Lamberton 1983, 9–11)

If we compare Porphyry's reading of Homer's Circe episode to
Sandys's reading of Ovid's version, we find Sandys to be well within
the main lines of the Neoplatonic reading, along with an attention
to cosmology or the "naturall sence" that also brings out the gender
discourse at hand. "But search wee a little higher," Sandys proposes, "and first into the naturall sence of this fable. *Circe* is feigned
to be begot by *Sol* on *Persis* [*Perseïs*], the daughter of *Oceanus;* in
that what ever hath being, is by the heat of the Sun and moisture
ingendred. *Circe* is so called of mixing, because the mixture of the
elements is necessary in generation which cannot bee performed
but by the motion of the Sun: *Persis,* or moisture supplying the
place of the female, and the Sun of the male, which gives forme to
the matter: wherefore that commixtion in generation is properly
Circe, the issue of these parents" (653).

Porphyry and Sandys both grasp Circe as "cyclical" and "mixed,"
an emblem of the receptacle of generative processes, an archetype of
the female or maternal daemonic.[12] In the Neoplatonic view, Circe's
metamorphic sorcery represents the devolution of souls into the
material world in the first place: "the witch's brew" of Circean genesis, Porphyry states, "truly mixes and brews together the immortal

and the mortal, the rational and the emotional, the Olympian and the terrestrial" (Lamberton 1986, 116). But what Porphyry has at least patronized as "the cyclical progress and rotation of metensomatosis," Sandys will abominate as "Lust," as in his exposition of Scylla as virginal (female) soul "polluted with the sorceries of *Circe*." In the Puritan reading, Circe is a sorceress surrounded by bestiality and mired in materiality, from which demonic status the entire misogynistic series then follows. Against the catastrophic fall from god to man to woman to beast, Odysseus as the type of the immortal (male) soul must ever draw his sword. Sandys's commentary continues:

> Yet *Ulysses* could not loose his shape with the rest, who being fortifyed by an immortall power, was not subject to mutation. For the divine & caelestiall soule, subsisting through the bounty of the Creator, can by no assault of nature be violated, nor can that bee converted into a beast, which so highly participates of reason.... *Circe* was said to bee the daughter of *Sol* and *Persis,* in that lust proceeds from heat and moisture, which naturally incites to luxury; and getting the dominion, deformes our soules with all bestial vices; alluring some to inordinate *Venus;* others to anger, cruelty, and every excesse of passion: the Swines, the Lyons, and the Wolves, produced by her sensuall charms; which are not to bee resisted, but by the divine assistance, Moly, the guift of *Mercury,* which signifies temperance. (654)

Taken as an allegorical emblem for temperance, Moly is the prescribed antidote to Circe's daemonic brew, proof against "lust," and ultimately, against mortality itself, the wheel of life, "the cyclical progress and rotation of metensomatosis" in its entirety. Both Porphyry and Sandys denude Hermes of his irreverent wiles, refurbishing his figure as the god of proper speech, "reason." As such, his "gift" loses its impropriety as well. The drug this Hermes gifts Odysseus with is no daemonic agent but the divine antidote to metamorphosis. The protective, solicitous Hermes of Porphyry and the counter-daemonic Mercury of Sandys are both Christ-ward revisions of the erstwhile stealthy thief, subversive son, and "eversmitten" trickster, the erotic Hermes that Keats will reinstate so dramatically in the beginning of *Lamia*.[13]

Perhaps one should continue to beware Greeks bearing gifts. One is reminded of something Odysseus gave Troy, the Trojan Horse. Troy took in what it took to be a gift, only to discover that it had swallowed a poison. By naming Moly allegorically as a remedy for intemperance, Sandys apprehends it directly in the midst of the *pharmakon* series Derrida has treated with regard to the *Phaedrus*. And Sandys's diction already points toward Derrida's exposition of Plato's use of the ambivalent *pharmakon,* insofar as the English "gift" is related to the German *Gift,* meaning "poison." Porphyry's "Hermes with his golden staff—in reality, reason (ὁ λόγος)" and Sandys's "Moly, the guift of *Mercury,* which signifies temperance" fit like hand in glove. Here is the Neoplatonic *pharmakon,* the philosophic word as antidote or remedy, transformed into the Christian Logos, the redeeming Word. This is a neat, quintessentially Neoplatonic allegorical maneuver, a chiasmus inverting the "gift" against itself, turning the poison of death into a remedy for life, transforming the Circean drug into the Neoplatonic antidote. But the maneuver lays bare its own subtext: metamorphosis is an allegory of (feminine) writing that produces the writing of (masculine) allegory. The only antidote to writing as a daemonic *pharmakon* (Circean metamorphosis) is Moly, the attribute of Hermes (temperance, reason, Logos), as a divine *pharmakon,* that is to say, writing. Thus a Platonic script—a romance of the soul deployed in Socratic dialogue for dialectical purposes—is transformed and fixed in the tradition of Neoplatonic literalism as the revelation of a metaphysical exile and homecoming. Doped with this Neoplatonic brew, the *Odyssey* undergoes a transcendental hard passage, and eventually, turns into a *Divine Comedy*.

The Changeling Boy

Like the *pharmakon* that slips out of semantic control in the moralization of the Circe story, a similarly ambivalent trope—the "changeling boy"—decenters the daemonic action of *A Midsummer Night's Dream*. On the one hand, Shakespeare adorns his erotic comedy with a lyrical gamut of names of generated forms, signs of natural growth and abundance. This profuse texture is one reason why, on the surface, the play is so good-natured:

> *Oberon.* I know a bank where the wild thyme blows,
> Where oxlips and the nodding violet grows,
> Quite over-canopied with luscious woodbine,
> With sweet musk-roses, and with eglantine.
> There sleeps Titania. . . . (*S* 2.1.249–53)

On the other hand, even good-natured mischief can be painful, as when Puck frightens Bottom's companions out of the woods, and his mock-horrific transformations out-proteus Proteus:

Puck. I'll follow you; I'll lead you about a round,
   Through bog, through bush, through brake, through
      brier.
Sometime a horse I'll be, sometime a hound,
   A hog, a headless bear, sometime a fire;
And neigh, and bark, and grunt, and roar, and burn,
Like horse, hound, hog, bear, fire, at every turn.
                                        (3.1.96–101)

Here Puck's declarative verbal metamorphoses set up a "round" or turning motion, a delirium of metaphor mimicking the primary process, the slipping of signifiers out of semantic control and proper relation.[14] The immediate outcome of Puck's metamorphic magic, of course, is the transformation of Bottom into a brief species catalogue, a fabulous monster, a man with the head of an ass.[15] Like the spirit with which he is introduced, Puck is marked by "miswandering," the *Verwandlung* of metamorphosis. But Puck's mischief makes a mockery of moralisms, "sad tales." Puck's "meaning" is conveyed in a key line—"My mistress with a monster is in love" (3.2.6)—that celebrates a triumph of misprision, the mock-incestuous liaison between the anointed Titania and the transformed Bottom. Concerning the confusions resulting from Puck's erotic mischief with the Athenian teenagers, Oberon objects:

What hast thou done? Thou hast mistaken quite
And laid the love-juice on some true-love's sight.
Of thy misprision must perforce ensue
Some true-love turned, and not a false turned true.
                                        (3.2.88–91)

Puck counters by affirming his own literary paradigm, the comic erotic daemonic represented by two lovers in interchangeable turmoil over one beloved:

Then will two at once woo one:
That must needs be sport alone;
And those things do best please me
That befall prepost'rously. (3.2.118–21)

The metamorphic business in this play is aggressive as well as erotic. Within the ironic frame but behind the comic screen, the disruptive and dispossessive overtones of metamorphosis are present in the "fairy quarreling" plot, through which Oberon uses Puck to humble Titania, tricking her into relinquishing "A lovely boy, stolen from an Indian king; / She never had so sweet a changeling"

(2.1.22–23). Oberon appears briefly in *Lamia* as well, prefiguring Apollonius as a paternal usurper of female possessions. Oberon's protests over Puck's metamorphic mischief are disingenuous, when he has been putting Robin Goodfellow up to all manner of daemonic stealth to recover this particular changeling boy. This is just to say that as fairy patriarch Oberon is above the law, outside the game he is playing (with Puck as his agent) on Titania.

The anger between the fairy king and queen is echoed at the broad scenic level by a reversal of natural seasonal progression: Oberon would have it that this blight on the land is a deviation from the proper nature of things and not simply from his own paternal prerogative. From Oberon's position, Titania's maternal willfulness is incestuous, hence monstrous, hence metamorphic, a travesty in which the parental figures as well as the seasons "change / Their wonted liveries."

> *Titania.* The seasons alter: hoary-headed frosts
> Fall in the fresh lap of the crimson rose,
> And on old Hiems' thin and icy crown
> An odorous chaplet of sweet summer buds
> Is, as in mockery, set. The spring, the summer,
> The childing autumn, angry winter change
> Their wonted liveries; and the mazèd world,
> By their increase, now knows not which is which.
> And this same progeny of evils comes
> From our debate, from our dissension;
> We are their parents and original.
> *Oberon.* Do you amend it then; it lies in you.
> Why should Titania cross her Oberon?
> I do but beg a little changeling boy
> To be my henchman. (2.1.107–21)

The absent center, the ultimate object of misprision in *A Midsummer Night's Dream,* is the changeling boy. This occulted figure is the true daemon of the plot. It is a talisman for its possessor, and Oberon sees no reason for Titania to possess hers beyond what he considers the proper season. Here the daemonic scene plays out an Imaginary scenario in which "two (parents) at once woo one (child)," and the one who is wooed is at once two—the bisexual child in the realm of the phallic mother.[16] Keyed at this level of archaic content or fabulous monstrosity, the changeling boy as hermaphroditic daemon is quite invisible, it exists only as absconded. Rather, we get multiple substitutes: the changeable, interchangeable Demetrius and Lysander, and the metamorphic Bottom, himself marked with a name figuring the ambivalent genitalia.

In *A Midsummer Night's Dream,* the metamorphic saturnalia concerns a disruption of and return to a patriarchally legitimate eros and fertility. Montrose (1986) seconds my previous remarks about the gender of metamorphosis in the *Golden Ass*—"within the changeling plot are embedded transformations of . . . male fantasies of motherhood" (75)—and also notes the ideological instability imported by metamorphic figures: "The festive conclusion of *A Midsummer Night's Dream,* its celebration of romantic and generative sexual union, depends upon the success of a process whereby the female pride and power manifested in misanthropic [Amazonian] warriors, possessive mothers, unruly wives, and willful daughters are brought under the control of husbands and lords. But while the dramatic structure articulates a patriarchal ideology, it also intermittently undermines its own comic propositions" (75–76). That is to say, in this comedy Shakespeare has worked an Apuleian parody against a Christian/Neoplatonic line of patriarchal allegory.

In this composite or ambivalent landscape, Titania is a Jocasta who has arrogated to herself a phallic son-consort, represented on the one hand by the "changeling boy" and on the other hand by the transformed Bottom. Bottom is both Sphinx—fabulous monster—and Oedipus, ending up in the bed of the Queen. Once again, now in a sophisticated Elizabethan farce, the themes of metamorphosis cluster around gender politics, here in a way that relates the incest taboo to a patriarchal interest in terminating a mother/son liaison. The rhetoric of metamorphosis in this play is focused most significantly on Oberon's efforts to persuade Titania to submit to his primacy by relinquishing her phallic consort. When he fails to persuade her with words, he resorts to magical wiles, but the comic daemonic business with the love potion (Oberon's *pharmakon*) remains rhetoric, ideological pressure, by other means.

We might interpret *A Midsummer Night's Dream* as encoding the slippages of patriarchal engendering. The dilemmas of the opening scene—Demetrius's desertion of Helena, Hermia's quarrel with Egeus, her determination to elope with Lysander, and so forth—represent the day's events; the day's residues are the vehement but unresolved erotic trends the lovers carry with them into the woods. The dream proper begins when the Fairies—the agents of the dreamwork performed upon the human lovers—emerge bearing transformative powers. All the "jangling" and "vexation" of the lovers' reversals is the dream distortion of their erotic relations, played for dramatic comedy: the lovers should be loving but they are fighting. But the "children" (the lovers) are quarreling because the "parents" (Oberon and Titania) are quarreling. The King and Queen of the Fairies are also the objects as well as the symbolic bearers of the infantile wishes. The subject of the infantile wishes is the changeling boy.

The quarrel of Oberon and Titania returns us to the latent infantile experiences driving the manifestations of the dream. In particular, the play screens a preoedipal child's experiences of uncertainty and divided loyalties within the nuclear family. The occulted changeling boy's primary libidinal trends are already distorted by displacements and reversals. On the one hand, the fairy parents' arguments over the son-figure correspond to a conscious desire—"I wish they would stop quarreling"—that laterally inflects Hermia's and Helena's anxieties over Demetrius's and Lysander's wrangling. On the other hand, as long as the fairy quarreling prevents parental intercourse, it produces a wishful separation, and Titania's refusal to relinquish the changeling boy fulfills his Oedipal desire: "I want to stay where I am and keep my mother as my lover." But this libidinal trend is unacceptable according to the patriarchal ego ideal that determines the manifest outcome of the dream—Oberon's theft/recovery of the changeling boy for masculine proprieties. Thus the primary latent wish of the changeling boy is displaced to another "changeling," the monstrous Bottom, through whom the metamorphic fantasy is played out to provide an illicit night of love in the bower of the mother. Once again, a metamorphic interlude allows for both a concealment and an exhibition of desire.

Lamia's First Life

Keats's Lamia, an uncanny changeling girl, cries to Hermes: "I was a woman, let me have once more / A woman's shape" (1.117–18). Is this a lie offered to the patron of liars, or not? Whatever the case, the serpentine Lamia's claim has a certain Platonic authority. In the palinode of the *Phaedrus,* Socrates stated that after a millennium of post-mortal reparation, "a human soul may pass into the life of a beast, and a soul which was once human, may pass again from a beast into a man. For the soul which has never seen the truth can never pass into human form" (*P* §249b). According to this doctrine, then, that Lamia does "pass into human form" argues that she had genuinely passed out of it once before. If Lamia *is* a human subject, if the "I" who implores awakening from a "wreathed tomb" signifies a captive or spellbound personhood and not merely a sinister principle or a cynical snare, then how did this person come to inform the body of a snake? Or less fabulously, what else might it mean that Keats has suggested for her a prior human existence disrupted by a rude metamorphosis?

If Lamia was human prior to her serpentine state, then her banishment and vanishing at the end of the poem represent at least a second alienation from the human, although into what cannot be said. This Lamia presents the figure of a vanisher, a perpetual exile who must take whatever form her circumstances permit.[17] In this, what does Lamia stand for, what has she had to put up with, such that her person becomes the scene of such fabulous suffering? To take seriously if not entirely literally at least this much of Keats's version of Lamia's story would be to credit the gender politics at play in the poem. The fate of Lamia in relation to Apollonius represents the dis-possession of the female and the casting out of the feminine from the masculine psyche.[18]

Critics of *Lamia* have had little to say about the role of gender in the poem. On this topic the discussion has not advanced much beyond the stereotypical moralization of gender in describing Keats's development as a stylist. So, for instance, Bush (1937) remarked on "the masculine and classic style of the sonnet on Chapman," commenting that "the manner of *Endymion* is largely that of *I Stood Tip-Toe* and *Sleep and Poetry,* luscious, half-feminine, and often beautiful" (88).[19] But all boundaries are shifty, especially those of gender identity. The *Herm* is placed at the boundary between two properties, because boundaries must always be bargained over, and the definition of boundaries is always subject to disingenuous motives. For instance, Apollonius identifies Lamia as a lamia—a treacherous female monster—when all along he knows that she is as human as he is (that is, they are both daemonic).

Stewart (1976) has given close attention to the problem of Lamia's past, carefully tracing Keats's allusions to Ariadne, Proserpine, and Circe, female figures who inflict or suffer desertion and transformation, rape and exile, metamorphosis: "Proserpine pines, like Lamia, for her proper bearing as an earthly woman.... 'Circean'... describes not Lamia's present appearance or powers so much as the lamented transformation which has brought her to this state" (13–14). And Lemprière's *Classical Dictionary,* one of Keats's standard references, has an entry on "LAMIAE" recording one tradition giving the Lamia a past to account for its reptilian state: "Certain monsters of Africa, who had the face and breast of a woman, and the rest of their body like that of a serpent. They allured strangers to come to them, that they might devour them...."

According to some, the fable of the Lamiae is derived from the amours of Jupiter with a certain beautiful woman called Lamia, whom the jealousy of Juno rendered deformed, and whose children she destroyed; upon which Lamia became insane, and so desperate that she eat up all the children that came in her way."[20]

Keats's suggestiveness concerning a prior life for Lamia may derive from his knowledge of this report, which in his verse would be transformed thus: "Her head was serpent, but ah, bitter-sweet! / She had a woman's mouth with all its pearls complete" (1.59–60). If we place Lemprière's report behind the Hermes episode Keats added to Burton's retelling of Philostratus, we can see the serpentine Lamia languishing in Crete as already the victim of a divine rape and retribution that have left her deformed, mad, and abandoned in Aphrodite's mythical outback. Jupiter's destructive dalliance here would be of a piece with the Olympian patriarchal prerogatives portrayed in Keats's parable of the "ever-smitten" Hermes's conquest of the nymph. Hermes's ambiguous dalliance with that daemon is present in the first place to intimate the tenor of Lamia's prior life.

> "When from this wreathed tomb shall I awake!
> When move in a sweet body fit for life,
> And love, and pleasure, and the ruddy strife
> Of hearts and lips! Ah, miserable me!" (1.35–41)

A metamorph speaking in figures calls out to Hermes in the first bold metaphor of the narrative. In fact, her cry is composed of two tropes: "this body is a tomb" and "being in this body is the sleep of death." The attribute "wreathed" refers literally to the coiled and knotted scales of her snakeskin, but figuratively reinforces the gist of her metaphors—that her metamorphosis is a kind of death—for a wreath is also the garland laid on a grave, the mark of a commemorative gesture for a departed soul. By her own account, Lamia is a spellbound outcast, transformed and held down by a curse. However derived, within her imprisonment Lamia has curious liberties, her clairvoyance and power over the nymph. But just as Hermes is powerless to discover the nymph without Lamia's consent, so is she powerless to liberate herself without his aid. Here is a strange bargain in the making.

Lamia has a stake to bargain with for her release, her genius for the scenic, the feminine artistry to body forth the invisible. Her possessive desires are twofold and both scenic in nature. "Place me where he is" reenacts "give me my woman's form": to be removed from the tomb of her serpentine form without being removed from the exile of Crete would be to no avail. Consequently the metamorphic formula is doubled—she desires a double displacement from her compound exile. Hermes is quick to swear a clean, binding oath: " 'Possess whatever bliss thou canst devise, / Telling me only where my nymph is fled' " (1.85–86). Lamia states her proposition:

> "... by my power is her beauty veil'd
> To keep it unaffronted, unassail'd....
> Thou shalt behold her, Hermes, thou alone,
> If thou wilt, as thou swearest, grant my boon!
> ... I was a woman, let me have once more
> A woman's shape, and charming as before.
> I love a youth of Corinth—O the bliss!
> Give me my woman's form, and place me where he is."
>   (1.100–20)

With regard to the nymph, Lamia is (Hermes) the spellbinder. But since this detail as well as the entire Hermes episode is absent from Philostratus's story of Lamia, why is Keats sharing out attributes between Hermes and Lamia?[21] In relation to the nymph Hermes desires, Lamia allegorizes the ambivalence or precariousness of the defenses a feminized psyche can muster under a patriarchal ideological regime. Perhaps Hermes and Lamia together compose an emblem for the participatory exchange of goods in free commerce, the legitimate counterpart of theft and dispossession.[22] But their commerce is also a fore-echo of Hermes's consumption of the nymph, the consummation between Hermes and the nymph that Keats leaves unwritten. In this role, Lamia appears both the pander and the pandered to; she prostitutes her power. Hermes and Lamia agree to swap possessions, to barter potencies, to enter into a momentary, entirely self-interested participation in the other's power. But for Lamia, whose power is circumscribed to her sexuality, only bad bargains are possible.

At the climax of the poem, as Apollonius bends his stare toward Lamia, at the same moment when Lycius unaccountably brings forth Lamia's name, he puts to her a question that her silence answers in the affirmative: " 'Lamia, what means this? Wherefore dost thou start? / Know'st thou that man?' Poor Lamia answer'd not" (2.254–55). Apollonius needed only to see Lamia's "royal porch" to conclude, "twas just as he foresaw" (2.155,162). She had previously implored Lycius not to invite Apollonius—"from him keep me hid" (2.101). And when the lovers had first arrived in Corinth, Lamia's trembling and coy inquiries concerning the identity of Apollonius were suspiciously nuanced: "tell me who / Is that old man? I cannot bring to mind / His features" (1.371–33), as though she ought to have known his name, and as though she were disingenuously testing Lycius's present loyalties. The déjà vu she shares with Apollonius is surely ironic. Manifestly it claims for Lamia a prior residence in Corinth; but implicitly it asserts that she knows Apollonius from some previous connection. The light shed on Lamia by the blight from Apollonius's "demon eyes" redefines the narrator's first attempt to identify Lamia:

> She seem'd, at once, some penanced lady elf,
> Some demon's mistress, or the demon's self. (1.55–56)

Having sketched out the numerous qualities that relate demon to mistress, let us concentrate on "some penanced lady elf." The *OED* notes that originally "elf" was masculine, "elven" feminine. Although in the 13th and 14th centuries the two seem to have been used indifferently of both sexes, in modern use "elf" chiefly, though not always, denotes a "male fairy." Keats's "lady elf" indicates his sensitivity to the masculine implication of "elf"; but the phrase effectively couples the genders together, as Stewart (1976) has noticed of the following line as well: "the confusion of gender between 'demon's mistress' and 'demon's self' is also of a piece with the discordant comprehension the snake evokes" (12). What about "penanced"? The term "penance" is ecclesiastical, signifying a spiritual authority's imposition upon a sinner of a period of penitential reparation. Granting Lamia a prior life makes sense of "penanced": her original metamorphosis into snake form is the result of a complex penance.

For instance, prime modes of penance are self-concealment or banishment, a hiding of the self for shame. "Penanced" suggests and contains the notion of "penned," enclosed or closed in, and Lamia's penance consists precisely of her exile to Crete and enclosure in an uncanny body. Concerning "penance" the *OED* offers these examples:

> 1653 H. COGAN tr. *Pinto's Trav.* vii 21 He shut himself up for fourteen days, by way of pennance, in a Pagod of an Idol.

> 1656 COWLEY *Pindar. Odes* Notes (1666) 9 The opinion . . . that souls past still from one body to another, till by length of time and many penances, they had purged away all their imperfections.

This last entry allows us to grasp the metamorphic allegory in the act of penance. Insofar as the departed soul is penitent beyond its connection with the fallen body, or more prosaically, insofar as shamed desires persist beyond their repression while undergoing severe qualitative transformations, penance will be a motive for metamorphosis, the casting out and transforming of the fallen self. Metamorphosis under the sign of "penance," then, characteristically involves a prior judgment and a thanatoptic moment—a movement of divorce and alienation between the body as the scene of sin and the soul as sinful agent. Penances ritually acknowledge this death and divorce by penning the repentant self anew in a confining space and burying it away, resulting in entombments such as Lamia's.

Further, one suffers penance when and if one repents, and it is curious to discover that in biology and zoology the adjective "repent"—pronounced REpent—denotes "creeping," the reptilian locomotion, as well as the gait of the repentant before the gaze of the judgmental. Lamia repents by becoming repent—she repeats regret by creeping. Her reptilian form concretizes her shame and abasement and signifies an implicit, perpetual apology to the spiritual authority who first authorized her penance. From this perspective, the presence of "penned" within "penanced" can be punned by "penned" meaning "written." Playing on an author's authority to authorize his characters, Keats "pens" his creation; but more importantly, the enforcement of Lamia's penance has un-penned or "written off" her prior mode of being, X'd out her "woman's shape."

Finally, if pen- is short for "penis," then "penanced" contains a strong suggestion of the phallus, echoed all along by Lamia's snake form. "Penanced lady," then, anticipates the bisexual configuration of "lady elf," and the entire series of phrases linguistically enacts the enclosing or concealing of feminine within masculine terms: "penanced(m) lady(f) elf(m)," "demon's(m) mistress(f) . . . self(m)." Adding all this up, "penanced" = (1) imposed upon to repent (2) enclosed—concealed, shamed (3) written (off), repressed (4) penised. "Some penanced lady elf" would thus convey "a repent (creeping, reptilian) metamorphosis (repression or outcasting) of a penitent, penised lady male fairy." Here then is the daemon of the poem in all its native colors. A stealthy Hermes and a jealous Aphrodite are brought together to engender a "penanced lady elf," a daemonic hermaphrodite then cast out by a spiritual authority. The complex apologia represented by Lamia's sufferings would bespeak the fate of the feminine within a patriarchal structure, or of any psyche inscribed or penned in an inappropriate form through the mortifications of an arbitrary spiritual authority.

The penised lady is (the child who views) the phallic mother, the ur-form of the commodity fetish, both the intermediate creature on whom the fantastic catastrophe of castration descends, and the uncanny empowered female at the center of preoedipal fantasies and post-Freudian speculations. The fraud addressed by the poem has its cryptic source in this occulted figure, for the phallic mother is at once a fraud, the victim of Oedipal fraud, and the uncanny memory of that victimization.[23] Lamia is an outcast that must hide itself for shame in doomed magical spaces, the fantastic figure of matriarchal power shamed and cast out by the revelation of its visible lack. Is the supposed feminine genius for the scenic, the cosmetic, the superficial manifestation, a perpetual atonement for this absence? Will Lamia ever have her own being, independent of the fantasies and prohibitions of some other agent? Tune in next week. The dilemma and as yet unresolved penance of the feminine and the female within a patriarchal culture is to be inescapably contaminated with male phallacies and prohibitions. That Keats could imagine for Lamia no ultimate escape from Apollonius dramatizes the tempered bewilderment of a poet who knew he needed to make his peace with the spirit and name of the fathers but could foresee only death as the outcome of that peace.

Keats had to find out for himself that at the extremities of metaphorical participation is the death drive, an urge to eliminate the self completely: "Now more than ever seems it rich to die" (*KP* 281).[24] At other times, however, as in Keats's visit with Jane Cox, his own generosity is reciprocated by the other's, in this case the implicit generosity of a self-possessed woman, a woman closer to Babylon than to Patmos:

> She is not a Cleopatra; but she is at least a Charmian. She has a rich eastern look; she has fine eyes and fine manners. When she comes into a room she makes an impression the same as the Beauty of a Leopardess. She is too fine and too conscious of her Self to repulse any Man who may address her—from habit she thinks that nothing *particular* [i.e., flirtatious]. I always find myself more at ease with such a woman; the picture before me always gives me a life and animation which I cannot possibly feel with anything inferiour—I am at such times too much occupied in admiring to be awkward or on a tremble. I forget myself entirely because I live in her. (*KL* 1:395)

How does the question of gender figure in these dynamics? *Lamia* ends in an impasse because Lamia cannot hold on to her own. Her unending tragedy is Lycius's as well, to remain the creature of Apollonius, their identities dissolved in his negativity. *Lamia* poses and leaves unresolved the Oedipal masculinist's perennial question: how can he participate in the feminine, how can he allow the female to participate, without losing his possessions? Keats's own impasse led to the stringent ironies of *Lamia*. That was a shame because he had found the clue he needed in Jane Cox. (Is her name a pun on the phallic woman, a female John Thomas?) The solution lies in dismantling the allegorical desire to erect a disingenuous masculine identity upon the submission or abjection of the female and the feminine.

The Vehicular Female

Metaphors and defenses, rhetoric and the moralization of rhetoric, are inseparable topics: witness the effect of Plato's ironic banishment of poetry from the ideal state bringing forth a whole literature of "Defenses" and "Apologies." In the *Republic*, Plato has Socrates personify poetry as a debilitating enchantress, a Lamia of sorts. Tzvetan Todorov has noted how another, more literal moral condemnation of poetry and rhetoric arose with the changeover in classical rhetoric from old to new eloquence. With the lapse of the Roman Republic and the coming of the Empire, and thus with the loss of empowered forums for political debate, the Roman pursuit of rhetoric turned its attention from instrumental to decorative ends. This revision led to a debasement of rhetorical discipline that abetted the dogmatic condemnation on principle of rhetorical practice. This classical note of moral disfavor illuminates the allegorical troping in *Jekyll and Hyde* because it comes in a clothes figure intended to express the inferiority of rhetorical "exteriors" to the "interior" signified thoughts:

> Quintilian cannot draw rhetoric into the celebration of language, for he sees not a celebration but an orgy. . . . Let us recall that the metaphors of the earlier rhetoric (from Aristotle to Cicero) referred to a relation of the means/end type. Now things are different; the means/end relation has been replaced by the form/content pair, or rather—and this is where the door is opened to devalorization—by the outside/inside pair. Thoughts or things are the interior, which is only covered over by a rhetorical wrapping. And, since language . . . is endlessly compared to the human body, with its gestures and its

> postures, rhetorical ornaments are the adornments of
> the body.
>   Such an identification implies two complementary
> positions: to use metaphors oneself is to cover the body;
> to understand them is to unveil it.[25]

The clothes figure as applied to rhetoric is thus an obvious
invitation to an erotics of discourse. To speak figuratively is to offer
one's meanings for undressing, but perhaps to cut one's phrases
more for their shape than for their significance. But once rhetoric
as a whole can be comprehended by figures of dress and adorn-
ment, such emphasis on the sensuous exterior opens the practice of
the discipline up to, in Todorov's words, "moral condemnations:
ornate discourse is like an easy woman, with glaring make-up"
(74). The devalorization attending this figure is that "clothing is of
less value than the body . . . an external envelope that must be
removed (even though this operation can be pleasurable). Further
evidence for this position is found in the frequent comparison of a
metaphor to a prostitute" (77). The moral condemnation of metaphor linguistically creates a sexual metamorphosis, summed up by
Todorov in this striking phrase: "rhetorical ornamentation changes
the sex of discourse" (75). If that is so, that change is obviously
from masculine to feminine, and stereotypically, from male essen-
tiality and inner virtue to female exteriority, transcience, and in-
terchangeability. The misogynist reduction of the female as "nothing
but" a prostitute asserts the merely vehicular, material status of
the female, and thus the feminine status of metaphorical discourse.
Concerning the new Roman eloquence, Todorov's conclusion is this:
"In the face of this contradictory requirement—that rhetoric be
concerned exclusively with the beauty of discourse but at the same
time that it must not valorize this beauty—there remains only one
possible attitude: that of bad conscience" (79).
    Thinking about the ornate rhetorical surface of *Jekyll and
Hyde* from this perspective, one might assess the connection between the language of Stevenson's narrators and the latent pa-
thologies of desire out of which Mr. Hyde emerges. In particular, in
his "Full Statement of the Case," Henry Jekyll's overwrought
figurations indicate that the very terms and tropes of his moral
discourse precipitated his transformative career. Henry Jekyll's
"almost morbid sense of shame" (*JH* 350) drives him to metamorphose himself into a metaphor for bad conscience itself, his motive
for metamorphosis being the attempt to escape from the moral
burdens of any sexual identity. Jekyll's moral terms, however,
underwrite that career with issues of gender differentiation that

the manifest text leaves unstated. The rhetoric of *Jekyll and Hyde* amply reinforces the thesis advanced in our discussion of Circe: to degrade the feminine by identification with the exteriority = inferiority equation to mere vehicular, passive, nonessential status, is necessarily to degrade the procreative body in general, not to mention the figures of rhetoric. To take the body as a mere outer vehicle or nonessential signifier for an inner agency of soul, and to take that soul as sole locus of value and identity, is ultimately to render the body invisible, or removable, like clothes or envelopes, which are all invisible once they have been removed, or like written words, once they have been erased.

Ostensibly, female characters are nonessential to this story. Jekyll's confession of Hyde's practices notoriously omits any reference to the sex of Hyde's presumably sexual objects.[26] But let us remark that to the extent that women literally appear as characters in this story, they have a part in its passion: they are either physically abused by Hyde or witnesses to Hyde's violence. Hyde "trampled calmly over the child's body and left her screaming on the ground" (*JH* 284); as Hyde "was trampling his victim [Sir Danver Carew] under foot and hailing down a storm of blows . . . at the horror of these sights and sounds, the maid fainted" (305); "a woman spoke to him," Jekyll recalls, "offering, I think, a box of lights. He smote her in the face, and she fled" (368). Concerning Jekyll's momentary hesitation here, Veeder has some incisive remarks: "A woman who walks the streets late at night asking men if they need a light is offering quite another type of box. And Jekyll (and Stevenson's readers) know it. Jekyll does not want to admit that the violence of Hyde's response is directed against female sexuality, for such an admission would confirm misogyny too starkly" (141).

In these passages Stevenson places Hyde adjacent to a series of violated females. Throughout the tale the feminine is invoked as vehicle for the narrators' meanings. The incidents as well as the narrators' rhetoric identify the female body with the bodily per se, and thus with the vehicle of Jekyll's metamorphoses into Mr. Hyde. In terms of patriarchal shame dynamics, this in-visibility of the feminine is a condition for the priority of a masculine identity. Although female characters are marginal in *Jekyll and Hyde*, that literal near-invisibility is textually countered by a series of moralized clothes figures that reinscribe the text with a gender dialectic. Taking the rhetoric of the narration to be part of the action, then, a debased configuration of the absconded feminine does makes a significant appearance. The literal prostitute whom Hyde abuses is countered by a figurative prostitute, a vehicular female projected upon a daemonic skyscape. Moreover, although it remains embedded in the narration, this literary daemon undergoes a drama that parallels the resolution of the tale's primary mystery, Utterson's discovery of Mr. Hyde's true identity.

The drama of the vehicular female begins as Mr. Utterson and a policeman are described sharing a cab moving through Victorian London's red-light district on the bleak morning of the murder of Sir Danver Carew. Projected by Utterson's dread onto the screen of the overcast sky, a veiled prostitute emerges from the figures of the narration:

> It was by this time about nine in the morning, and the first fog of the season. A great chocolate-coloured pall lowered over heaven, but the wind was continually charging and routing these embattled vapours; so that as the cab crawled from street to street, Mr. Utterson beheld a marvelous number of degrees and hues of twilight; for here it would be dark like the back-end of evening; and there would be a glow of a rich, lurid brown, like the light of some strange conflagration; and here, for a moment, the fog would be quite broken up, and a haggard shaft of daylight would glance in between the swirling wreaths. The dismal quarter of Soho seen under these changing glimpses, with its muddy ways, and slatternly passengers, and its lamps, which had never been extinguished or had been kindled afresh to combat this mournful reinvasion of darkness, seemed, in the lawyer's eyes, like a district of some city in a nightmare. The thoughts of his mind, besides, were of the gloomiest dye; and when he glanced at the companion of his drive, he was conscious of some touch of that terror of the law and the law's officers, which may at times assail the most honest. (307)

The terms of Jekyll's inner struggle appear here, projected by the figures of Utterson's patriarchal conscience. In this passage, the clothes figure that we noted earlier as the bearer of allegorical investments reappears in the clouds, cloaking the sky with a "pall." The foggy sky is modulated into sexual allegory by a series of Neoplatonic moral dualisms cast off by Utterson into a daemonic space, the ethereal horizon where the terrestrial wars with the transcendental.[27] Utterson's skyscape reflects a moralized commerce between spirit and flesh—the wind and the fog, shafts of light and swirling wreaths, dry and clear masculinity and opaque or impure feminine moisture. As in the Neoplatonic cosmos expounded by

Porphyry et al, the masculine spirit is transparent and divinely potent, above the clouds, forceful, dry, and phallic, like wind and sunbeams, whereas the feminine body is opaque, an inert, earthy back-end, like mud, yielding but possessive.[28] Thus a note of misogynist disgust is present in vaguely excremental qualities like "chocolate-coloured . . . lurid brown," tones that bring out the image of a painted woman whose lurid exterior hides a degraded interior: "marvelous . . . hues . . . lurid . . . muddy. . . slattern-" (cf. Veeder 1988, 114).

The "swirling wreaths" of fog condense to reveal a lost woman, a prostitute clothed in metaphor, a vapory slattern routed by the wind, momentarily pierced by a "haggard shaft of daylight." Utterson confronts this scene as an upright bachelor ought, as a discreet professional and connoisseur of exteriors who looks but does not touch—as a voyeur: "Mr. Utterson beheld . . . the back-end of evening . . . would glance . . . these changing glimpses . . . slatternly passengers." But once the shaft of daylight pierces the wreath of fog, Utterson responds immediately to this projected scene of consummated sexual desire with anxiety and self-accusation: "mournful reinvasion of darkness . . . nightmare . . . terror of the law." The note of "nightmare" marks a transgression; "terror" conveys the defensive repercussions, the guilty conscience even of a man whose transgressions are strictly imaginary. Throughout this story, then, Jekyll's bad conscience, his "almost morbid sense of shame," is measured against Utterson's pride in his own integrity, Jekyll's craven impulsiveness against Utterson's granite self-control.

Utterson's ultimate payoff (Jekyll is said to be worth a quarter million late-Victorian pounds) is the economic counterpart of a previous climax, the libidinal payoff that resolves his relation to Hyde. On the fatal night when Utterson follows the butler Poole into Jekyll's house and laboratory, Utterson's curiosity is finally satisfied. Jekyll's death enables Utterson to have his voyeuristic climax. Now another skyscape sets the scene, and once again a sexualized drama unfolds upon it:

> It was a wild, cold, seasonable night of March, with a pale moon, lying on her back as though the wind had tilted her, and a flying wrack of the most diaphanous and lawny texture. The wind made talking difficult, and flecked the blood into the face. It seemed to have swept the streets unusually bare of passengers, besides; for Mr. Utterson thought he had never seen that part of London so deserted. He could have wished it otherwise; never in his life had he been conscious of so sharp a wish to see

and touch his fellow creatures; for struggle as he might, there was borne in upon his mind a crushing anticipation of calamity. (326)

Although here the swirling fog is gone, it leaves just the trace of a "flying wrack." The wind reappears, strengthened, this time "tilting" a "pale moon, lying on her back."[29] Here again is a startling image of the penetration of a female figure, again followed immediately by a description of gloom, here, evacuation and absence: "unusually bare . . . so deserted." The winds of the death drive blow through these repetitious patriarchal metaphors: intercourse with the female = evacuation of essence = loss of soul = death. This sense of emptiness precedes the discovery that within Jekyll's cabinet, within his very body, the usual inhabitant has also fled, as too the "lost soul" of Hyde is about to fly its "clay continent." As Utterson prepares to break into Jekyll's sanctum, only to discover the corpse of Hyde, the sky signals that the deed of darkness is done: "The scud had banked over the moon, and it was now quite dark" (334). And in this moment suspended just before the revelation of the wreck and evacuation of Jekyll, while listening to "the sounds of a footfall moving to and fro along the cabinet floor," Utterson and Poole have a conversation drawing up into manifest terms the vehicular female embedded in the text:

> "Once I heard it weeping!"
> "Weeping? how's that?" said the lawyer, conscious of a sudden chill of horror.
> "Weeping like a woman or a lost soul," said the butler. (334)

As we noted in the Circe episode in the *Odyssey*, weeping is the affective mark of the post-metamorphic moment. But here Jekyll is not weeping for joy. Instead, he cries in mortal as well as moral terror because he has finally trapped himself irrevocably within his own metamorphic refuge. He has lost for good the ability to pretend that there is any difference between his proper and his daemonic self. Despite the appearance of the suicidal corpse Utterson is about to discover, there is no Mr. Hyde, really. Rather, Hyde is the distorted and suppositious emblem of the vehicular female, Jekyll's abjected femininity. In the end as in the beginning, there is only Henry Jekyll, grieving for the loss of the affective possibilities he had allowed himself to indulge only behind an allegorical mask.

The Crone

Crone, *sb*. . . . [In the sense 'old ewe' the word appears to be related to early mod.Du. *kronje, karonje*, 'adasia, ouis vetula, rejecula' (Kilian), believed to be the same word as *karonje, kronje*, MDu. *caroonje, croonje* carcass, a. NFr. *carogne* carcass: see CARRION. As applied to a woman, it may be an Eng. transferred application of 'old ewe' . . . ; but it was more probably taken directly from ONF. *carogne* (Picard *carone*, Walloon *coronie*) 'a cantankerous or mischievous woman', cited by Littré from 14th c.App. rare in the 18th c., till revived by Southey, Scott and their contemporaries]
   1. A withered old woman. . . .
   2. An old ewe; a sheep whose teeth are broken off. Also *crone sheep*. . . .
   Crone, *v. Obs*. [f. the sb.] *trans*. To pick out and reject (the old sheep) from a flock. (*OED*)

Gregor Samsa's affectionate investment in his sister, Grete, need not be belabored. By doubling Gregor's filial presumption, arrogating to herself the maternal role as caretaker of the monstrous brother, Grete takes up the interest Gregor has renounced with regard to his mother. But eventually, as Gregor had grown weary of discharging his father's role, Grete tires of her corresponding parental chores. She turns Gregor over to another mother. In a way, the whole story tends back to the bosom of this nameless crone. It is the "gigantic bony charwoman," who appears in the third section of the story, and into whose ultimate care Gregor is consigned:

> Who could find time, in this overworked and tired-out family, to bother about Gregor more than was absolutely needful? The household was reduced more and more; the servant girl was turned off; a gigantic bony charwoman with white hair flying round her head came in morning and evening to do the rough work. . . . This old widow, whose strong bony frame had enabled her to survive the worst a long life could offer, by no means recoiled from Gregor. (*M* 91, 97)

The crone figure recurs in metamorphic stories from Apuleius to García Márquez, in the bandits' cook, the anonymous old woman who narrates the story of Cupid and Psyche, and in Úrsula, the

matriarch of the Buendías, who withers magnificently before she
dies: "Little by little she was shrinking, turning into a fetus, becoming mummified in life to the point that in her last months she
was a cherry raisin lost inside of her nightgown, and the arm that
she always kept raised looked like the paw of a marimonda mon-
key" (*GM* 315). Who is this Crone metamorphic allegories call upon?
Who carts off the carcass of Gregor Samsa? In mythic terms, with
broom in hand, she is Hecate, the terrible face of the Great Mother,
the goddess of crossroads, the subterranean patroness of witches
and their potions, the mistress of the *pharmakon,* the old wife cast
out of the flock and banished to the roadside, the cave, the dark of
the night.[30] Hecate is a prime type of the outcast or superannuated
term, the term daemonized by exclusion. The Crone is woman transformed by fertility and motherhood, metamorphosed by natural commerce with an aging and procreating body, and then, thrown away,
rejected from the house.[31] Kafka's Crone is thus a metamorph in her
own right, another sign and metonymy of Oedipal victimization.

As an obscure emblem of systemic atrocity, the Crone suffers
cultural as well as natural abuse. Kafka's stories typically turn on
inscrutable atrocities, to which his protagonists ultimately, if ironically, submit. In the *Metamorphosis,* Gregor ultimately submits to
Grete's desire: "the decision that he must disappear was one that
he held to even more strongly than his sister, if that were possible"
(117). Gregor "disappears" because he is persuaded to his own
nonentity through identification with the discourse of the Other, in
this case, his sister's desire. In a way, he disappears into the sister,
or transfers his identity into hers, and so fulfills his own desire: "at
the end of their journey their daughter sprang to her feet first and
stretched her young body" (127). Perhaps, like Plato's cicadas, he
just sang until he died. Nevertheless, he doesn't disappear altogether. He leaves the corpse of the daemonic form. This monstrous
display underlines how Kafka's modernist allegory parodies Baroque emblematics as well as classical mythology, for here there is
the ostentatious display of a corpse, surrounded by no mourning:

> "Dead?" said Mrs. Samsa, looking questioningly at the
> charwoman, although she could have investigated for
> herself, and the fact was obvious enough without inves-
> tigation. "I should say so," said the charwoman, proving
> her words by pushing Gregor's corpse a long way to one
> side with her broomstick. Mrs. Samsa made a movement
> as if to stop her, but checked it. "Well," said Mr. Samsa,
> "now thanks be to God." He crossed himself, and the
> three women followed his example. (119, 121)

No burial is performed for Gregor, the family proper having lost their faith in his sentient existence. So Kafka rolls in the char-woman, to carry his burial out. While he still lives, she treats him like a "dung beetle," and uses his room as a dump for the family's trash, but at least she takes him seriously enough to credit "him with every kind of intelligence" (119). Cast out by the family, Gregor falls at last under the sway of another outcast, the bag-lady of metamorphic allegory. Somehow, these two know each other.

In the landscape of literary metamorphosis, the crone and the insect go together like mother and child, an archaic dyad driven together by the death drive's attempt to restore an earlier state of things. Compare the 1943 production of "Frankenstein Meets the Wolf Man," where Lon Chaney, Jr.—the Wolf Man—goes in quest of Maria Ouspenskaya—a gypsy crone (an outcast twice over)—whose son, now dead, was the werewolf that had bit and trans-formed him. The crone had helped her doomed son to die. Thus, the Wolf Man thinks, she will possess the wisdom to help him achieve his sole desire: to die (again). The charwoman and the dead Gregor form a Baroque pieta, an emblem of defiant mourning for yet an-other deferral of the body held down beneath the patriarchal word.

NOTES

Preface

1. Walter Benjamin, *The Origin of German Tragic Drama*, trans. John Osbourne (London: Verso, 1985), 184; Rita Copeland and Stephen Melville, "Allegory and Allegoresis, Rhetoric and Hermeneutics," *Exemplaria* 3:1 (March 1991), 185; Fredric Jameson, *Postmodernism, or, The Cultural Logic of Late Capitalism* (Durham: Duke University Press, 1991), 168.

2. Hans-Georg Gadamer, *Truth and Method*, 2nd rev. ed., trans. Joel Weinsheimer and Donald G. Marshall (New York: Crossroad, 1989); Paul de Man, "The Rhetoric of Temporality," in Charles S. Singleton, ed., *Interpretation: Theory and Practice* (Baltimore: Johns Hopkins University Press, 1969), 173–209.

3. Angus Fletcher, *Allegory: The Theory of a Symbolic Mode* (Ithaca: Cornell University Press, 1964), 23.

1. Writing as the Daemonic

1. The current canon of full-length works in English devoted to aspects of metamorphosis in literature is Leonard Barkan, *The Gods Made Flesh: Metamorphosis and the Pursuit of Paganism* (Yale University Press, 1986); Nancy Gray Díaz, *The Radical Self: Metamorphosis to Animal Form in Modern Latin American Narrative* (Columbia: University of Missouri Press, 1988); Irving Massey, *The Gaping Pig: Literature and Metamorphosis* (Berkeley: University of California Press, 1976); Harold Skulsky, *Metamorphosis: The Mind in Exile* (Cambridge: Harvard University Press, 1981); and Charles Tomlinson, *Poetry and Metamorphosis* (New York: Cambridge University Press, 1983.) Other important discussions are Mikhail M. Bakhtin, *The Dialogic Imagination: Four Essays*, trans. Caryl Emerson and Michael Holquist (Austin: University of Texas Press, 1981), 111–29; Jean Baudrillard, *The Ecstasy of Communication*, trans. Bernard and Caroline Schutze, ed. Sylvere Lotringer (Brooklyn: Autonomedia, 1988), 45–56; Leo Bersani, *A Future for Astyanax: Character and Desire in Literature* (Boston: Little, Brown, 1976), 189–229; William C. Carroll, *The Metamorphoses of Shakespearean Comedy* (Princeton: Princeton University Press, 1985), 7–40; Stanley Corngold, *Franz Kafka: The Necessity of Form* (Ithaca: Cornell University Press, 1988), 47–89; Rosemary Jackson, *Fantasy: The Literature of Subversion* (New York: Methuen, 1981), 72–82; and Tzvetan Todorov, *The Fantastic: A Structural Approach to a Literary*

Genre, trans. Richard Howard (Ithaca: Cornell University Press, 1980), 169–72.

2. See Bainard Cowan, "Walter Benjamin's Theory of Allegory," *New German Critique* 22 (Winter 1981): 109–22; Michael Jennings, "Between Allegory and Aura: Walter Benjamin's 1938 Reading of Kafka," *Journal of the Kafka Society of America* 1–2:1 (June 1988): 42–50; and Samuel Weber, "Genealogy of Modernity: History, Myth, and Allegory in Benjamin's *Origin of German Tragic Drama,*" *MLN* 106:3 (April 1991): 465–500

3. More than one recent author has compared literary translation to metamorphosis by reincarnation. Translation is an act of "literary metempsychosis. . . . In translating poetry you are either 'transfus'd' by the soul of your original or you are nowhere," Charles Tomlinson, *Poetry and Metamorphosis* (New York: Cambridge University Press, 1983), 73. Cf. Lydia Davis's "A Note on the Translation," reflecting on her rendering Blanchot's French into English: "when the translator wins, the text wins too, and when the translator loses, what wins is the demon inhabiting the space between languages. . . . The act of translation: the 'idea' takes off in wild flight, and the translator pursues it every way he can . . . as he tries to bend it into another language: the soul of the text crossing from one body to another," in Maurice Blanchot, *The Gaze of Orpheus and Other Literary Essays,* trans. Lydia Davis, ed. P. Adams Sitney (Barrytown, NY: Station Hill, 1981), xiii. See also Elinor S. Shaffer, "Translation as metamorphosis and cultural transmission," *Comparative Criticism: An Annual Journal* 6 (1984): xiii–xxvii.

4. A contemporary translation is given in Charles Boer, trans., *The Homeric Hymns* (Chicago: Swallow, 1970), 26–61.

5. Jacques Derrida, *Plato's Pharmacy,* in *Dissemination,* trans. Barbara Johnson (Chicago: University of Chicago Press, 1981), 88.

6. "Hermes is the hero of *stealthy* appropriation," Norman O. Brown remarks in *Hermes the Thief* (New York: Vintage, 1969), putting the accent more on the stealth than on the appropriation; "when the Greek tragedians describe Hermes as 'tricky' or as 'the trickster,' they have in mind not a patron of theft or any other type of misappropriation, but a patron of stealthy action in general" (7, 8). For more on Hermes's connection with trickster figures and *pharmakoi,* see Paul Allen Miller, "Epos and Iambos or Archilochus Meets the Wolfman," *Lyric Texts and Lyric Consciousness* (New York: Routledge, 1994), 9–36.

7. The metamorphosis of Bottom's top into an ass's head recalls Octavio Paz's remarks about the tragicomic metaphor between the ass and the face: "our face laughs at our ass and thus retraces the dividing line between the body and the spirit. . . . A burst of laughter is also a metaphor: the face becomes a phallus, a vulva, or an ass," *Conjunctions and Disjunctions,* trans. Helen R. Lane (New York: Viking, 1974), 5–6. As Mikhail

Bakhtin comments, "the essential priciple of grotesque realism is degradation, that is, the lowering of all that is high, spiritual, ideal, abstract; it is a transfer to the material level, to the sphere of earth and body in their indissoluble unity," *Rabelais and His World,* trans. Hélène Iswolsky (Bloomington: Indiana University Press, 1984), 19–20.

8. Louis A. Montrose, "*A Midsummer Night's Dream* and the Shaping Fantasies of Elizabethan Culture: Gender, Power, Form," in Margaret W. Ferguson, Maureen Quilligan, and Nancy J. Vickers, ed., *Rewriting the Renaissance: The Discourses of Sexual Difference in Early Modern Europe* (Chicago: University of Chicago Press, 1986), reads the daemonic/erotic origin of "love-in-idleness": "Cupid's shaft violates the flower when it [the shaft] has been deflected from the vestal: Oberon's purple passion flower is procreated in a displaced and literalized defloration" (83).

9. Karl Kerenyi, *Hermes: Guide of Souls,* trans. Murray Stein (Zurich: Spring, 1976), 15.

10. Jane Ellen Harrison, *Mythology* (New York: Harcourt, Brace & World, 1963), 5, 9.

11. "Because of his power to bind and to release, Hermes was the god who prevented the souls of the dead from leaving the tomb," Brown 1969, 13. See Derrida on writing, psychoanalysis, and the crypt: "Whatever one might write upon them, the crypt's parietal surfaces do not simply separate an inner forum from an outer forum. The inner forum is (a) safe, an outcast outside inside the inside. . . . Is this strange space *hermetically* sealed? . . . What is at stake here is what takes place secretly, or takes a secret place, in order to keep itself *safe* somewhere in a self," "Fors," *The Georgia Review* 31:1 (Spring 1977), 68. Compare Jacques Lacan: "Thus the symbol manifests itself first of all as the murder of the thing, and this death constitutes in the subject the eternalization of his desire. The first symbol in which we recognize humanity in its vestigial traces is the sepulture, and the intermediary of death can be recognized in every relation in which man comes to the life of his history," "The Function and Field of Speech and Language in Psychoanalysis," *Ecrits: A Selection,* trans. Alan Sheridan (New York: Norton, 1977), 104.

12. Cf. Coleridge on the Hermes of *Promethus Bound:* "Hermes, the impersonation of interest with the entrancing and serpentine Caduceus. . . . The Hermes impersonates the eloquence of cupidity, the cajolement of power regnant; and, in a larger sense, the irrational in language. . . . He is the messenger, the inter-nuncio, in the low but expressive phrase, the go-between, to beguile or insult": "On the Prometheus of Aeschylus," *The Literary Remains of Samuel Taylor Coleridge,* ed. Henry Nelson Coleridge, 2 vols. (London: William Pickering, 1836; rp. New York: AMS Press, 1967), 2:355–56.

13. Derrida (1981) develops one of the anthropomorphic metaphors for writing Plato gives to Socrates in the *Phaedrus* ("every word, when

once it is written . . . always needs its father to help it" [*P* §275e]): "This signifier of little, this discourse that doesn't amount to much, is like all ghosts: errant. It rolls (kulindeitai) this way and that like someone who has lost his way, who doesn't know where he is going, having strayed from the correct path, the right direction, the rule of rectitude, the norm; but also like someone who has lost his rights, an outlaw, a pervert, a bad seed, a vagrant, an adventurer, a bum. Wandering in the streets, he doesn't even know who he is, what his identity—if he has one—might be, what his name is, what his father's name is" (143).

14. On "reification" in allegory theory, see Stephen A. Barney, *Allegories of History, Allegories of Love* (Hamden, CN: Archon Books, 1978), 30–38.

15. My erstwhile colleague Laurie Churchill tells me that in Greek the name "Thelyphron" appears to come out as "weak wit." "Thelyphron treats his own *animus* as a separate entity: 'I was assuaging my *animus*,' 'nursing my *animus*'. . . . Thelyphron means, 'I assumed an attitude of manly courage,' but the words are also a play on his own name, which in Greek means 'female *animus*.' (We will not discuss whether 'female *animus*' suggests *psyche*, or Psyche, who also takes on a 'masculine *animus*')," John J. Winkler, *Auctor & Actor: A Narratological Reading of Apuleius's Golden Ass* (Berkeley: University of California Press, 1985), 115.

16. In a word or two, in order to get money, Thelypron enters a house haunted by witches, where he is disfigured by a pun. Disfigurement during sleep and a pun on a name recalls the Cyclops episode in the *Odyssey*, where Polyphemus also gets it in the face and falls for a false name, when Odysseus claims to be Outis, or No-man. Perhaps Apuleius, Joyce-like, is travestying the *Odyssey* here, as he is said to be doing in general: "Lucius, instead of mastering the world around him, is approaching an experience that will remove him from that world altogether. In this sense, his odyssey is a mockery of the original *Odyssey*, and he himself is a mockery of that poem's hero," James Tatum, *Apuleius and The Golden Ass* (Ithaca: Cornell University Press, 1979), 76.

17. The authors in William Veeder and Gordon Hirsch, ed., *Dr Jekyll and Mr Hyde After One Hundred Years* (Chicago: University of Chicago Press, 1988), touch variously on the grammatological dynamics in the text: "A signature identifying a body or 'self' *as* itself is another indication that the self is constituted by its otherness or figurality, its relentless transfiguration into a display of signs (its signature) that is read by others into one or more contexts where a univocal self is thoroughly dispersed," Jerrold E. Hogle, "The Struggle for a Dichotomy: Abjection in Jekyll and his Interpreters," Veeder and Hirsch 1988, 188; "Two objects remain behind to take the place of the vanished narrator: the text of the narrative itself and the 'body of the self-destroyer' called Hyde. The two are, in important ways, the same thing. . . . Hyde is from the outset the product of Jekyll's pen," Ronald R. Thomas, "The Strange Voices of the Strange Case: Dr. Jekyll, Mr. Hyde, and the Voices of Modern Fiction," Veeder and Hirsch 1988, 78.

18. The seminal statement of this logic is the chapter " '. . . *That Dangerous Supplement . . . ,* ' " Jacques Derrida, *Of Grammatology,* trans. Gayatri Chakravorty Spivak (Baltimore: Johns Hopkins University Press, 1976), 141–64. Craig Owens remarks: "the allegorical supplement is not only an addition, but also a replacement. . . . If allegory is identified as a supplement, then it is also aligned with writing, insofar as writing is conceived as supplementary to speech," "The Allegorical Impulse: Toward a Theory of Postmodernism," *October* 12 (Spring 1980): 84; an expanded version appears in Craig Owens, *Beyond Recognition: Representation, Power, and Culture* (Berkeley: University of California Press, 1992). Commenting that "by reading the text as allegory, allegoresis in effect *supplies* the *integumentum* or veil with which to cover the text; it recuperates the text through concealment of it," Copeland and Melville (1991) note that their word *supplies* carries "the French overtones of the word, because we are indeed within what Derrida has called 'the logic of the supplement' " (171). The allegorical veiling of the text is parallel to the metamorphic "sheathing" of the proper body.

19. The daemonic as an allegory of communication has affinities with Michel Serres's "demon," which emerges from considerations of thermodynamics and information theory, systemic noise [le parasite] and its exclusion: "Serres called this included/excluded third man the demon. . . . The parasite, like the demon and the third man, is an integral part of the system. By experiencing a perturbation and subsequently integrating it, the system passes from a simple to a more complex state. Thus, by virtue of its power to perturb, the parasite ultimately constitutes, like the *clinamen* and the demon, the *condition of possibility of the system.* In this way the parasite attests from within order the primacy of disorder; it produces by way of disorder a more complex order," Josué V. Harari and David F. Bell, "Introduction: Journal à plusieurs voies," in Michel Serres, *Hermes: Literature, Science, Philosophy*, ed. Josué V. Harari and David F. Bell (Baltimore: Johns Hopkins University Press, 1982), xxvi–xxvii.

20. For some authors, the daemonic as the "spiritual" is simply subsumed by the divine, leaving the Judeo-Christian "demonic" as a side-topic. In literary discussions the daemonic has traditionally been approached as a religious or philosophical datum. For instance, R. D. Stock develops his treatment of the daemonic in the frame of "numinous experience": "The personal daemon is analogous to the numen as wholly other. . . . The daemonic, either in its personal or transcendental sense, is mysterious, energetic, non-rational, non-moral. Otto suggests that at an early stage of religious consciousness the daemonic may be closely joined with the numinous as expressing the Numen's horrendousness and ethically amibiguous vitality," *The Holy and the Daemonic from Sir Thomas Browne to William Blake* (Princeton: Princeton University Press, 1982), 18–19. Stock expands his focus to include pagan religious consciousness in *The Flutes of Dionysus: Daemonic Enthrallment in Literature* (Lincoln: University of Nebraska Press, 1989). But closer to my sense of the daemonic is

Tobin Siebers's discussion of the structural logic of the sacred: "The sacred is always characterized by oscillating polarities, ambivalence, and reversibility. It presents uncanny mixtures," *The Mirror of Medusa* (Berkeley: University of California Press, 1983), 18. Discussions of the daemonic in literature are J. B. Beer, *Coleridge the Visionary* (London: Chatto & Windus, 1959), 99–132; and Charles I. Patterson, Jr., *The Daemonic in the Poetry of John Keats* (Urbana: University of Illinois Press, 1970). For the daemonic in Platonic dialogue, see Ronna Burger, *Plato's Phaedrus: A Defense of a Philosophic Art of Writing* (University: University of Alabama Press, 1980), 44–69.

21. "Apuleius often obscures the wider distinction between gods and demons themselves by applying the term 'god' (deus) [as in the "god" of Socrates] in different contexts to demons never embodied, demons after embodiment, and demons currently embodied," Stephen Gersh, *Middle Platonism and Neoplatonism: The Latin Tradition*, 2 vols. (Notre Dame: University of Notre Dame Press, 1986), 1:315, n.367.

22. "Apuleius is once again drawing together into a systematic form scattered doctrines in Plato's writings. Thus, the notion that the human soul is a demon is based upon the *Timaeus* where the rational part of the soul is described as something 'which God has bestowed as a demon on each individual,'" Gersh 1986, 1:235. See also Plutarch, "On the Sign of Socrates," in *Plutarch's Moralia in Fifteen Volumes*, trans. Phillip H. de Lacy and Benedict Einarson (Cambridge: Harvard University Press, 1959), 7:361–509

23. From *Dichtung und Wahrheit*, cited in Patterson 1970, 8–9. On Goethe's role in the critical agon between allegory and the symbol, see "The Limits of Erlebniskunst and the Rehabilitation of Allegory," Gadamer 1989, 70–81. The Romantic revival of the daemonic significantly anticipated modern psychology: "the demonic ceased to be a supernatural category and developed into a much more equivocal notion, suggesting that alienation, metamorphosis, doubling, transformation of the subject, were expressions of unconscious desire," Jackson 1981, 62.

24. See Montrose (1986), where a careful attention to the verbal texture of the fairy dialogue produces powerful results. See C. L. Barber, *Shakespeare's Festive Comedy: A Study of Dramatic Form in its Relation to Social Custom* (New York: Meridian, 1967), on the Saturnalian and Aristophanic backgrounds of *Dream,* and the connection to classical psychoanalysis. "It is a fundamental structural principle of the play that the creatures of the dream world enact literally what is undergone figuratively or metaphorically by the citizens of the court," Marjorie B. Garber, *Dream in Shakespeare: From Metaphor to Metamorphosis* (New Haven: Yale University Press, 1974), 77. In fact, the entire play pivots on the fairy plot that turns it from stock melodrama toward metamorphic allegory. The changeability of Demetrius in Act 1 is already a repercussion of the fairy quarreling just offstage. Relative to the fairy plot the human plots are comically superficial.

25. "When you equate two terms, either can replace the other, which is to say that the equating of two terms prepares the way for eliminating one of them," Kenneth Burke, *A Grammar of Motives* (Berkeley: University of California Press, 1969), 469.

26. Steven Knapp, *Personification and the Sublime: Milton to Coleridge* (Cambridge: Harvard University Press, 1985), 60.

27. Peter de Bolla has located the trope of reverse personification in another context: "in the Wordsworth poem the disturbance is marked by the reversal of personification so that an animate being is seen in terms of an inanimate object. . . . In 'A slumber' a human presence, 'she,' is described as a 'thing'. This is what I term a reverse prosopoeia," *Harold Bloom: Towards Historical Rhetorics* (New York: Routledge, 1988), 137–38.

28. Theresa M. Kelley, " 'Fantastic Shapes': From Classical Rhetoric to Romantic Allegory," *Texas Studies in Literature and Language* 33:2 (Summer 1991): 225–60, underscores the anxiety bound up with this aspect of allegorical agency, that its magical animation may turn uncanny or horrific: "what later detractors of allegory may fear most [is] the possibility that its hybrid of abstraction and visualizable shapes might come to life" (231).

29. "The basic intention of the art of hospitality was to transform the *stranger* into a *guest*. . . . It was a strategy of accommodation by re-nomination, a virtual metamorphosing of the alien presence. . . . The failure to transform, tame, familiarize, or domesticate the ambiguous presence from 'the outside' (another territory, another world—or just another house) is one of the permanently generative themes of Western literature," Tony Tanner, *Adultery in the Novel* (Baltimore: Johns Hopkins University Press, 1979), 24–26.

30. See Richard J. Durocher, "Satan's Metamorphoses and Ovidian Counterheroism," *Milton and Ovid* (Ithaca: Cornell University Press, 1985), 111–47.

31. In their spirited polemic against thematizing, theologizing, and psychologizing Kafka criticism, Gilles Deleuze and Félix Guattari declare, "We won't try to find archetypes that would represent Kafka's imaginary, his dynamic, or his bestiary (the archetype works by assimilation, homogenization, and thematics, whereas our method works only where a rupturing and heterogenous line appears)," *Kafka: Toward a Minor Literature*, trans. Dana Polan (Minneapolis: University of Minnesota Press, 1986), 7.

32. Walter Benjamin, *Illuminations,* ed. Hannah Arendt, trans. Harry Zohn (London: Fontana, 1982), 117.

33. It is worth noting that Hermes is the patron of Ulysses's grandfather, Autolycos (*Odyssey* 19:394–96). For more on this connection, see Jenny Strauss Clay, *The Wrath of Athena* (Princeton: Princeton University Press, 1983), 82–83; and John Peradotto, *Man in the Middle Voice: Name and Narration in the Odyssey* (Princeton: Princeton University Press, 1990), 129.

34. "Franz Kafka: On the Tenth Anniversary of His Death," Benjamin 1982, 111–40, is treated in detail in Henry Sussman, "The Herald: An Introduction," *Franz Kafka: Geometrician of Metaphor* (Madison: Coda Press, 1979), 1–41. See also Charles Bernheimer, "Crossing Over: Kafka's Metatextual Parable," *Flaubert and Kafka: Studies in Psychopoetic Structure* (New Haven: Yale University Press, 1982), 45–55; Corngold 1988, 47–89; and Skulsky 1981, 171–94. For a collection of recent work on Kafka, see Alan Udoff, ed., *Kafka and the Contemporary Critical Performance: Centenary Readings* (Bloomington: Indiana University Press, 1987).

35. "The writing of allegory depends upon a condemnation of and distancing from mere allegoresis (... we see this ... in the traps writers like Spenser and Hawthorne lay for the allegorizing imaginations of their readers ...)," Copeland and Melville 1991, 184–85.

36. Deleuze and Guattari (1986) treat Kafka's bureaucracies in the context of an alternative "triangulation" that offers to displace a reductive fixation on the Oedipal triangle: "Sometimes, one of the terms of the family triangle finds itself replaced by another term that is enough to defamiliarize the whole thing.... Sometimes, it's the whole triangle that changes its form and its characters and reveals itself to be judiciary or economic or bureaucratic or political" (11). They recover a daemonic reading of the bureaucracy in the following passage: "the becomings-animal have value only in terms of the assemblages that inspire them—assemblages where the animals function like pieces of a musical machine or of a science machine, a bureaucratic machine, and so on, and so on. And the letters [to Felice] are already part of a machinic assemblage where fluxes are exchanged and where the postman plays the erotic role of an indispensible cog of the machine, a bureaucratic mediator without whom the epistolary pact would be unable to operate" (40). These remarks parallel the epistolary daemonic in Jacques Derrida, *The Post Card: From Socrates to Freud and Beyond,* trans. Alan Bass (Chicago: University of Chicago Press, 1987).

37. Franz Kafka, *Parables and Paradoxes* (New York: Schocken, 1958), 85.

38. "Recalling Freud's suggestion that children are often figured in dreams as insects, we should probably find the clearest representation of the mysterious, troubled communication between father and son as different 'kinds of being' expressed most directly in the story, *Metamorphosis,* about a son who was a monster cockroach. Rhetorically, we may note that, in this very disgrace of the offspring, there is a desperate vengeance against the parent from which it was descended," Kenneth Burke, *A Rhetoric of Motives* (Berkeley: University of California Press, 1969), 242.

39. See Walter H. Sokel, "From Marx to Myth: The Structure and Function of Self-Alienation in Kafka's *Metamorphosis,*" *Literary Review* 26:4 (Summer 1983), 488.

2. History of Metamorphic Allegory

1. On the cultural distance between Homer and Plato as an effect of the transition from orality to writing, see Eric A. Havelock, *Preface to Plato* (Cambridge: Harvard University Press, 1963). Miller (1994) relates the emergence of lyric consciousness to the technology of writing (2–3).

2. Edwin Honig details the emergence of allegorical reading in classical Greek culture in *Dark Conceit: The Making of Allegory* (Evanston: Northwestern University Press, 1959), 19–31. See also Fletcher 1964, 231–33.

3. Its origins are typically defensive—whether to defend the letter of a text by supplying it with a nonliteral sense, or to defend the poet against philosophical or philistine attack. Allegorical techniques, applied by adherents of diverse sects, flourished in Greece. "Allegorization began early in Greece (the end of the 6th century B.C.). . . . Along with the wish to rescue the ancient poets from the charge of moral baseness and defamation of the gods, a charge which became more insistent in the fifth and fourth centuries (e.g. Xenophanes and Plato), there was the understandable impulse to exploit the sanctity of certain ancient texts for the purpose of furthering philosophical or religious views to which the interpreter was personally committed": James A. Coulter, *The Literary Microcosm: Theories of Interpretation of the Later Neoplatonists* (Leiden: E. J. Brill, 1977), 26. "The need to articulate the truth thought to be contained in the *Iliad* and *Odyssey* can be traced to two primary motives: the desire of the interpreters to use the prestige of the Homeric poems to support their own views and the desire to defend Homer against his detractors," Lamberton 1986, 15.

4. Cf. Michel Foucault, *The Use of Pleasure: The History of Sexuality,* vol. 2, trans. Robert Hurley (New York: Vintage, 1985), 230–46. See also Charles Altieri, "Plato's Performative Sublime and the Ends of Reading," *NLH* 16:2 (Winter 1985): 251–73.

5. "The authoritative text which most occupied the attention of the Neoplatonists was the *Timaeus,*" Lamberton 1983, 6.

6. On Plato's revaluations of Pythagorean doctrines on the soul, see Ronna Burger, *The Phaedo: A Platonic Labyrinth* (New Haven: Yale University Press, 1984): "The attempt to reinterpret the meaning of 'separation' [of the psyche from the body], and in so doing to reverse the Pythagorean position, is, one might say, the fundamental intention of the *Phaedo*" (7). "In Plato and Aristotle the instruments of philosophical constructions . . . impose themselves on the subject of inquiry so that the whole of nature and the ethical life seem to be pressed into shape by the doctrinal instruments," Honig 1959, 28. See also Charles L. Griswold, Jr., *Self-Knowledge in Plato's Phaedrus* (New Haven: Yale University Press, 1986).

7. In *Myth and Language* (Bloomington: Indiana University Press, 1980), Albert Cook shows that the aphorisms of Heraclitus achieve a kind

Notes

of literary synthesis crucial for the philosophical transumption of mythic discourse by classical Greek thought (69–107).

8. On Socratic irony, see Gregory Vlastos, *Socrates: Ironist and Moral Philospher* (Ithaca: Cornell University Press, 1991), 21–44.

9. Ovid's conventionalized portrait of Pythagoras appears in Book 15 of *The Metamorphoses*: "Our souls / Are deathless; always, when they leave our bodies, / They find new dwelling-places. I myself, / I well remember, in the Trojan War / Was Panthous' son, Euphorbus.... All things are always changing, / But nothing dies. The spirit comes and goes, / Is housed wherever it wills, shifts residence / From beasts to men, from men to beasts, but always / It keeps on living.... Full sail, I voyage / Over the boundless ocean, and I tell you / Nothing is permanent in all the world. / All things are fluent; every image forms, / Wandering through change," *OH* 15.156–80.

10. See Robert A. Kantra, "Practical Wisdom and Satiric Humor in Philosophic Fictions," *Mosaic* 22:3 (Summer 1989): 85–100, for a discussion of Socrates as comedian and hermetic satirist: "Socrates's philosophic intention can seem as duplicitous as Hermes's intellectual reputation" (86).

11. "Just how kosmos is the essential type of an allegorical image will appear as soon as the term is defined. It signifies (1) a universe, and (2) a symbol that implies a rank in a hierarchy.... As in English, the Greek term *kosmos* has a double meaning, since it denotes both a *large-scale order* (macrocosmos) and the small-scale *sign of that order* (microcosmos)," Fletcher 1964, 109–10.

12. Italo Calvino, *The Uses of Literature: Essays*, trans. Patrick Creagh (New York: Harvest/HBJ, 1986), 157.

13. On Ovid's chronology, see Sara Mack, *Ovid* (New Haven: Yale University Press, 1988), 26–27. "Ovid, it is thought, knew his Lucretius perfectly well": George Depue Hadzsits, *Lucretius and His Influence* (New York: Longmans, Green, 1935), 54. Horace Gregory goes further: "There is not much doubt that the source of his inspiration [for the opening of Book I] is in the first book of Lucretius's *De Rerum Natura* with its statements on the indestructibility of matter. In no sense does Ovid directly imitate Lucretius.... Ovid's imagination has none of Lucretius's bent toward darkness": *Ovid: The Metamorphoses*, trans. Horace Gregory (New York: Viking, 1958), 2. See also "Lucretius: Science and Religion," Serres 1982, 98–124; and Warren F. Motte, Jr., "Clinamen Redux," *Comparative Literature Studies* 23:4 (Winter 1986): 263–81.

14. Fergus Millar, "The World of the *Golden Ass*," *Journal of Roman Studies* 71 (1981): 66.

15. As Bakhtin (1981) comments on the Western novel in general, "Parodic stylizations of canonized genres and styles occupy an essential place in the novel[, as do] parodies and travesties of all the high genres (parodies precisely of genres, and not of individual authors or schools)" (6).

16. "That the hero of Apuleius' book dies in the odor of sanctity would make him only the more acceptable to the Middle Ages [whereas the] last part of the *Golden Ass* . . . is a huge parody of the mystic rites," Ezra Pound, *The Spirit of Romance* (Norfolk, CN: New Directions, 1929), 18.

17. Winkler (1985) reviews the major historical trends in *Golden Ass* interpretation, by way of proposing his own brilliant narratological attentions, in "The Question of Reading" (1–22). He puts Apuleius's stylistic virtuosity this way: "Borges and Nabokov have nothing on Apuleius" (vii). See Tatum 1979, esp. "An African Socrates" (105–34). For a traditional, somewhat outdated, but lively overview of Apuelius's times, career, and influence on literature and art, see Elizabeth Hazelton Haight, *Apuleius and His Influence* (New York: Longmans, Green, 1927). For a Jungian approach, see Marie-Louise von Franz, *An Interpretation of Apuleius' Golden Ass*, 2nd. ed. (Irving, TX: Spring, 1980); for a study of Apuleius's influence on the English literary tradition through Shakespeare, see J. J. M. Tobin, *Shakespeare's Favorite Novel: A Study of The Golden Asse As Prime Source* (New York: University Press of America, 1984).

18. William Adlington, trans., *The Golden Asse, being the Metamorphoses of Lucius Apuleius* (1566), rev. S. Gaselee (Cambridge: Harvard University Press, 1915).

19. A. D. Nock, *Conversion: The Old and the New in Religion from Alexander the Great to Augustine of Hippo* (Oxford: Clarendon Press, 1933), 138, 155. A recent, less emphatic theological reading is offered by Carl Schlam, *The Metamorphoses of Apuleius: On Making an Ass of Oneself* (Chapel Hill: University of North Carolina Press, 1992): "Some vision of an ordered cosmos under divine providence forms part of the comic entertainment offered" (4).

20. Steven Heller, "Apuleius, Platonic Dualism, and Eleven," *American Journal of Philology* 104:4 (Winter 1983): 324. See Haight's (1927) discussion of Apuleius's Platonism and the literary influence of *On the God of Socrates;* cf. Joseph G. DeFilippo, "*Curiositas* and the Platonism of Apuleius's *The Golden Ass*," *American Journal of Philology* 111:4 (1990): 471–92. For more on the Isis cult in relation to Apuleius, see J. Gwyn Griffiths, *The Isis-Book (Metamorphoses, Book XI)* (Leiden: E. J. Brill, 1975); and Winkler 1985, 204–27.

21. Gersh 1986 sets out the following classifications of classical Platonism: "(i) 'Pagan Ancient Platonic,' (ii) 'Christian Middle Platonic,' (iii) 'Pagan Middle Platonic,' (iv) 'Christian Neoplatonic,' and (v) 'Pagan Neoplatonic'" (1:25).

22. On the early Christian reception of Apuleius, see Robert Graves's introduction (*GA* xvii). Cf. Augustine, *The City of God*, trans. Marcus Dods, D.D., 2 vols (New York: Hafner, 1948). In Book 18, sections 16–18, Augustine addresses stories of human transformation, including Varro's relation of the Odysseus/Circe story. Section 18 is "What we should believe concerning the transformations which seem to happen to men through the art of

demons." Augustine relates that, "Indeed we ourselves, when in Italy, heard such things about a certain region there, where landladies of inns, imbued with these wicked arts, were said to be in the habit of giving to such travellers as they chose, or could manage, something in a piece of cheese by which they were changed on the spot into beasts of burden . . . just as Apuleius, in the books he wrote with the title of *The Golden Ass,* has told, or feigned, that it happened to his own self that, on taking poison, he became an ass, while retaining his human mind. These things are either false, or so extraordinary as to be with good reason disbelieved. But it is to be most firmly believed that Almighty God can do whatever he pleases" (2:236).

23. See Benjamin 1985, 217ff., on the Christian transumption of pagan allegory.

24. Joel F. Wilcox, "Ficino's Commentary on Plato's *Ion* and Chapman's Inspired Poet in the *Odyssey,*" *Philological Quarterly* 64:2 (Spring 1985): 195–209, addresses Chapman's debt to Ficino's commentaries on Plato, and cites Chapman's allegorized rendering of the story of Aphrodite's adultery with Ares: "One can feel Chapman straining to invent the allegorical suggestion that by adultery the lovers have caused their 'sound lims' to turn 'lame,' only to be restored when the lame Vulcan shames them" (202). In his annotation to the opening of the *Odyssey,* Chapman represents Odysseus in traditional Neoplatonic fashion: "The information or fashion of an absolute man, and necessarie (or fatal) passage through many afflictions (according with the most sacred Letter) to his naturall haven and countrey, is the whole argument and scope of this inimitable and miraculous Poeme": Allardyce Nicoll, ed., *Chapman's Homer,* 2 vols. (New York: Pantheon, 1956), 2:11. For a strain of British Romantic Neoplatonism with which Blake and Coleridge came into contact, see Kathleen Raine and George Mills Harper, ed., *Thomas Taylor the Platonist: Selected Writings* (Princeton: Princeton University Press, 1969). "Neoplatonism stems from one side of Plato—all that he inherited, through Pythagoras and the Orphic tradition, from the 'revealed' wisdom of antiquity. Blake is neither the first nor the last reader of Plato's works to have been bewildered by the presence of two, in many respects contradictory, aspects of his thought—logos and mythos": Kathleen Raine, *Blake and Tradition,* 2 vols. (Princeton: Princeton University Press, 1968), 1:73. Derrida (1981) has termed this Blakean bewilderment "the general problematic of the relations between the mythemes and the philosophemes that lie at the origin of western *logos.* That is to say, of a history—or rather, of History—which has been produced in its entirety in the *philosophical* difference between *mythos* and *logos,* blindly sinking down into that difference as the natural obviousness of its own element" (86).

25. Gersh (1986) notes, "It has been generally accepted for at least a hundred years that Plato's thought and Neoplatonism are two different things," but then goes on to challenge this view (1:26–50). Clearly, how one

reads Plato will hinge on the status one accords the myths within the dialogues. See Burger 1984 concerning the *Phaedrus* and the *Phaedo*, esp. 1–7.

26. "In the fourth century, the 'Platonists' formed the nucleus of the last opposition to the triumph of the Church . . . [which] before the time of Proclus . . . had become the real heir of Platonic philosophy. . . . The writings of the so-called 'Dionysius the Areopagite,' which laid the foundations of mediaeval angelology . . . [are] only a superficially Christianized version of Proclus. . . . The Plato who thus influenced theology is primarily Plato seen through the medium of Plotinus": Alfred Edward Taylor, *Platonism and its Influence* (New York: Cooper Square, 1963), 13–20. Lamberton (1983) has described the congruence between Neoplatonic and Protestant allegorical transcendentalism: "like the Puritans, the Neoplatonists of late antiquity lived in a world whose provisional configurations were real only to the extent that they functioned as symbols, as prefigurations, of a non-material and unchanging reality" (4).

27. Lamberton (1986) has noted that Plato's own allegorical activity is creative rather than hermeneutical: "Plato is certainly aware of the possibilities opened up by the interpretation of epic according to 'second meanings,' yet he seldom feels the need to enter into that activity. The obvious reason for this is that Plato himself is mythopoeic: when he abandons dialectic to 'theologize,' he does so not by interpreting existing texts or stories but by generating new myths" (25). As Nietzsche rather blandly stated a century ago, "the mythic component in the dialogues is the rhetorical": Friedrich Nietzsche, "Nietzsche's Lecture Notes on Rhetoric," trans. Carole Blair, *Philosophy and Rhetoric* 16:2 (1983): 99.

28. On the history of Ovid's *Metamorphoses* in English translation, see Lee T. Pearcy, *The Mediated Muse: English Translations of Ovid 1560–1700* (Hamden, CN: Archon, 1984); and Tomlinson 1983, 1–22.

29. The breadth of Apuleius's influence on European literature, art, and philosophy is discussed in Haight 1927, 90–181; Tobin 1984, xi–xxiv; and John F. D'Amico, "The Progress of Renaissance Latin Prose: The Case of Apuleianism," *Renaissance Quarterly* 37:3 (Autumn 1984): 351–92.

30. For Ovid's influence on Shakespeare, see the essays collected under the heading "Ovidian Transformations" in Maurice Charney, ed., *Shakespearean Comedy*, in *New York Literary Forum* 5–6 (1980): 47–96; and Carroll 1985. "It is a temptation to try to find in *A Midsummer Night's Dream* some sure reminiscence of the *Metamorphoses* of Apuleius. . . . But I can find no evidence of direct debt to Apuleius on Shakespeare's part," Haight 1927, 140; cf. D. T. Starnes, "Shakespeare and Apuleius," *PMLA* 60 (1945): 1021–50. Tobin 1984 shows that Shakespeare called upon Apuleius throughout his plays, but that his debt was not directly to Apuleius but rather to the text of Adlington's translation. On *A Midsummer Night's Dream*, see Tobin 1984, 31–40.

31. This is part of the melancholy turn modern allegory takes, epitomized in the Baroque theatre studied by Benjamin (1985): "the allegorization of the physis can only be carried through in all its vigour in respect of the corpse" (217).

32. Regina Janes, *Gabriel García Márquez: Revolutions in Wonderland* (Columbia: University of Missouri Press, 1981), 7. See also Laurence M. Porter and Laurel Porter, "Relations with the Dead in *Cien años de soledad*," *Mosaic* 15:1 (Winter 1982): 119–27; and Nina M. Scott, "Vital Space in the House of Buendía," *STCL* 8:2 (Spring 1984): 265–72.

33. Stuart M. Sperry notes in *Keats the Poet* (Princeton: Princeton University Press, 1973) how "many of Keats's favorite words for referring to poetry or the process by which it is created—'abstract' and 'abstraction,' 'spirit' and 'spiritual,' 'essence' and 'essential,' 'instense' and 'intensity,' 'distill' and 'distillation,' 'empyreal,' 'ethereal,' 'sublime'—have more or less exact meanings in the chemistry of his day" (37). Cf. Marjorie Levinson, *Keats's Life of Allegory: The Origins of a Style* (New York: Basil Blackwell, 1988): "'Lamia' is the closest thing we have in the Romantic repertoire to a scientific poem" (28).

34. "Both the mystery and potential tragedy of her sudden disintegration are comically subverted by the realization, if only implicit, of the virtually scientific logic that dominates the phases of her various transformations," Sperry 1973, 304.

35. Lesley Milne, *Mikhail Bulgakov: A Critical Biography* (New York: Cambridge University Press, 1990), 63.

36. The gory denouement of "The Fly" appears to parody Book 2 of *Paradise Lost,* where the incestuous coupling of Satan with his daughter Sin produces Death, who then couples with his mother to produce the hounds of Hell.

37. See David Porush, "Cybernetic Fiction and Postmodern Science," *New Literary History* 20:2 (Winter 1989): 373–96; and N. Katherine Hayles, "The Materiality of Informatics," *Configurations* 1:1 (Winter 1993): 147–70.

38. Hans Moravec, *Mind Children: The Future of Robot and Human Intelligence* (Cambridge: Harvard University Press, 1988).

39. O. B. Hardison, Jr., *Disappearing Through the Skylight: Culture and Technology in the Twentieth Century* (New York: Viking, 1989).

3. Metamorphic Subjects

1. "Even if it only appears under this name (the subject) with the rise of bourgeois ideology, above all with the rise of legal ideology, the

category of the subject (which may function under other names: e.g., as the soul in Plato, as God, etc.) is the constitutive category of all ideology . . . *insofar as all ideology has the function (which defines it) of 'constituting' concrete individuals as subjects*": Louis Althusser, *Lenin and Philosophy and Other Essays*, trans. Ben Brewster (New York: Monthly Review Press, 1971), 170–71. Kaja Silverman adapts Althusser's classical formulas to Lacanian feminism in "Subjectivity and Ideological Belief," *Male Subjectivity at the Margins* (New York: Routledge, 1992), 16–23.

2. "If the symbolic is (overhastily) assimiliated to various organic conceptions of the work of art and of culture itself, then the return of the repressed of its various opposites, and of a whole range of overt or covert theories of the allegorical, can be characterized by a generalized sensitivity, in our own time, to breaks and discontinuities, to the heterogeneous (not merely in works of art), to Difference rather than Identity, to gaps and holes rather than seamless webs and triumphant narrative progressions, to social differentiation rather than Society as such and its 'totality,' in which older doctrines of the monumental work and the 'concrete universal' bathed and reflected themselves," Jameson 1991, 167–68.

3. "When Lacan makes the subject an effect of the signifier, when he defines the unconscious as the 'discourse of the Other' (let us note, a direct translation of the etymology of allegory: ἄλλος, other; ἀγορεύω, to speak), he establishes psychoanalysis as precisely that science whose concern is the split in the subject occasioned by the subject's accession to language": Joel Fineman, "The Structure of Allegorical Desire," *The Subjectivity Effect in Western Literary Tradition: Essays Toward the Release of Shakespeare's Will* (Cambridge: MIT Press, 1991), 20.

4. Anna Freud, *The Ego and the Mechanisms of Defense*, rev. ed. (New York: International Universities Press, 1966), 32.

5. On the absolute evacuation of affect posited by the death drive, see Jean Laplanche, *Life and Death in Psychoanalysis*, trans. Jeffrey Mehlman (Baltimore: Johns Hopkins University Press, 1976), 103–24. "As Derrida has suggested, in 'White Mythology,' and Harold Bloom in *Poetry and Repression*, en-tropy, the absence of linguistic tropes, became an important theme in aesthetics and epistemology at about the same time the thermodynamic theories were advanced in geology and physics": Kathryne V. Lindberg, *Reading Pound Reading: Modernism After Nietzsche* (New York: Oxford University Press, 1987), 255–56. Cf. Harold Bloom's formulation: "The repressed rhetorical formula of Freud's discourse in *Beyond the Pleasure Principle* can be stated thus: *literal meaning equals anteriority equals an earlier state of meaning equals an earlier state of things equals death equals literal meaning.* Only one escape is possible from such a formula, and it is a simpler formula: *Eros equals figurative meaning*": "Freud and the Sublime," *Agon: Towards a Theory of Revisionism* (New York: Oxford University Press, 1982), 107; Bloom's italics. Structural psychoanalysis treats the death drive as a function not of the organism but of the letter in the unconscious: see *French Freud: Struc-*

tural Studies in Psychoanalysis, Yale French Studies 48 (1972; rp. Kraus, 1976).

6. "Fantasy, with its tendency to dissolve structures, moves towards an ideal of undifferentiation . . . close to the instinct which Freud identified in *Beyond the Pleasure Principle* (1920), and in his late works, as the most fundamental drive in man: a drive towards a state of inorganicism. . . . Modern fantasy makes explicit this attraction towards an entropic state. . . . Metamorphosis, with its stress upon the instability of natural forms, obviously plays a large part in fantastic literature for this reason," Jackson 1981, 72, 73, 81.

7. See also Raine 1968, 1:63–64, 91–92; and Lamberton 1983, 33–34. For other approaches to the figure of Proteus, see Massey 1976, 20–22, and Carroll 1985, 31–35. Cf. Eric Gould, *Mythical Intentions in Modern Literature* (Princeton: Princeton University Press, 1981), 86, on the interplay between mythic cosmology and Freudian metapsychology.

8. The obvious example in this regard is Athena's behavior and Odysseus's imitation of it throughout the *Odyssey*: see Clay 1983, and Peradotto 1990. Closely related to the metamorphosis of affect is the ego's investment in disguise. Discussing the psychoanalytical theory of narcissism, Laplanche (1976) states: "what is at stake here, in Freud's hesitations is, in fact, the actually ambiguous status of the ego: the ego, even though it is a reservoir of the libido cathecting it, can appear to be a source; it is not the subject of desires and wishes, not even the site in which the drive originates (a site represented by the id), but it can pass itself off as such" (74).

9. On Baroque melancholy, see Benjamin 1985, 138–58: "Whereas the Aristotelian insights into the physical duality of the melancholy complexion and the antithetical nature of the influence of Saturn had given way, in the middle ages, to a purely demonic representation of both, such as conformed with Christian speculation; with the Renaissance the whole wealth of ancient meditations re-emerged from the sources . . . [reinterpreting] saturnine melancholy as a theory of genius" (150).

10. "The phallus is the privileged signifier of that mark in which the role of the logos is joined with the advent of desire. . . . It can play its role only when veiled, that is to say, as itself a sign of the latency with which any signifiable is struck, when it is raised (*aufgehoben*) to the function of signifier. The phallus is the signifier of this *Aufhebung* itself, which it inaugurates (initiates) by its disappearance. That is why the demon of Αἰδώς (*Scham*, shame) arises at the very moment when, in the ancient mysteries, the phallus is unveiled. . . . It then becomes the bar which, at the hands of this demon, strikes the signified, marking it as the bastard offspring of this signifying concatenation": Lacan 1977, 287–88. Cf. Jane Gallop, *The Daughter's Seduction: Feminism and Psychoanalysis* (Ithaca: Cornell University Press, 1982), 98ff.

11. Léon Wurmser, *The Mask of Shame* (Baltimore: Johns Hopkins University Press, 1981), 84. In "The Theme of the Three Caskets," during

a discussion touching upon but not directed at certain metamorphic episodes in Grimm's *Fairy Tales,* Freud interprets the metamorphic commonplaces of both aphasia ("dumbness") and disappearance as death-symbols: "the dumbness in the dream represented death. Hiding and being unfindable . . . is another unmistakable symbol of death in dreams," *SE* 12:295.

12. Discussing the broad field of shame affects from an ego-analytical perspective, Wurmser (1981) notes that they are "interwoven with issues of narcissism—though the two realms are by no means identical. . . . Narcissism is a drive term, whereas the current trend has been to give not only clinical, but also theoretical precedence to the role of affects over that of instinctual drives" (16–17). Wurmser explains how shame dynamics connect judgmental with perceptual processes: "This power struggle and power limitation looming behind shame and guilt show archaic aspects of these affects: The area encircled by the inner boundary [the inscription of shame] may indeed be derived from the original ideal self, a self still partly fused with the omnipotent other. To lose this core of the self would mean annihilation. Primordial exchange through looking and appearing may be assumed to have built up this core of identity, presumably during the first months of life. . . . To be rejected in one's inmost area means that the other turns away in contempt and disappears. Ultimately radical abandonment by the other also means disappearance of the self" (62–63).

13. "The Story of Actaeon," *OH* 3.139ff.; see Barkan 1986, 44–47. "The idea of discovery, of revelation, includes an idea of appropriative enjoyment. What is seen is possessed; to see is to deflower . . . Every investigation implies the idea of a nudity which one brings out into the open by clearing away the obstacles which cover it, just as Actaeon clears away the branches so that he can have a better view of Diana at her bath": Jean-Paul Sartre on the "Actaeon complex," in *Being and Nothingness*, trans. Hazel E. Barnes (New York: Washington Square Press, 1966), 738.

14. DeFilippo (1990) argues that the prominence of the curiosity theme shows the novel to be espousing dogmatic Platonism. I agree rather with Graham Anderson: "Apuleius need not be playing the professional Platonist, as opposed to the Platonic connoisseur on holiday. . . . Nor are Apuleius' *philosophica* themselves consistently serious or free from literary diversion," *Eros Sophistes: Ancient Novelists at Play* (Chico, CA: Scholars Press, 1982), 157.

15. "Small animals and vermin represent small children": Sigmund Freud, *The Interpretation of Dreams*, trans. James Strachey (New York: Avon, 1969), 392. As far as I know, the anagrammatic identity of "incest" and "insect" is unique to English.

16. Cf. John Incledon's Derridean reading, "Writing and Incest in *One Hundred Years of Solitude*," in Bradley A. Shaw and Nora Vera-Godwin,

ed., *Critical Perspectives on Gabriel García Márquez* (Lincoln: Society of Spanish and Spanish-American Studies, 1986), 51–64. It may be significant that the incest here, like that in *The Metamorphosis*, is what Deleuze and Guattari (1986) term "schizo-incest," which "is opposed in numerous ways to a neurotic Oedipal incest. The Oedipal incest occurs, or imagines that it occurs, or is interpreted as if it occurs, as an incest with the mother, who is a territoriality, a reterritorialization. Schizo-incest takes place with the sister, who is not a substitute for the mother, but who is on the other side of the class struggle, the side of maids and whores, the incest of deterritorialization" (67).

17. See Gene H. Bell-Villada, "Banana Strike and Military Massacre: *One Hundred Years of Solitude* and What Happened in 1928," in Gene H. Bell-Villada, Antonio Giménez, and George Pistorius, ed., *From Dante to García Márquez: Studies in Romance Literatures and Linguistics* (Williamstown: Williams College, 1987), 391–403.

18. Lewis Thomas has noted a parallel instance at the immunological level: "We still think of human disease as the work of an organized, modernized kind of demonology. . . . However . . . disease usually results from inconclusive negotiations for symbiosis . . . a biologic misinterpretation of borders. . . . Our arsenals for fighting off bacteria are so powerful, and involve so many different defense mechanisms, that we are more in danger from them than from the invaders," *The Lives of a Cell: Notes of a Biology Watcher* (New York: Bantam, 1975), 88–92.

19. Karl Marx, *A Contribution to the Critique of Political Economy*, ed. Maurice Dobb (New York: International Publishers, 1972), 86.

20. With the work of Marx and George Simmel in mind, Levinson (1988) discusses metamorphic elements in Keats's *Lamia* in terms similar to those I am using to discuss the *Golden Ass*: "the contradictions within the money form . . . drive it not only to 'breed' but to undergo a fixed sequence of metamorphoses. We shall see that Lamia's changes (those she suffers and those she engenders) emplot this economic sequence" (261).

21. Cf. Raine 1968 on Blake and the Neoplatonic *Odyssey* as revived by "the English Pagan . . . professed Platonist, polytheist, and anti-Christian" Thomas Taylor: "The stripping off of the ragged garments of mortality is an aspect of the symbol that Taylor often stressed; and the many instances in Blake's writings in which the body is compared to ragged or filthy garments, and that which is experienced in the body to 'the rotten rags of memory,' seem to echo Taylor's many allusions to the beggar's rags of which Odysseus divested himself when he returned to Ithaca," 1:67, 80, alluding to Porphyry's *On the Cave of the Nymphs*. As Sartre (1966) notes: "To be sure, I can *grasp* the Other, grab hold of him, knock him down. . . . But everything happens as if I wished to get hold of a man who runs away and leaves only his coat in my hands. It is the coat, it is the outer shell which I possess" (511). Cf. Burke 1969a on the clothes figure as applied to capitalism: "in the pragmatism and Puritanism of science and

business, . . . one *clothes oneself* in the severe promises of future yield, *donning* the idealizations of what one would like to be, *dressing up* in the symbols of lien and bond (we mean: *'investing'*)" (333).

22. On allegorical veiling or *integumentum,* see Copeland and Melville 1991, 169–73.

23. Irving R. Saposnik, "The Anatomy of Dr. Jekyll and Mr. Hyde," *SEL* 11:4 (Autumn 1971): 725.

24. "Buildings, localities, and landscapes are employed as symbolic representations of the body, and in particular (with constant reiteration) of the genitals," Freud 1969, 401. In "The 'Uncanny,'" Freud mentions "a joking saying that 'Love is home-sickness'; and whenever a man dreams of a place or a country and says to himself, while he is still dreaming: 'this place is familiar to me, I've been here before,' we may interpret the place as being his mother's genitals or her body," *SE* 17:245. Cf. Marcia Ian, *Remembering the Phallic Mother: Psychoanalysis, Modernism, and the Fetish* (Ithaca: Cornell University Press, 1993), 37.

25. This episode travesties the archaic concept of justice Nietzsche (1968) discusses in section 2.4 of *On the Genealogy of Morals*—"the idea that every injury has its *equivalent* and can actually be paid back, even if only through the *pain* of the culprit"; on this relation of guilt (*Schuld*) to debts (*Schulden*), Nietzsche comments, "this primeval, deeply rooted, perhaps by now ineradicable idea . . . of an equivalence between injury and pain" draws its power from "the contractual relationship between *creditor* and *debtor,* which is as old as the idea of 'legal subjects' and in turn points back to the fundamental forms of buying, selling, barter, trade, and traffic" (499). That is, the Pythias episode in the *Golden Ass* is another parable of Hermetic "trade." The entire Second Essay, " 'Guilt,' 'Bad Conscience,' and the Like," is of the highest interest here, as is the analysis of affect throughout the *Genealogy.*

26. In *On the God of Socrates,* Apuleius amplifies the Platonic metaphor by which the daemon of conscience is described as an advocate before a judge, that is, like Utterson, as a lawyer. Here again, as I am about to argue, Utterson is a daemonic figure. See Winkler 1985, 60–93, and Gordon Hirsch, "Frankenstein, Detective Fiction, and *Jekyll and Hyde,*" in Veeder and Hirsch 1988, 223–46. Metamorphic narratives call forth detection motifs because bodily metamorphoses effectively conceal identities. The metamorphic body can serve as a "hyde-out."

4. Fabulous Monsters

1. See James J. Paxson, *The Poetics of Personification* (New York: Cambridge University Press, 1994). Paxson makes a significant distinction between anthropomorphism and personification in this passage: "The

substantialized abstractions Vergil places at the mouth of the Underworld . . . are often treated . . . as seminal models of formal personification. But they are utterly mute. . . . [Here is] no prosopopoeia because the figures possess no human voices, and therefore, no *prosopa* or 'faces.' . . . The figural operator [here] is anthropomorphism" (44–45).

2. *The Aeneid of Virgil,* trans. Rolfe Humphries, ed. Brian Wilkie (New York: Macmillan, 1987), 132.

3. N. K. Sandars, trans., *The Epic of Gilgamesh* (New York: Penguin, 1985), 106–7.

4. Clive Bloom comments on Donne's "The Flea" in the context of the daemonic in literature in *The "Occult" Experience and the New Criticism: Daemonism, Sexuality and the Hidden in Literature* (Totowa, NJ: Barnes & Noble, 1987), 1–3. Lewis W. Leadbeater, "Aristophanes and Kafka: The Dung Beetle Connection," *Studies in Short Fiction* 23:2 (Spring 1986): 169–78, traces Kafka's *Mistkäfer* to Aristophanes's play *Peace,* which involves "the ascent of a dung beetle and his master . . . to the heights of Olympus to resurrect the goddess Peace" (171), and offers a reading that sees the final resurrection of Grete as modeled on the redemptive pattern in Aristophanes's drama and the folklore of the divine scarab. I think Leadbeater quite misses the truly Aristophanic line of scurrilous travesty in Kafka's tale, but he does plausibly connect Gregor's metamorphic appearance to classical allegory.

5. Anne Carson, *Eros the Bittersweet: An Essay* (Princeton: Princeton University Press, 1986), treats the temporal dimension of this allegory: "The cicadas can be read as an image of the fundamental erotic dilemma [in the *Phaedrus*]. They are creatures pulled into confrontation with time by their own desire. . . . Passing time and its transitions do not affect them. They are stranded in a living death of pleasure" (139).

6. "There is also another species of demons . . . and this is the human soul, after it has performed its duties in the present life, and quitted the body: I find that this is called in the ancient Latin language by the name of Lemur. . . . But those who, having no fixed habitation of their own, are punished with vague wandering, as with a kind of exile, on account of the evil deeds of their life, are usually called 'Larvae' " (*GS* 364).

7. On butterflies and bees as images of the poet and the writing of poetry, see Sharon Nell, "A Bee in Pindar's Bonnet: Humanistic Imitation in Ronsard, La Fontaine, and Rococo Style," in *New Perspectives on Renaissance Humanism,* ed. Diane S. Wood and Paul Allen Miller (Knoxville: New Paradigm Press, 1995).

8. Cited from *The Random House Dictionary of the English Language, College Edition,* 1st ed. In the same edition, the definition of the entomological sense of "metamorphosis" is illustrated with drawings of the metamorphic developmental stages of the fly and the mosquito. The *OED*

is a bit less specific about the maturation of the genitalia: "Imago . . . *Entom.*
The final or perfect stage or form of an insect after it has undergone all
its metamorphoses; the 'perfect insect'"; "Nymph . . . 3. An insect in that
stage of development which intervenes between the larva and the imago;
a pupa. . . . 1747 GOULD *Eng. Ants* 44 They are called Nymphs in allusion
to Brides, because when they leave this state, they are often arrayed in
Gayety and Splendour."

9. On the historical Apollonius of Tyana, see Philostratus, *Life of
Apollonius*, trans. C. P. Jones, ed. G. W. Bowersock (Baltimore: Penguin,
1970).

10. *OED:* "Some have thought that ident-(i) was taken from the L.
adv. identidem 'over and over again, repeatedly.'" On the ego, repetition,
and the death drive, see Freud, *Beyond the Pleasure Principle* (*SE* 18:1–
64), and Derrida 1987.

11. Garrett Stewart, "*Lamia* and the Language of Metamorphosis,"
Studies in Romanticism 15:1 (Winter 1976): 33.

12. Jorge Luis Borges with Margaritta Guerro, *The Book of Imaginary Beings*, trans. Norman Thomas di Giovanni (New York: Avon, 1970),
43–44.

13. See Martin Wallen, ed., *Coleridge's* Ancient Mariner: *An Experimental Edition of Texts and Revisions 1798–1828* (Barrytown, NY: Station
Hill, 1993), for commentary and complete critical references on the changes
of this "metamorphic" text.

14. John Bunyan, *The Pilgrim's Progress from this World to That
which is to Come*, ed. James Blanton Wharey (Oxford: Clarendon Press,
1928), 80, 125.

15. See Jerome J. McGann, "The Meaning of the Ancient Mariner,"
Critical Inquiry 8:1 (Autumn 1981): 35–67, for a sociohistorical analysis
of the narrative voices introduced into the poem by the addition of the
gloss.

16. Knapp (1985) devotes a chapter to these particular figures and
their reception, "Milton's Allegory of Sin and Death in Eighteenth-Century
Criticism" (51–65).

17. Coleridge underscores his abiding attention to Milton's Sin
and Death in the famous section of his Shakespeare lectures where he
cites this passage of *Paradise Lost* as producing "a middle state of mind
more strictly appropriate to the imagination than any other, where it is,
as it were, hovering between images," cited in Joseph Anthony Wittreich,
Jr., *The Romantics of Milton: Formal Essays and Critical Asides* (Cleveland: Case Western Reserve University Press, 1970), 200–201. See also
John Gatta, Jr., "Coleridge and Allegory," *MLQ* 38:1 (March 1977): 62–
77.

18. For a different reading of this passage, see Susan Buck-Morss, *The Dialectics of Seeing: Walter Benjamin and the Arcades Project* (Cambridge: MIT Press, 1989), 175.

19. See Chris Baldick, *In Frankenstein's Shadow: Myth, Monstrosity, and Nineteenth-Century Writing* (Clarendon: Oxford University Press, 1987).

20. See Frank Dietz, "The Image of Medicine in Utopian and Dystopian Fiction," in Bruce Clarke and Wendell Aycock, ed., *The Body and the Text: Comparative Essays in Literature and Medicine* (Lubbock: Texas Tech University Press, 1990), 115–26, for a brief treatment of *Heart of a Dog* in the context of "dystopian" fiction: "we find a decidedly conservative stance in most dystopian novels. What utopias regarded as progress, they regard as interference with human nature bound to have disastrous consequences. As it affects the 'natural state' on the most basic, physical level, medicine becomes one of the main culprits" (121).

21. Lucretius "undoubtedly proposes his theory of the clinamen literally rather than analogically: in his materialist vision, the mind itself is composed of atoms, and the *clinamen atomorum* functions as a cause whose effect is an act of will. . . . The pivotal point lies in the assumption that the clinamen is nonprogrammatic, that it is an element distinct from the system, intervening in aleatory fashion; its function is on the contrary to subvert the control mechanism," Motte 1986, 264–65.

22. Motte (1986) develops the controversy between Michel Serres and René Thom over the proper roles of chance and noise in scientific rationality and of figurative language in scientific discourse. Motte's sympathies in this debate are with Serres. See also William R. Paulson, *The Noise of Culture: Literary Texts in a World of Information* (Ithaca: Cornell University Press, 1988), 30–52. For a strong counter-statement, see Hayles 1990, 196–208.

23. James Gleick, *Chaos: Making a New Science* (New York: Penguin, 1987), 3. Gleick goes on to invoke "the demon of nonlinearity" (24). Attending to this characteristic of Gleick's narrative, David Porush, "Making Chaos: Two Views of a New Science," in Murdo William McRae, ed., *The Literature of Science: Perspectives on Popular Scientific Writing* (Athens: University of Georgia Press, 1993), has argued that due to Gleick's investment in Kuhnian paradigms, his book *Chaos* "reads as a sort of postmodern mythology. . . . Chaos, like Beowulf, 'emerged from a backwater' " (153). I take it that Porush is referring to Grendel, Beowulf's monstrous adversary.

24. Ivars Peterson, *The Mathematical Tourist: Snapshots of Modern Mathematics* (New York: W. H. Freeman, 1988), 162.

25. "As singular boundaries between two realms of existence, phase transitions tend to be highly nonlinear in their mathematics. The smooth and predictable behavior of matter in any one phase tends to be little help in understanding the transitions," Gleick 1987, 160.

26. For a treatment of Calvino's literary uses of the Lucretian notion of the *clinamen,* see Paul A. Harris, "Italo Calvino: The Code, the Clinamen and Cities," *Mosaic* 23:4 (Fall 1990): 67–85. See also John Gery, "Love and Annihilation in Calvino's Qfwfq Tales," *Critique: Studies in Contemporary Fiction* 30:1 (Fall 1988): 59–68; and Kathryn Hume, "Italo Calvino's Cosmic Comedy: Mythography for the Scientific Age," *Papers on Literature and Language* 20:1 (Winter 1984): 80–95, and "Science and Imagination in Calvino's *Cosmicomics,*" *Mosaic* 15:4 (December 1982): 47–58.

27. Ernest L. Fontana, "Metamorphoses of Proteus: Calvino's *Cosmicomics,*" *Perspectives on Contemporary Literature* 5 (1979): 147.

28. "Cybernetics is the paradigmatic postmodern science. It views the universe as a set of interconnected systems of energy, matter, space, and time all of which can be described in terms of (or reduced to) how much information those systems transmit or contain. To put it another way, *cybernetics is the quintessential science of narrativity,* if you accept that any exchange of information creates a narrative. . . . Of the many authors of cybernetic fiction, none has more explicitly addressed the attractions and power of cybernetics than Italo Calvino": Porush 1989, 379, 383.

29. Calvino meditates meta-fictively on this structural arrangement in "The Origin of the Birds" (*TZ* 14–27).

30. In what came to called the Demon, Maxwell imagined a being capable of a microscopic sorting activity that effectively overcame the rule of thermodynamic entropy. "If we conceive a being whose faculties are so sharpened that he can follow every molecule in its course, such a being, whose attributes are still as essentially finite as our own, would be able to do what is at present impossible for us": James Clerk Maxwell, *Theory of Heat,* 9th ed. (New York: Longmans, Green, 1888), 328.

31. Mitosis as metamorphic origin echoes Ovid's erotic cosmogony and subsequent text of metamorphic anecdotes denoting the multiple origins of natural things. As a metamorphic narrator, Qfwfq is also reminiscent of Lucius's first-person account of fantastic subjectivity in the *Golden Ass,* narrating in minute detail and from the inside an experience of bodily transformation. In fact, before his mitosis Qfwfq is roughly equivalent to the pre-metamorphic Lucius in youthful development: "Physically I was an individual in his full flowering . . . young, healthy, at the peak of my strength" (*TZ* 64).

5. The Gender of Metamorphosis

1. Lucius's priesthood under Isis can be read "either as a pro-Isiac message (e.g., 'Her unspeakable wisdom transcends human language') or

as an anti-Isiac message (e.g., 'The final state of Lucius as a bald eccentric in Rome, impoverished by greedy priests, is the ultimate folly')," Winkler 1985, 127. Cf. Massey 1976: after resuming human form and converting to Isis, Lucius "is still in a passive role . . . still involved with puzzles. . . . His detachment from other people has been elevated into a principle" (44).

2. Anderson (1982) has noted how the *Symposium* as well as the *Phaedrus* corresponds to the first tale in the *Golden Ass*: in the *Symposium*, "Plato offers a second-hand account of how Socrates did not reach the party in time, because he was lost in meditation along the way—of course waylaid by his *daimon*. Is it coincidence that the *Metamorphoses* opens with a second-hand account of how *a* Socrates was waylaid—by a witch? . . . The author has woven an eccentric pot-pourri of magical slapstick from several easily recognizable Platonic features, twisted or turned upside-down at will: Apuleius begins with a *divertissement* in Platonic black magic" (80).

3. According to Carl C. Schlam, *Cupid and Psyche: Apuleius and the Monuments* (University Park, Penn.: American Philological Association, 1976), "the basic plot of the story of Cupid and Psyche has been shown to be a stable type of folk tale. J. Swahn in his investigation of Aarne-Thompson Type 425, 'The Search for the Lost Husband,' and a few closely related types, analyzes some eleven hundred recorded versions in which the main motif is that of marriage between a human and a supernatural being combined with a special taboo. Swahn classifies the Apuleian tale as the oldest example of his sub-type A, in which the heroine, in the course of her search, comes to the house of a witch who gives her seemingly impossible tasks to perform. It is only in the Apuleian version, however, that the principals are identified as Cupid and Psyche" (2–3).

4. Samuel Taylor Coleridge, "Allegory," *Coleridge's Miscellaneous Criticism,* ed. T. M. Raysor (Cambridge: Harvard University Press, 1936), 30. Over a century ago, J. J. Bachofen, a Swiss historian of archaic law, unearthed textual traces of the Neolithic matriarchies and reinterpreted certain myths after these findings. His reading of Psyche's story as an allegory of feminine psychological development was picked up and extended by Jung, and in detail by Erich Neumann in *Amor and Psyche: The Psychic Development of the Feminine,* trans. Ralph Manheim (Princeton: Princeton University Press, 1971). Von Franz (1980) sketches the tradition of Jungian treatment of the story, reconnecting it with masculine psychology, and referring it to Apuleius's *On the God of Socrates* (61–70). For feminist readings of the tale, see Rachel Blau DuPlessis, "Psyche, or Wholeness," *Massachusetts Review* 20:1 (Spring 1979): 77–96; and Lee R. Edwards, *Psyche as Hero: Female Heroism and Fictional Form* (Middletown, CN: Wesleyan University Press, 1984); for a refutation of Neumann's (1971) reading of the feminine, see DuPlessis 1979. See also the remarks scattered in Winkler 1985 concerning the ways that Apuleius's "Cupid and Psyche" has been uprooted from its context.

5. In the *Golden Ass,* the Socrates of the *Phaedrus* invoked by travesty at the beginning of the novel is unfolded into both the daemonic Cupid and the mortal Psyche. Page duBois argues in "Phallocentrism and its Subversion in Plato's *Phaedrus,*" *Arethusa* 18:1 (1985): 91–103, that the *Phaedrus* "engages in erotic metamorphosis which threatens to erase the evident misogyny in Greek culture. . . . Socrates speaks his first discourse *enkalupsamenos* (237a), veiled as one near death, or as a woman. . . . Veiled, Socrates is a woman, both seductive and chaste; with head bared, he is both a violated woman and a man" (96–98).

6. I take this information from *AM,* which translates every name in the text. Bakhtin (1981) offers a folkloric allegory of the prominence of "everyday life" in the *Golden Ass:* "the time spent by Lucius in everyday life coincides with his presumed death (his family considers him dead), and his leaving that life is his resurrection. The ancient folkloric core of Lucius' metamorphosis is in fact precisely death; the passage to the nether regions and resurrection. In this instance everyday life corresponds to the nether regions, to the grave" (121).

7. Emphasizing that "Cupid and Psyche" is constructed like a detective fiction (and complaining that the mystery is given away when the episode is titled "Cupid and Psyche"), Winkler (1985) arrives at an original perspective on Psyche's sisters: "Because [Cupid's monstrosity] is a lie and wickedly motivated, most readers (I think) miss its intellectual power as a hypothesis. In fact the sisters' conjecture makes more sense of this story than anything else offered so far" (92).

8. On the thematics of activity/passivity in the *Phaedrus* and the Platonic erotic, see Burger 1980; and David M. Halperin, "Plato and Erotic Reciprocity," *Classical Antiquity* 5:1 (April 1986): 60–80: "To be an *erastes,* an aggressor in love, is to begin to make progress in the quest for immortality—or, as Socrates puts it in a moment of greater earnestness in the *Phaedrus,* to begin to grow the wings of the soul. Just as one cannot desire another person without desiring that portion of transcendent beauty embodied by him . . . , so also one cannot seek wisdom without first being possessed by the *mania* of erotic desire. Wisdom will not come to us of its own accord: we have to desire it in order to pursue it" (74). Clearly what Halperin says here corresponds entirely to Psyche's story. I would just add that although wisdom will not come unless pursued, Love comes whether we will or not, as with Psyche, and it is then up to us to redeem that ambivalent catastrophe through wisdom and desire.

9. On the "curse of Eve," see my "The Eye and the Soul: A Moment of Clairvoyance in *The Plumed Serpent,*" *Southern Review* 19:2 (Spring 1983), 289–301. Discussing Keats's "Ode to Psyche," Harold Bloom, *A Map of Misreading* (New York: Oxford University Press, 1975), remarks, "in some sense Keats says Cupid and Psyche but means Adam and Eve" (153); see Donald C. Goellnicht, " 'In Some Untrodden Region of My Mind': Double Discourse in Keats's 'Ode to Psyche,' " *Mosaic* 21:2–3 (Spring 1988): 91–103.

10. Although Massey (1976) does not take up "Cupid and Psyche" in his discussion of the *Golden Ass,* Psyche's relentless curiosity, establishing identity while inducing unconsciousness, relates to what Massey calls the "element of ignorance" that founds human thought: "although we may come to understand our motives by hindsight, we do not know why we are as we are. The random element in every dialectic is the element of ignorance in the creative process, and is perhaps an element of sanity itself. The Gods may see everything clearly, but *we* must include the recognition of our blindness in all accounts that we give of our experience; it is the silent portion of our answer to every question" (54–55).

11. A fragment of Empedocles (B 126 D-K) cited in Lamberton 1986, 116. For Plotinus, "Odysseus has become explicitly a hero of the renunciation of the material world, along with the pleasures and beauties accessible to the senses, in favor of the transcendent, eternal beauty," Lamberton 1986, 107. Lamberton minutely investigates the development of this Neoplatonic reading of the Circe episode from the second to the fifth century, and discusses possible contributions to the ideas in Porphyry's fragment (c. 275) by Pseudo-Plutarch, Numenius, and Plotinus.

12. The term genesis (γένεσις) in its Neoplatonic provenance names "the sub-lunar sphere characterized by birth, change, and death," Lamberton 1986, 353.

13. "The fact that λόγος is here identified with the Hermes of the myth . . . [points] to later developments of the same identification that lead, for example, to the identification, by the Naassenian Gnostics of the first and second centuries, of Hermes the Psychopomp (*Od.*24.1–14) with the creative and redeeming λόγος—that is, with Christ," Lamberton 1986, 42.

14. Shakespeare "came close to dramatizing Freud's hydraulic theory about the flow of libidinal cathexis which blindly drives the unconscious will from object to object, when he showed the lovers blindly 'transferring' their loves from object to object in the forest, though he saw, instead of a flow of cathexis, a flow of juice from the flower 'love-in-idleness' ": Meredith Anne Skura, *The Literary Use of the Psychoanalytic Process* (New Haven: Yale University Press, 1981), 37.

15. Cf. René Girard, "Bottom's One-Man Show," in Clayton Koelb and Virgil Lokke, ed., *The Current in Criticism: Essays on the Present and Future of Literary Theory* (West Lafayette: Purdue University Press, 1987), 99–122: "the 'translation' of Bottom and the intervention of the 'fairies' mark the culmination of the dynamic process triggered by the collective decision to perform a play. It is not a magical irruption, a sudden and inexplicable disturbance in a static situation of bucolic peace among people going peacefully about their business of acting, it is the climax of successive structural transformations" (107). The dramatic becomes daemonic when the game of role-playing becomes contagious and generates its own metamorphic momentum.

16. On Freud's ambivalence toward the concept of bisexuality within his own theory, see Ian 1993, 2–4.

17. Cf. D. H. Lawrence, *Apocalypse* (New York: Cambridge University Press, 1980), on the pagan Magna Mater exiled by the Christian era: "She has been in the desert ever since, the great cosmic Mother crowned with all the signs of the zodiac. Since she fled, we have had nothing but virgins and harlots, half-women: the half-women of the Christian era. For the great Woman of the pagan cosmos was driven into the wilderness at the end of the old epoch, and she has never been called back" (121).

18. My premise is that the "daemonic ambivalence" in the symbol of the serpent allegorizes ambivalences of gender identity generally: "This 'daemonic ambivalence' can be traced in a good deal of the mythology concerning serpents, where the serpent appears sometimes as a good figure, sometimes as a bad. The mythologists of Coleridge's day were fond of pointing out that the Hebrew word S'R'PH could signify either a serpent or an angelic being," Beer 1959, 127. The theme of abjection in *Lamia* is amenable to Kristeva's theories of gender construction and maintenance: for an overview of Kristeva in this context, see Hogle 1988. For an attack on Kristeva's gender theories, see Ian (1993), 27–31, who might prefer to read Lamia's serpentine form as a fantasy of the umbilical cord (29–40).

19. This line of discussion ends up moralizing Keats's development as the struggle to discover a capable masculine poetic identity, as this is thought to be traced in his crossover from effeminate, narcissistic lyrical to more robust ironic and comprehensive dramatic modes. Again in Bush's (1937) loaded phrases for Keats's later self-questionings: "If [the poet's] existence is justified, can he allow his imagination to be self-centered, in the large sense 'lyrical,' or should it be dramatic and rooted in the heart of man and human life?" (82).

20. John Lemprière, *A Classical Dictionary; Containing a Copious Account of all the Proper Names Mentioned in Ancient Authors*, 11th ed. (London: T. Cadell and W. Davies, 1820), 389–90.

21. Unlike the patrician Apollo, Hermes was a patron of the relatively powerless and impoverished, and yet was too urbane for the conservative Hesiod, who disdained him as a promoter of stealthy deceit and "feminine wiles," Brown 1969, 9. Lamia's ability to withhold and bring forth the nymph is typical Hermetic magic: "Hermes [stealing] Ares out of the brazen pot . . . belongs to the folk-tale type of the 'demon caught in a bottle or other receptacle'. . . . In this type of story both the imprisonment and the release of the demon are magical exercises," Brown 1969, 13.

22. In this light the Hermes/Lamia relation is analogous to the erotic sophistry of Lysias in the *Phaedrus,* the reduction of eros to economics: "The relationship of exchange for the mutual benefit of two contracting parties, which Lysias praises in the name of the nonlover, is grounded on the principles of exchange in the economic sphere," Burger 1980, 25. Cf.

Levinson 1988: "Lycius's project is to turn his beloved into that monstrous thing, the commodity. That this potential was implicit in Lamia all along (or, that the [economic] allegory is operating at a fairly deliberate level) is suggested by Keats's description of her original value form, the serpent body, as a congeries of precious stones and metals" (278).

23. See Sigmund Freud, "Femininity," *New Introductory Lectures on Psychoanalysis*, trans. James Strachey (New York: Norton, 1965), 99–119; Lacan 1977, 207; Julia Kristeva, *Powers of Horror: An Essay on Abjection*, trans. Leon S. Roudiez (New York: Columbia University Press, 1982), 90–112; and Ian 1993. Norman O. Brown, *Love's Body* (New York: Random House, 1966), explicitly identifies the Whore of Babylon with the phallic mother (75). Whereas Ian (1993) reads the phallic mother as a mere fraud, Gallop (1982) nuances the topic more subtly in "The Phallic Mother: Fraudian Analysis": "it is more usual and more comfortable to associate the phallic with the Father. A feminist protest might be lodged that to speak of a 'phallic mother' is to subsume female experience into male categories. Kristeva, however, hangs on to the phallic categories. Perhaps it is this insistence on the seemingly paradoxical term 'phallic mother' which can most work to undo the supposedly natural logic of the ideological solidarity between phallus, father, power, and man. The Phallic Mother is undeniably a fraud, yet one to which we are infantilely susceptible. If the phallus were understood as the veiled attribute of the Mother, then perhaps this logical scandal could expose the joint imposture of both Phallus and Mother" (117).

24. For an overview of the deconstructive alignment of metaphor and metonymy with regard to Freud's Eros and the death drive, see Bernheimer 1982, 33–44.

25. Tzvetan Todorov, *Theories of the Symbol*, trans. Catherine Porter (Ithaca: Cornell University Press, 1982), 73.

26. For other treatments of the feminine and the maternal in this and other works by Stevenson, see William Veeder, "Children of the Night: Stevenson and Patriarchy," in Veeder and Hirsch 1988, 139–48; and Hogle 1988.

27. Cf. Apuleius's comparison of the bodies of daemons to clouds in *On the God of Socrates*. Mark M. Hennelly, Jr., "Stevenson's 'Silent Symbols' of the 'Fatal Cross Roads' in *Dr. Jekyll and Mr. Hyde*," *Gothic* 1 (1979): 10–16, cites most of this passage from Stevenson but, in my opinion, misreads it by subscribing too closely to the manifest moralizations of the characters themselves: "the wasteland battleground between the natural and the artificial is most obviously contested between the fresh, animating wind and the polluting, stagnant fog" (15). Cf. Silverman 1983: "Stevenson provides us with a densely coded narrative, whose obsessive antitheses and preoccupations would enable us to exhume Christianity. . . . [It is] organized at every level by mutually reinforcing antitheses, of which

light/darkness, groomed/ungroomed, day/night, soul/body, humanity/besti-
ality, Jekyll/Hyde, and good/evil are only the most evident. The last of
these represents the central symbolic opposition, that which gives rise to
and supports the others" (275). I would suggest that the antithesis male/
female, anterior to its patriarchal moralization into good/evil, is the most
central in the text.

28. Cf. Sartre's (1966) gendered ruminations on "Quality as a Revelation of Being," concerning the concept of slime (*le visqueux*): "I open my
hands, I want to let go of the slimy and it sticks to me, it draws me, it
sucks at me. . . . It is a soft, yielding action, a moist and feminine sucking,
it lives obscurely under my finders, and I sense it like a dizziness. . . . In
the very apprehension of the slimy there is a gluey substance, compromis-
ing and without equilibrium, like the haunting memory of a *metamorphosis*" (776–77). Ricks (1984) comments that these passages from Sartre "are
to me the best criticism of Keats ever written not about him" (139).

29. Both Veeder 1988 and Hogle 1988 remark the "night woman" in
the sky over Jekyll's house when Utterson breaks into Jekyll's cabinet, and
Veeder grasps the clothes figure inscribed on the clouds of that sky and
Utterson's penchant for projection: "the erotic evocation of diaphanous
nightwear is complicated by the violence of describing clouds as a 'flying
wrack,' " Veeder 1988, 142; cf. Hogle 1988, 180.

30. See Julia Reinhard Lupton and Kenneth Reinhard, *After Oedipus: Shakespeare in Psychoanalysis* (Ithaca: Cornell University Press, 1993),
on Benjamin's idea that mourning " 'is at once the mother of the allegories
and their content [*die Mutter der Allegorien und ihr Gehalt*]'. . . . Benjamin's
choice of metaphor manifests through the very act of figuration the role of
the 'Mother' in the mutual constitution of allegory and mourning. . . . The
origin of allegory can only be presented in an allegory of origin *as allegory,*
a paradox embodied and gendered in Benjamin's use of the mother as
figure of originary loss" (62).

31. The abject Crone shares the lost landscape of metamorphic allegory with the phallic mother. Gallop (1982) works carefully through this
difficult thicket of notions, playing Kristeva off Irigaray and both of them
off Lacan: "Perhaps the conflict is always between body—as the inad-
equate name of some uncommanded diversity of drives and contradictions—and Power, between body and Law, between body and Phallus, even
between body and Body" (121). Cf. Lacan (1977) on the phallic mother in
"The signification of the phallus": the phallic stage "seems to exclude in
both sexes, until the end of this stage, that is, to the decline of the Oedipal
stage, all instinctual mapping of the vagina as locus of genital penetration.
This ignorance is suspiciously like *méconnaissance* in the technical sense
of the term—all the more so in that it is sometimes quite false. Does this
not bear out the fable in which Longus shows us the initiation of Daphnis
and Chloe subordinated to the explanations of an old woman?" (282–83).

BIBLIOGRAPHY

Adlington, William, trans. *The Golden Asse, being the Metamorphoses of Lucius Apuleius* (1566). Rev. S. Gaselee. Cambridge: Harvard University Press, 1915.

Althusser, Louis. *Lenin and Philosophy and Other Essays*. Trans. Ben Brewster. New York: Monthly Review Press, 1971.

Altieri, Charles. "Plato's Performative Sublime and the Ends of Reading." *NLH* 16:2 (Winter 1985): 251–73.

Anderson, Graham. *Eros Sophistes: Ancient Novelists at Play*. Chico, CA: Scholars Press, 1982.

Augustine. *The City of God*. Trans. Marcus Dods, D.D. 2 vols. New York: Hafner, 1948.

Bachofen, J. J. *Myth, Religion, and Mother Right*. Trans. Ralph Manheim. Princeton: Princeton University Press, 1967.

Bakhtin, Mikhail M. *The Dialogic Imagination: Four Essays*. Trans. Caryl Emerson and Michael Holquist. Austin: University of Texas Press, 1981.

———. *Rabelais and His World*. Trans. Hélène Iswolsky. Bloomington: Indiana University Press, 1984.

Baldick, Chris. *In Frankenstein's Shadow: Myth, Monstrosity, and Nineteenth-Century Writing*. Clarendon: Oxford University Press, 1987.

Barber, C. L. *Shakespeare's Festive Comedy: A Study of Dramatic Form in its Relation to Social Custom*. New York: Meridian, 1967.

Barkan, Leonard. *The Gods Made Flesh: Metamorphosis and the Pursuit of Paganism*. Yale University Press, 1986.

Barney, Stephen A. *Allegories of History, Allegories of Love*. Hamden, CN: Archon Books, 1978.

Baudrillard, Jean. *The Ecstasy of Communication*. Trans. Bernard and Caroline Schutze. Ed. Sylvere Lotringer. Brooklyn: Autonomedia, 1988.

Beer, J. B. *Coleridge the Visionary*. London: Chatto & Windus, 1959.

Bell-Villada, Gene H. "Banana Strike and Military Massacre: *One Hundred Years of Solitude* and What Happened in 1928." In Gene H. Bell-Villada, Antonio Giménez, and George Pistorius, ed. *From Dante to García Márquez: Studies in Romance Literatures and Linguistics*. Williamstown: Williams College, 1987, 391–403.

Benjamin, Walter. *Illuminations*. Ed. Hannah Arendt. Trans. Harry Zohn. London: Fontana, 1982.

———. *The Origin of German Tragic Drama*. Trans. John Osbourne. London: Verso, 1985.

Bernheimer, Charles. *Flaubert and Kafka: Studies in Psychopoetic Structure*. New Haven: Yale University Press, 1982.

Bersani, Leo. *A Future for Astyanax: Character and Desire in Literature*. Boston: Little, Brown, 1976.

Blanchot, Maurice. *The Gaze of Orpheus and Other Literary Essays*. Trans. Lydia Davis. Ed. P. Adams Sitney. Barrytown, NY: Station Hill, 1981.

Bloom, Clive. *The "Occult" Experience and the New Criticism: Daemonism, Sexuality and the Hidden in Literature*. Totowa, NJ: Barnes & Noble, 1987.

Bloom, Harold. *Agon: Towards a Theory of Revisionism*. New York: Oxford University Press, 1982.

———. *A Map of Misreading*. New York: Oxford University Press, 1975.

Boer, Charles, trans. *The Homeric Hymns*. Chicago: Swallow, 1970.

Borges, Jorge Luis, with Margaritta Guerro. *The Book of Imaginary Beings*. Trans. Norman Thomas di Giovanni. New York: Avon, 1970.

Brown, Norman O. *Hermes the Thief*. New York: Vintage, 1969.

———. *Love's Body*. New York: Random House, 1966.

Buck-Morss, Susan. *The Dialectics of Seeing: Walter Benjamin and the Arcades Project*. Cambridge: MIT Press, 1989.

Bunyan, John. *The Pilgrim's Progress from this World to That which is to Come*. Ed. James Blanton Wharey. Oxford: Clarendon Press, 1928.

Burger, Ronna. *The Phaedo: A Platonic Labyrinth*. New Haven: Yale University Press, 1984.

———. *Plato's Phaedrus: A Defense of a Philosophic Art of Writing*. University: University of Alabama Press, 1980.

Burke, Kenneth. *A Grammar of Motives*. Berkeley: University of California Press, 1969a.

———. *A Rhetoric of Motives*. Berkeley: University of California Press, 1969b.

Bush, Douglas. *Mythology and the Romantic Tradition in English Poetry*. Cambridge: Harvard University Press, 1937.

Calvino, Italo. *The Uses of Literature: Essays*. Trans. Patrick Creagh. New York: Harvest/HBJ, 1986.

Carroll, William C. *The Metamorphoses of Shakespearean Comedy.* Princeton: Princeton University Press, 1985.

Carson, Anne. *Eros the Bittersweet: An Essay.* Princeton: Princeton University Press, 1986.

Charney, Maurice, ed. *Shakespearean Comedy.* In *New York Literary Forum* 5–6 (1980).

Clarke, Bruce. "The Eye and the Soul: A Moment of Clairvoyance in *The Plumed Serpent.*" *The Southern Review* 19:2 (Spring 1983), 289–301.

Clarke, Bruce, and Wendell Aycock, ed. *The Body and the Text: Comparative Essays in Literature and Medicine.* Lubbock: Texas Tech University Press, 1990.

Clay, Jenny Strauss. *The Wrath of Athena.* Princeton: Princeton University Press, 1983.

Coleridge, Samuel Taylor. *Coleridge's Miscellaneous Criticism.* Ed. T. M. Raysor. Cambridge: Harvard University Press, 1936.

———. *The Literary Remains of Samuel Taylor Coleridge.* Ed. Henry Nelson Coleridge. 2 vols. London: William Pickering, 1836; rp. New York: AMS Press, 1967.

Cook, Albert. *Myth and Language.* Bloomington: Indiana University Press, 1980.

Copeland, Rita, and Stephen Melville. "Allegory and Allegoresis, Rhetoric and Hermeneutics." *Exemplaria* 3:1 (March 1991): 159–87.

Corngold, Stanley. *Franz Kafka: The Necessity of Form.* Ithaca: Cornell University Press, 1988.

Coulter, James A. *The Literary Microcosm: Theories of Interpretation of the Later Neoplatonists.* Leiden: E. J. Brill, 1977.

Cowan, Bainard. "Walter Benjamin's Theory of Allegory." *New German Critique* 22 (Winter 1981): 109–22.

D'Amico, John F. "The Progress of Renaissance Latin Prose: The Case of Apuleianism." *Renaissance Quarterly* 37:3 (Autumn 1984): 351–92.

De Bolla, Peter. *Harold Bloom: Towards Historical Rhetorics.* New York: Routledge, 1988.

DeFilippo, Joseph G. "*Curiositas* and the Platonism of Apuleius's *The Golden Ass.*" *American Journal of Philology* 111:4 (1990): 471–92.

Deleuze, Gilles, and Félix Guattari. *Kafka: Toward a Minor Literature.* Trans. Dana Polan. Minneapolis: University of Minnesota Press, 1986.

de Man, Paul. *Allegories of Reading: Figural Language in Rousseau, Nietzsche, Rilke, and Proust.* New Haven: Yale University Press, 1979.

———. "The Rhetoric of Temporality." In Charles S. Singleton, ed. *Interpretation: Theory and Practice*. Baltimore: Johns Hopkins University Press, 1969, 173–209.

Derrida, Jacques. "Fors." *The Georgia Review* 31:1 (Spring 1977): 64–116.

———. *Of Grammatology*. Trans. Gayatri Chakravorty Spivak. Baltimore: Johns Hopkins University Press, 1976.

———. *Plato's Pharmacy*. In *Dissemination*. Trans. Barbara Johnson. Chicago: University of Chicago Press, 1981, 63–169.

———. *The Post Card: From Socrates to Freud and Beyond*. Trans. Alan Bass. Chicago: University of Chicago Press, 1987.

Díaz, Nancy Gray. *The Radical Self: Metamorphosis to Animal Form in Modern Latin American Narrative*. Columbia: University of Missouri Press, 1988.

Dietz, Frank. "The Image of Medicine in Utopian and Dystopian Fiction." Clarke and Aycock, 115–26.

duBois, Page. "Phallocentrism and its Subversion in Plato's *Phaedrus*." *Arethusa* 18:1 (1985): 91–103.

DuPlessis, Rachel Blau. "Psyche, or Wholeness." *Massachusetts Review* 20:1 (Spring 1979): 77–96.

Durocher, Richard J. *Milton and Ovid*. Ithaca: Cornell University Press, 1985.

Edwards, Lee R. *Psyche as Hero: Female Heroism and Fictional Form*. Middletown, CN: Wesleyan University Press, 1984.

Fenichel, Otto. *The Collected Papers of Otto Fenichel*. 2nd. series. New York: Norton, 1954.

Fineman, Joel. "The Structure of Allegorical Desire." In *The Subjectivity Effect in Western Literary Tradition: Essays Toward the Release of Shakespeare's Will*. Cambridge: MIT Press, 1991, 3–31.

Fletcher, Angus. *Allegory: The Theory of a Symbolic Mode*. Ithaca: Cornell University Press, 1964.

Fontana, Ernest L. "Metamorphoses of Proteus: Calvino's *Cosmicomics*." *Perspectives on Contemporary Literature* 5 (1979): 147–54.

Foucault, Michel. *The Use of Pleasure: The History of Sexuality*, vol. 2. Trans. Robert Hurley. New York: Vintage, 1985.

French Freud: Structural Studies in Psychoanalysis, Yale French Studies 48 (1972; rp. Kraus, 1976).

Freud, Anna. *The Ego and the Mechanisms of Defense*. Rev. ed. New York: International Universities Press, 1966.

Freud, Sigmund. *Beyond the Pleasure Principle. SE* 18:1–64.

————. *Gesammelte Werke.* Vol. 10. London: Imago, 1949.

————. *The Interpretation of Dreams.* Trans. James Strachey. New York: Avon, 1969.

————. *New Introductory Lectures on Psychoanalysis.* Trans. James Strachey. New York: Norton, 1965.

————. "Repression." *SE* 14:141–58.

————. "The Theme of the Three Caskets." *SE* 12:289–301.

————. "The 'Uncanny.'" *SE* 17:217–56.

————. "The Unconscious." *SE* 14:159–215.

Gadamer, Hans-Georg. *Truth and Method.* 2nd rev. ed. Trans. Joel Weinsheimer and Donald G. Marshall. New York: Crossroad, 1989.

Gallop, Jane. *The Daughter's Seduction: Feminism and Psychoanalysis.* Ithaca: Cornell University Press, 1982.

Garber, Marjorie B. *Dream in Shakespeare: From Metaphor to Metamorphosis.* New Haven: Yale University Press, 1974.

Garrett, Peter K. "Cries and Voices: Reading Jekyll and Hyde." In Veeder and Hirsch, 59–72.

Gatta, John, Jr. "Coleridge and Allegory." *MLQ* 38:1 (March 1977): 62–77.

Gersh, Stephen. *Middle Platonism and Neoplatonism: The Latin Tradition.* 2 vols. Notre Dame: University of Notre Dame Press, 1986.

Gery, John. "Love and Annihilation in Calvino's Qfwfq Tales." *Critique: Studies in Contemporary Fiction* 30:1 (Fall 1988): 59–68.

Girard, René. "Bottom's One-Man Show." In Clayton Koelb and Virgil Lokke, ed. *The Current in Criticism: Essays on the Present and Future of Literary Theory.* West Lafayette: Purdue University Press, 1987, 99–122.

Gleick, James. *Chaos: Making a New Science.* New York: Penguin, 1987.

Goellnicht, Donald C. " 'In Some Untrodden Region of My Mind': Double Discourse in Keats's 'Ode to Psyche.' " *Mosaic* 21:2–3 (Spring 1988): 91–103.

Gould, Eric. *Mythical Intentions in Modern Literature.* Princeton: Princeton University Press, 1981.

Graves, Robert. *The Greek Myths.* 2 vols. Baltimore: Penguin Books, 1969.

Gregory, Horace, trans. *Ovid: The Metamorphoses.* New York: Viking, 1958.

Griffiths, J. Gwyn. *The Isis-Book (Metamorphoses, Book XI)*. Leiden: E. J. Brill, 1975.

Griswold, Charles L., Jr. *Self-Knowledge in Plato's Phaedrus*. New Haven: Yale University Press, 1986.

Hadzsits, George Depue. *Lucretius and His Influence*. New York: Longmans, Green, 1935.

Haight, Elizabeth Hazelton. *Apuleius and His Influence*. New York: Longmans, Green, 1927.

Halperin, David M. "Plato and Erotic Reciprocity." *Classical Antiquity* 5:1 (April 1986): 60–80.

Harari, Josué V., and David F. Bell. "Introduction: Journal à plusieurs voies." In Serres ix–xl.

Hardison, O. B., Jr. *Disappearing Through the Skylight: Culture and Technology in the Twentieth Century*. New York: Viking, 1989.

Harris, Paul A. "Italo Calvino: The Code, the Clinamen and Cities." *Mosaic* 23:4 (Fall 1990): 67–85.

Harrison, Jane Ellen. *Mythology*. New York: Harcourt, Brace & World, 1963.

Havelock, Eric A. *Preface to Plato*. Cambridge: Harvard University Press, 1963.

Hayles, N. Katherine. *Chaos Bound: Orderly Disorder in Contemporary Literature and Science*. Ithaca: Cornell University Press, 1990.

———. "The Materiality of Informatics." *Configurations* 1:1 (Winter 1993): 147–70.

Heller, Steven. "Apuleius, Platonic Dualism, and Eleven." *American Journal of Philology* 104:4 (Winter 1983): 321–39.

Hennelly, Mark M., Jr. "Stevenson's 'Silent Symbols' of the 'Fatal Cross Roads' in *Dr. Jekyll and Mr. Hyde*." *Gothic* 1 (1979): 10–16.

Hesiod. *The Works and Days, Theogony, The Shield of Herakles*. Trans. Richmond Lattimore. Ann Arbor: University of Michigan Press, 1959.

Hirsch, Gordon. "Frankenstein, Detective Fiction, and *Jekyll and Hyde*." In Veeder and Hirsch, 223–46.

Hogle, Jerrold E. "The Struggle for a Dichotomy: Abjection in Jekyll and his Interpreters." In Veeder and Hirsch, 161–207.

Honig, Edwin. *Dark Conceit: The Making of Allegory*. Evanston: Northwestern University Press, 1959.

Hume, Kathryn. "Italo Calvino's Cosmic Comedy: Mythography for the Scientific Age." *Papers on Literature and Language* 20:1 (Winter 1984): 80–95.

———. "Science and Imagination in Calvino's *Cosmicomics*." *Mosaic* 15:4 (December 1982): 47–58.

Ian, Marcia. *Remembering the Phallic Mother: Psychoanalysis, Modernism, and the Fetish*. Ithaca: Cornell University Press, 1993.

Incledon, John. "Writing and Incest in *One Hundred Years of Solitude*." In Bradley A. Shaw and Nora Vera-Godwin, ed. *Critical Perspectives on Gabriel García Márquez*. Lincoln: Society of Spanish and Spanish-American Studies, 1986, 51–64.

Jackson, Rosemary. *Fantasy: The Literature of Subversion*. New York: Methuen, 1981.

Jameson, Fredric. "Utopianism After the End of Utopia." In *Postmodernism, or, The Cultural Logic of Late Capitalism*. Durham : Duke University Press, 1991, 154–80.

Janes, Regina. *Gabriel García Márquez: Revolutions in Wonderland*. Columbia: University of Missouri Press, 1981.

Jennings, Michael. "Between Allegory and Aura: Walter Benjamin's 1938 Reading of Kafka." *Journal of the Kafka Society of America* 1–2:1 (June 1988): 42–50.

Kantra, Robert A. "Practical Wisdom and Satiric Humor in Philosophic Fictions." *Mosaic* 22:3 (Summer 1989): 85–100.

Kelley, Theresa M. " 'Fantastic Shapes': From Classical Rhetoric to Romantic Allegory." *Texas Studies in Literature and Language* 33:2 (Summer 1991): 225–60.

Kerenyi, Karl. *Hermes: Guide of Souls*. Trans. Murray Stein. Zurich: Spring, 1976.

Knapp, Steven. *Personification and the Sublime: Milton to Coleridge*. Cambridge: Harvard University Press, 1985.

Kristeva, Julia. *Powers of Horror: An Essay on Abjection*. Trans. Leon S. Roudiez. New York: Columbia University Press, 1982.

Lacan, Jacques. *Ecrits: A Selection*. Trans. Alan Sheridan. New York: Norton, 1977.

Lamberton, Robert. *Homer the Theologian: Neoplatonic Allegorical Reading and the Growth of the Epic Tradition*. Berkeley: University of California Press, 1986.

———, trans. *Porphyry: On the Cave of the Nymphs*. Barrytown, NY: Station Hill Press, 1983.

Laplanche, Jean. *Life and Death in Psychoanalysis*. Trans. Jeffrey Mehlman. Baltimore: Johns Hopkins University Press, 1976.

Lawrence, D. H. *Apocalypse*. New York: Cambridge University Press, 1980.

Leadbeater, Lewis W. "Aristophanes and Kafka: The Dung Beetle Connection." *Studies in Short Fiction* 23:2 (Spring 1986): 169–78.

Lemprière, John. *A Classical Dictionary; Containing a Copious Account of all the Proper Names Mentioned in Ancient Authors.* 11th ed. London: T. Cadell and W. Davies, 1820.

Levinson, Marjorie. *Keats's Life of Allegory: The Origins of a Style.* New York: Basil Blackwell, 1988.

Lindberg, Kathryne V. *Reading Pound Reading: Modernism After Nietzsche.* New York: Oxford University Press, 1987.

Lucretius. *The Nature of Things.* Trans. Frank O. Copley. New York: Norton, 1977.

Lupton, Julia Reinhard, and Kenneth Reinhard. *After Oedipus: Shakespeare in Psychoanalysis.* Ithaca: Cornell University Press, 1993.

Mack, Sara. *Ovid.* New Haven: Yale University Press, 1988.

Madsen, Deborah L. *The Postmodernist Allegories of Thomas Pynchon.* New York: St. Martin's Press, 1991.

Marx, Karl. *A Contribution to the Critique of Political Economy.* Ed. Maurice Dobb. New York: International Publishers, 1972.

Massey, Irving. *The Gaping Pig: Literature and Metamorphosis.* Berkeley: University of California Press, 1976.

Maxwell, James Clerk. *Theory of Heat.* 9th ed. New York: Longmans, Green, 1888.

McHale, Brian. "Tropological Worlds." In *Postmodern Fiction.* New York: Methuen, 1987, 133–47.

McRae, Murdo William, ed. *The Literature of Science: Perspectives on Popular Scientific Writing.* Athens: University of Georgia Press, 1993.

Millar, Fergus. "The World of the *Golden Ass.*" *Journal of Roman Studies* 71 (1981): 63–75.

Miller, Paul Allen. *Lyric Texts and Lyric Consciousness.* New York: Routledge, 1994.

Milne, Lesley. *Mikhail Bulgakov: A Critical Biography.* New York: Cambridge University Press, 1990.

Montrose, Louis A. "*A Midsummer Night's Dream* and the Shaping Fantasies of Elizabethan Culture: Gender, Power, Form." In Margaret W. Ferguson, Maureen Quilligan, and Nancy J. Vickers, ed. *Rewriting the Renaissance: The Discourses of Sexual Difference in Early Modern Europe.* Chicago: University of Chicago Press, 1986, 65–87.

Moravec, Hans. *Mind Children: The Future of Robot and Human Intelligence.* Cambridge: Harvard University Press, 1988.

Motte, Warren F., Jr. "Clinamen Redux." *Comparative Literature Studies* 23:4 (Winter 1986): 263–81.

Nell, Sharon Diane. "A Bee in Pindar's Bonnet: Humanistic Imitation in Ronsard, La Fontaine, and Rococo Style." In Diane S. Wood and Paul Allen Miller, ed. *New Perspectives on Renaissance Humanism.* Knoxville: New Paradigm Press, 1995.

Neumann, Erich. *Amor and Psyche: The Psychic Development of the Feminine.* Trans. Ralph Manheim. Princeton: Princeton University Press, 1971.

Nietzsche, Friedrich. *Basic Writings of Nietzsche.* Trans. Walter Kaufmann. New York: Modern Library, 1968.

———. "Nietzsche's Lecture Notes on Rhetoric." Trans. Carole Blair. *Philosophy and Rhetoric* 16:2 (1983): 94–129.

Nock, A. D. *Conversion: The Old and the New in Religion from Alexander the Great to Augustine of Hippo.* Oxford: Clarendon Press, 1933.

Ovid. *The Metamorphoses.* Trans. Horace Gregory. New York: Viking, 1958.

Owens, Craig. "The Allegorical Impulse: Toward a Theory of Postmodernism." *October* 12 (Spring 1980): 67–86.

———. *Beyond Recognition: Representation, Power, and Culture.* Berkeley: University of California Press, 1992.

Patterson, Charles I., Jr. *The Daemonic in the Poetry of John Keats.* Urbana: University of Illinois Press, 1970.

Paulson, William R. *The Noise of Culture: Literary Texts in a World of Information.* Ithaca: Cornell University Press, 1988.

Paxson, James J. *The Poetics of Personification.* New York: Cambridge University Press, 1994.

Paz, Octavio. *Conjunctions and Disjunctions.* Trans. Helen R. Lane. New York: Viking, 1974.

Pearcy, Lee T. *The Mediated Muse: English Translations of Ovid 1560–1700.* Hamden, CN: Archon, 1984.

Peradotto, John. *Man in the Middle Voice: Name and Narration in the Odyssey.* Princeton: Princeton University Press, 1990.

Peterson, Ivars. *The Mathematical Tourist: Snapshots of Modern Mathematics.* New York: W. H. Freeman, 1988.

Philostratus. *Life of Apollonius.* Trans. C. P. Jones. Ed. G. W. Bowersock. Baltimore: Penguin, 1970.

Plato. *Phaedrus*. Trans. W. C. Helmbold and W. G. Rabinowitz. Indianapolis: Bobbs-Merrill, 1975.

———. *Plato's Phaedrus*. Trans. R. Hackforth. Cambridge: Cambridge University Press, 1972.

Plutarch. "On the Sign of Socrates." In *Plutarch's Moralia in Fifteen Volumes*. Vol. 7. Trans. Phillip H. de Lacy and Benedict Einarson. Cambridge: Harvard University Press, 1959, 361–509.

Porter, Laurence M. and Laurel Porter, "Relations with the Dead in *Cien años de soledad*." *Mosaic* 15:1 (Winter 1982): 119–27.

Porush, David. "Cybernetic Fiction and Postmodern Science." *New Literary History* 20:2 (Winter 1989): 373–96.

———. "Making Chaos: Two Views of a New Science." In McRae, 152–68.

Pound, Ezra. *The Spirit of Romance*. Norfolk, CN: New Directions, 1929.

Quilligan, Maureen. *The Language of Allegory: Defining the Genre*. Ithaca: Cornell University Press, 1979.

Raine, Kathleen. *Blake and Tradition*. 2 vols. Princeton: Princeton University Press, 1968.

Raine, Kathleen, and George Mills Harper, ed. *Thomas Taylor the Platonist: Selected Writings*. Princeton: Princeton University Press, 1969.

Ricks, Christopher. *Keats and Embarrassment*. 2nd. ed. Oxford: Clarendon Press, 1984.

Sandars, N. K., trans. *The Epic of Gilgamesh*. New York: Penguin, 1985.

Saposnik, Irving R. "The Anatomy of Dr. Jekyll and Mr. Hyde." *SEL* 11:4 (Autumn 1971): 715–31.

Sartre, Jean-Paul. *Being and Nothingness*. Trans. Hazel E. Barnes. New York: Washington Square Press, 1966.

Schlam, Carl C. *Cupid and Psyche: Apuleius and the Monuments*. University Park, PA: American Philological Association, 1976.

———. *The Metamorphoses of Apuleius: On Making an Ass of Oneself*. Chapel Hill: University of North Carolina Press, 1992.

Scott, Nina M. "Vital Space in the House of Buendía." *STCL* 8:2 (Spring 1984): 265–72.

Serres, Michel. *Hermes: Literature, Science, Philosophy*. Ed. Josué V. Harari and David F. Bell. Baltimore: Johns Hopkins University Press, 1982.

Shaffer, Elinor S. "Translation as metamorphosis and cultural transmission." *Comparative Criticism: An Annual Journal* 6 (1984): xiii–xxvii.

Shelley, Mary. *Frankenstein or, The Modern Prometheus*. New York: New American Library, 1983.

Siebers, Tobin. *The Mirror of Medusa*. Berkeley: University of California Press, 1983.

Silverman, Kaja. *Male Subjectivity at the Margins*. New York: Routledge, 1992.

———. *The Subject of Semiotics*. New York: Oxford University Press, 1983.

Skulsky, Harold. *Metamorphosis: The Mind in Exile*. Cambridge: Harvard University Press, 1981.

Skura, Meredith Anne. *The Literary Use of the Psychoanalytic Process*. New Haven: Yale University Press, 1981.

Sokel, Walter H. "From Marx to Myth: The Structure and Function of Self-Alienation in Kafka's *Metamorphosis*." *The Literary Review* 26:4 (Summer 1983): 485–95.

Sperry, Stuart M. *Keats the Poet*. Princeton: Princeton University Press, 1973; rp. 1994.

Starnes, D. T. "Shakespeare and Apuleius." *PMLA* 60 (1945): 1021–50.

Stewart, Garrett. "*Lamia* and the Language of Metamorphosis." *Studies in Romanticism* 15:1 (Winter 1976): 3–41.

Stock, R. D. *The Flutes of Dionysus: Daemonic Enthrallment in Literature*. Lincoln: University of Nebraska Press, 1989.

———. *The Holy and the Daemonic from Sir Thomas Browne to William Blake*. Princeton: Princeton University Press, 1982.

Sussman, Henry. *Franz Kafka: Geometrician of Metaphor*. Madison: Coda Press, 1979.

Tanner, Tony. *Adultery in the Novel*. Baltimore: Johns Hopkins University Press, 1979.

Tatum, James. *Apuleius and The Golden Ass*. Ithaca: Cornell University Press, 1979.

Tave, Katherine Bruner. *The Demon and the Poet: An Interpretation of "The Rime of the Ancient Mariner" According to Coleridge's Demonological Sources*. Salzburg: Institut für Anglistik und Amerikanistic, 1983.

Taylor, Alfred Edward. *Platonism and its Influence*. New York: Cooper Square, 1963.

Thomas, Lewis. *The Lives of a Cell: Notes of a Biology Watcher*. New York: Bantam, 1975.

Thomas, Ronald R. "The Strange Voices of the Strange Case: Dr. Jekyll, Mr. Hyde, and the Voices of Modern Fiction." In Veeder and Hirsch, 73–93.

Tobin, J. J. M. *Shakespeare's Favorite Novel: A Study of The Golden Asse As Prime Source*. New York: University Press of America, 1984.

Todorov, Tzvetan. *The Fantastic: A Structural Approach to a Literary Genre.* Trans. Richard Howard. Ithaca: Cornell University Press, 1980.

———. *Theories of the Symbol.* Trans. Catherine Porter. Ithaca: Cornell University Press, 1982.

Tomlinson, Charles. *Poetry and Metamorphosis.* New York: Cambridge University Press, 1983.

Udoff, Alan, ed. *Kafka and the Contemporary Critical Performance: Centenary Readings.* Bloomington: Indiana University Press, 1987.

Veeder, William. "Children of the Night: Stevenson and Patriarchy." In Veeder and Hirsch, 108–60.

Veeder, William, and Gordon Hirsch, ed. *Dr Jekyll and Mr Hyde After One Hundred Years.* Chicago: University of Chicago Press, 1988.

Virgil. *The Aeneid of Virgil.* Trans. Rolfe Humphries. Ed. Brian Wilkie. New York: Macmillan, 1987.

Vlastos, Gregory. *Socrates: Ironist and Moral Philospher.* Ithaca: Cornell University Press, 1991.

von Franz, Marie-Louise. *An Interpretation of Apuleius' Golden Ass.* 2nd. ed. Irving, TX: Spring, 1980.

Wallen, Martin, ed. *Coleridge's* Ancient Mariner: *An Experimental Edition of Texts and Revisions 1798–1828.* Barrytown, NY: Station Hill, 1993.

Weber, Samuel. "Genealogy of Modernity: History, Myth, and Allegory in Benjamin's *Origin of German Tragic Drama*." *MLN* 106:3 (April 1991): 465–500.

Wilcox, Joel F. "Ficino's Commentary on Plato's *Ion* and Chapman's Inspired Poet in the *Odyssey*." *Philological Quarterly* 64:2 (Spring 1985): 195–209.

Winkler, John J. *Auctor & Actor: A Narratological Reading of Apuleius's Golden Ass.* Berkeley: University of California Press, 1985.

Wittreich, Joseph Anthony, Jr. *The Romantics on Milton: Formal Essays and Critical Asides.* Cleveland: Case Western Reserve University Press, 1970.

Wurmser, Léon. *The Mask of Shame.* Baltimore: Johns Hopkins University Press, 1981.

INDEX

Adlington, William, 37–38, 43, 44
Aeneid (Virgil), 83
affect, affectivity
  the daemonic as, 11
  guilt, 165n. 12, 167n. 25
  loss of, 144
  melancholy, 1, 63, 64, 162n. 31,
    164n. 9
  moral, xi
  in the *Odyssey*, 58–63
  pride, 77, 143
  shame, 164n. 10, 165n. 12
    as economic figuration, 77–78
    as female attribute, 66–67,
      114
    in *Jekyll and Hyde*, 80, 140–
      141
    as keynote of metamorphic
      affect, 63–67
    in *One Hundred Years of
      Solitude*, 70
    in Ovid's *Metamorphoses*, 61
    and penance, 136–138
    in *Phaedrus*, 11, 116
    transcendence of, 121
  transformation of, 56–63, 79,
    164n. 8
  weeping, 61–62, 144
agent
  metamorphic. *See* metamorph
  human, 16, 46, 80
ahistoricism, x
alchemy, 70
allegoresis, ix, 5, 42, 92, 115–117
  detachability of, 117
  and the supplement, 153n. 18
allegory
  abuse of, 119
  archetypal form of, 41
  baroque, 1, 63, 64, 96, 146–147,
    162n. 31

and cosmos, 30–31
as cultural mediation, 23
daemonic agency in, 53, 155n.
  28
as defense, 11, 42, 124, 157n. 3
demotion of, 13, 91
irony in, 1, 19, 41
and metamorphosis
  relations between, x–xi, 2,
    10, 21, 47
  thematic fields of, 57
and mourning, 147, 177n. 30
pagan, 13, 19, 103
patriarchal, 122, 124, 131
as redemptive, 101
as regressive, 53
as revisionary reading, 23, 24
structure of, 23–24, 53, 94, 96,
  163n. 3
subversion of, xi, 81, 84, 131
temporality of, ix, x, 23–24,
  168n. 5
theory of, ix, 1, 2, 10, 54, 83,
  152n. 14
typography of, 92
typology in, 93
allegory of writing
  in *Ancient Mariner*, 93
  clinamen as, 103
  cybernetics as, 23
  Golden Ass as, 73
  in *Heart of a Dog*, 97, 100
  Jekyll and Hyde as, 9, 152n. 17
  Lamia as, 4–6
  metamorphosis as, 2, 21, 23,
    51, 59, 107–108, 128
  The Metamorphosis as, 1
  One Hundred Years of Solitude
    as, 71
  pharmakon as, 6
  in *t zero*, 108

191

Althusser, Louis, 53, 100, 163n. 1
A Midsummer Night's Dream
(Shakespeare)
"changeling boy" in, 128–132
classical influences on, 43–44
daemonic figuration in, 14–16
misreading in, 3–4
as parody of the daemonic, 13–14, 46
pharmakon in, 6
See also faery
Ancient Mariner (Coleridge), 91–96
Anderson, Graham, 165n. 14,
172n. 2
androgyne, androgyny, 4. *See also*
bisexuality
anthropomorphism, 83, 97
apocalypse, 71
Apollonius of Tyana, 169n. 9
Apuleius
Augustine on, 160n. 22
and the daemonic, 11–12
depictions of women by, 114–115, 145
modern influences of, 43–44
and Plato, 11–12, 19–20, 25,
30, 38–39, 41–42, 172n. 2
relations to Neoplatonism, 38–39, 41–42, 165n. 14
as satirist of Roman imperialism, 37, 72–74
See also Cupid and Psyche,
Golden Ass, On the God of
Socrates
archetype, 18, 155n. 31
Aristophanes, 168n. 4
Aristotle, 139, 157n. 6, 164n. 9
Augustine, 13, 37–38, 40, 159n. 22
autonomy. *See* subject, human

Bachofen, J. J., 172n. 4
Bakhtin, Mikhail, 31–32, 35–37,
117, 151n. 7, 159n. 15, 173n. 6
Barber, C. L., 154n. 24
Barkan, Leonard, 13, 34, 42, 113,
119
Barney, Stephen A., 151n. 14
basilisk, 90–91

Bataille, Georges, 106
Baudrillard, Jean, 49
beauty, 28–29
Beer, J. B., 175n. 18
Benjamin, Walter
on baroque allegory, 1, 24,
162n. 31, 164n. 9
on evil and allegory, 83, 96
on Kafka, 19
on mourning and allegory,
177n. 30
on writing and allegory, 2
Bernheimer, Charles, 176n. 24
bisexuality, 130, 137, 175n. 16
Blake, William, 160n. 24, 166n. 21
Bloom, Clive, 168n. 4
Bloom, Harold, 163n. 5, 173n. 9
body, the
human, 21, 28, 32, 49–50, 78,
139–141, 147
metamorphic, x, 9, 18, 76,
167n. 26
transmission of, 49
Brown, Norman O., 5, 150n. 6,
151n. 11, 175n. 21, 176n. 23
Bulgakov, Mikhail, 47–48, 96–102.
See also Heart of a Dog
Bunyan, John, 92
bureaucracy, 19–20, 156n. 36
Burger, Ronna, 157n. 6, 173n. 8,
176n. 22
Burke, Kenneth, 155n. 25, 156n.
38, 167n. 21
Burnet, Thomas, 92
Burton, Robert, 90, 134
Bush, Douglas, 123, 133

Calvino, Italo
"The Aquatic Uncle," 105
"At Daybreak," 105
and the *clinamen*, 103, 171n.
26
and cybernetics, 171n. 28
"The Distance of the Moon,"
105
"The Form of Space," 103
"The Origin of the Birds," 171n.
29

on affect, 56
Beyond the Pleasure Principle, 163n. 5, 164n. 6
on cathexis, 174n. 14
"Theme of the Three Caskets," 165n. 11
See also psychoanalysis

Gadamer, Hans–Georg, x, 154n. 23
Gallop, Jane, 176n. 23, 177n. 31
Garber, Marjorie B., 154n. 24
García Márquez, Gabriel, 71, 72, 113, 145. *See also One Hundred Years of Solitude*
Gauttari, Félix, 19, 55, 87, 155n. 31, 156n. 36, 166n. 16
gender
  confusion of, 136
  in *Cupid and Psyche*, 115
  economics of, 78
  metamorphosis as allegory of, 113
  Neoplatonic moralization of, 124
  psychopolitics of, 131–133, 138–139
  reversal of, 120, 130, 140
  and rhetoric, 140
  and shame, 66
genitalia, 64, 131
Gersh, Stephen, 154nn. 21, 22, 159n. 21, 161n. 25
Gilgamesh, Epic of, 24, 84, 113
Girard, René, 174n. 15
Gleick, James, 170n. 23, 171n. 25
Goethe, Johann, 13, 113, 154n. 23
Golden Ass (Apuleius)
  Adlington on, 38
  Bakhtin on, 36–37, 173n. 6
  critical debates about, 38–39
  and economics, 75–76, 78–79
  linguistic devices in, 6–7
  as metamorphic comedy, 37, 64–66
  misreading in, 3, 65–66
  as parody of mystery religion, 159n. 16, 172n. 1
  as parody of *Odyssey*, 152n. 16
  as parody of patriarchy, 114–

115
  relations to *Cupid and Psyche*, 117–118
  relations to *Phaedrus*, 30, 118
  revisions of Plato in, 30, 39, 41–42, 172n. 2, 173n. 5
  satire on colonialism in, 74
  shame dynamics in, 64–68, 78–79
Gothic, 94
Gould, Eric, 164n. 7
Gregory, Horace, 45, 158n. 13

Hadzits, George Depue, 158n. 13
Haight, Elizabeth H., 161n. 30
Halperin, David M., 173n. 8
Hardison, O. B., Jr., 49–50
Harris, Paul A., 171n. 26
Harrison, Jane, 5
Havelock, Eric A., 157n. 1
Heart of a Dog (Bulgakov), 45, 47–49, 96–102, 170n. 20
Hecate, 118, 146
Heliodorus, 42
Heller, Stephen, 39
Hennelly, Mark M., Jr., 176n. 27
Heraclitus, 27, 75, 158n. 7
Hermaphroditus, 4
hermeneutics, 5
Hermes
  and Christianity, 174n. 13
  Coleridge on, 151n. 12
  and the crypt, 151n. 11
  daemonic complexion of, 3–5, 175n. 21
  in *Lamia*, 4–5, 66, 88, 132, 134–135
  in Neoplatonic allegory, 127–128
  in *Odyssey*, 61–62, 155n. 33
  as trickster, 19
Hesiod, 24, 25, 31, 33, 35, 36
history, ix, x, 1, 23, 96
  relation to allegorical structure, 23–24, 96
Homer
  and Neoplatonism, 40–42, 58, 124–126, 157nn. 1, 3
  and Plato, 24–25, 157n. 1

162n. 36
scapegoat (*pharmakos*), 5, 48,
150n. 6
Schlam, Carl C., 159n. 19, 172n. 3
science
biology, 49, 86, 106–110, 166n.
18
chaos theory, x, 103–104,
170nn. 22, 23, 171n. 25
cybernetics, 49–51, 105–106,
110–111, 171n. 28
genetics, 107–111
information theory, 103, 153n.
19
in modern metamorphic
allegory, 45–48, 98–102
physics, 49, 103, 106, 153n. 19,
163n. 5, 171n. 30
in postmodern metamorphic
allegory, 49–51, 102–111
in premodern metamorphic
allegory, 42–43
self. *See* subject, the human
Serres, Michel, 153n. 19, 170n. 22
sexuality
in *Jekyll and Hyde*, 140–141,
143–144
Oedipal, 68
politics of, 135
and repression, 70
reproductive, 109–111
and witchcraft, 67–68
Shakespeare, William, xi, 44, 46,
169n. 17, 174n. 14
shame. *See* affect
Siebers, Tobin, 154n. 20
sign, the
in *Ancient Mariner*, 93–96
and the daemonic, 11, 110
Hermes and, 4–5
and the logos, 164n. 10
structural model of, 2
and the subject, 16, 21, 163n. 3
Thoth and, 4–5
signification, 59
signature, 7–9, 43
Silverman, Kaja, 77, 81, 163n. 1,
177n. 27

Simmel, George, 166n. 20
Sin, 17, 94–96, 104, 162n. 36,
169n. 17
Skulsky, Harold, 54, 122–123
Skura, Meredith Anne, 174n. 14
slime (*le visqueux*), 177n. 28
Socrates
Bakhtin on, 35–36
and the daemonic, 11–12, 42,
115, 172n. 2
and the erotic, 173nn. 5, 8
as ironist, 26, 39, 158n. 10
and metamorphosis, 25–30
and Psyche, 116, 121
soul, the human
and the daemonic, 12, 168n. 6
eros and, 121
fall of, 123
as "gold," 76
immateriality of, 101, 122, 141
in Plato, 26–28
in Porphyry, 125–126
Sperry, Stuart M., 46, 162nn. 33,
34
state, political, 70–72, 100
Stevenson, Robert Louis, 113
Stewart, Garrett, 89, 133
Stock, R. D., 153n. 20
*Strange Case of Dr. Jekyll and Mr.
Hyde. See Jekyll and Hyde*
subject, the human
autonomy of, 53–55
catastrophic origin of, 16
ironies of, 44, 54, 132–133
structural determination of, 53,
55, 88, 109–110, 113, 163nn.
1, 3
supernatural, 46, 72, 93
superstition, 53
supplement, 9–10, 14, 113, 153n.
18
symbol, x, 13, 29, 92, 154n. 23,
163n. 2

t zero, 47, 49, 105–111
Tanner, Tony, 155n. 29
Tatum, James, 39, 152n. 16
Taylor, Alfred E., 161n. 26